KARATEDO PARADIGM SHIFT

空手道
パラダイム
シフト

Karatedo Paradigm Shift

空手道 パラダイム シフト

The Path to Rediscovering Budo Karate

Kousaku Yokota

横田耕作

ISBN: 978-0-9982236-1-2

This book was printed in the United States of America.

To order additional copies of this book, contact:
Azami Press
1-765-242-7988
www.AzamiPress.com
Info@AzamiPress.com

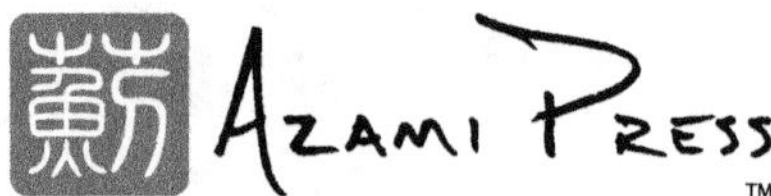

Dedication
奉納

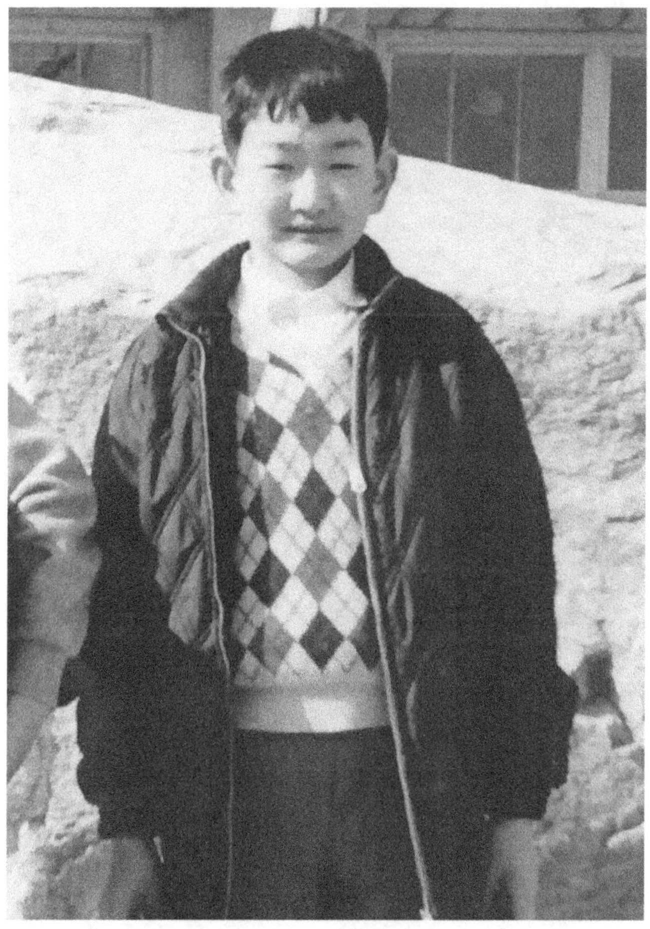

I dedicate this book to my deceased brother, Takuji Yokota (横田卓治, 1954–1972). He took his own life when he was a mere eighteen years old. It is a very painful memory, even though it happened more than forty years ago. He was a sweet and good young man who practiced kendo in his high school days. By dedicating this book to him, I wish to show that I still remember him. He was the only brother I had, and he had a strong impact on my life. I hope he rests in peace and is happy with our parents, who are also in the spirit world now.

Kousaku Yokota Biography
経歴

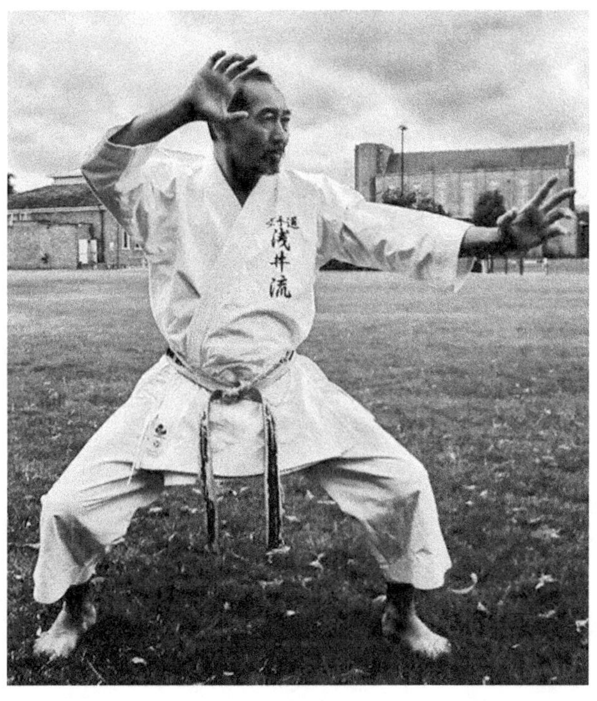

Shihan Kousaku Yokota (横田耕作), eighth *dan*, is a professional *karateka* with extensive experience in various martial arts. With over fifty years of training in Shotokan karate (松濤館空手), he specializes in Asai Ryu Bujutsu karate (浅井流武術空手). His wide range of experience includes training in *kobudo* (*nanas-etsuben* and nunchaku), in the art of ki, and in the breathing method by Nishino Ryu Kikojutsu (西野流気功術). He was a member of the JKA for forty years and then joined the JKS for seven years. In 2013, he founded his organization, ASAI (Asai Shotokan Association International [www.asaikarate.com]), to honor Master Tetsuhiko Asai (浅井哲彦). Shihan Yokota travels extensively around the world to share the knowledge and techniques of Asai Ryu karate. He is also a main contributor at Karate Coaching (www.karatecoaching.com), where he extends his karate teaching through Internet media.

Acknowledgments
感謝の言葉

Many people are responsible for making the creation of this book, *Karatedo Paradigm Shift*, possible. I want to extend my gratitude to all those who have so generously contributed their time and experience to the creation of this book and to all those who have purchased it.

I wish to dedicate this book to my younger brother, Takuji, who decided to leave this world when he was only eighteen years old. I want to thank him for leaving me many wonderful memories. Our time together was short, but he still lives within me.

I also want to thank the cultural heritage of Japan and that of Shotokan *karatedo* as these have taught me honor and respect. I must give my sincere thanks to all my instructors and students, past and present, for giving me the knowledge and understanding of this great karate style, Shotokan. Out of all the sensei I have had in the past, I must credit Master Tetsuhiko Asai with having shown me not only the techniques but also the lifestyle of *budo* karate.

In the past, I learned from my sensei and my *senpai*. Today, though my sensei have passed, my students and other *karateka* are my new teachers. Without all of you, my karate would not be where it is today, and this book would probably not have materialized. Master Funakoshi, the founder of Shotokan said, "Karate training is a lifetime endeavor." I am still training and learning every day, yet I have not seen the summit of karate.

I also want to thank you, the reader of this book. I hope you enjoy reading it as much as I have enjoyed writing it. I also hope that I get to meet you and train with you in the future, regardless of your organization or style. True enjoyment of karate is found in doing it. I dream of a day when all karate practitioners can train together without worrying about politics. On that day, I am sure that Funakoshi Sensei and Asai Sensei will be truly pleased.

From the bottom of my heart, I want to say, "Thank you very much to all of you."

皆様に心より御礼申し上げます。

Minasama ni kokoro yori orei mōshiagemasu.

Foreword

By Simon Dodd
Yondan, Welsh Karate Union
Wales, United Kingdom

Fel ymarferydd o *karatedo* a jiwdo, a fel ymchwilydd academaidd o crefft ymladd a chwaraeon brwydro, mae e'n fraint arbennig i mi cael gofyn i ysgrifennu rhagair y gyhoeddiad hon. Cafais y lwc dda i gwrdd a Yokota Sensei ar ol ddarllen eu gwaith gynharach, a chafais argraff arbennig o dda o'i nod i hyrwyddo rhinweddau *budo* dros y byd. Ers ei'n ohebiaith gyntaf tan i ni gwrdd o'r diwedd yn bersonol, dw'i wedi ddod i barchu y ddyn ysbrydoledig yma am ei wybodaeth, feddwl agored ac ymroddiad i achos teilwng, a rydw i'n falch iawn i gefnogi e yn y nod hon. Yn ei ffordd hoffus, wnaeth e ddisgrifio ei hun wedi 'hanner-ymddeoli', ond mae ei hymroddiad i'r bywyd karate yn ymddangos i fod yn swydd llawn amser; rheoli gohebiaethau, seminarau rhyngwladol, ysgrifennu ei blog, a gyhoeddi.

Mae cysylltiadau Yokota Sensei i rhyngwladoli karate wedi gadael e weld yn uniongyrchol sut mae karate a'i canfyddiad wedi ddatblygu dros y byd. Ar ol hynny, mae e wedi ysgrifennu yn eang am yr arfer, ddywilliant, ac effeithiau cymdeithasol o *budo* i geisio chwalu'r chwedlon sydd wedi datblygu, yn enwedig yn Y Gorllewin, or gwmpas y crefft ymladd *budo*. Credaf fod ddylai karate ddatblygu gyda amser, cyn belled a dyw e ddim yn colli ei egwyddorion a gwerthoedd sylfaenol. Fodd bynnag, achai'r perygl o gamddefnyddio diwylliannol arwain at y wanhau o'r ymarferydd rydym yn cynnal yn annwyl. Yn ei ymdrell i atal hyn, mae e'n bleser i weld yr ansawdd a hyd o waith Kousaka Yokota gwella ac ymhelaethu, a mae'r llyfr hon yn cynrychioli gyd o'i waith galed hyd yma.

Fel chrefftwyr ymladd, rydym yn cymryd yn ganiataol yr arferion rydym yn cymryd rhan yn ac yn hyrwyddo, ac yn rhai achosion glynu at syniadau a tybiaethau anghywyr. Dyw Kousaku Yokota byth yn ofn i ddrafod bwnciau anodd neu ddadleuol i ysgogi trafodaeth a myfyrdod yn y gymyned crefft ymladd ehangach. Mae'r gwaith hon yn cynnwys pynciau yn gwmpasu biomecaneg, defnyddio technoleg, datblygion diwyllianol a cymdeithasol, a dealltwriaeth hanesyddol ac athronyddol. Gallwll mwynhau penodau yn gynnwys rhai ar y dull hyfforddi enwog o'r 'squat kick' a os, yng ngoleini dealltwriaeth meddygol, os bod e'n arfer peryglys, un arall ar y syniad o rhoi'r gorau i arfer *bunkai*, a un bellach am yr elfen mwyaf pwysig yn ymarfer karate *budo*. Nid oes amheuaeth bydd y pynciau yma yn achosi ymateb sylweddol o ymarferydd crefft ymladd, ac yn briodol felly.

Fel awdur, mae arddull ysgrifennu Yokota Sensei yn hoffus iawn ac yn aml yn deimlo fel mae'r ddarllenydd yn ddarn o sgwrs ddiddorol a nid yn ddarllen geiriau ar y tudalen. Fe'u hanogaf ymarferydd crefft ymladd o fob brofiad cymerud yr amser i fwynhau'r llyfr yma, i drafod e, i ddadlu e, a hyd yn oed i anghytuno efo fe. Beth sy'n bwysig yw bod y broses yn annog ddysgu a dealltwriaeth bydd yn fudd i cenedlaethau'r dyfodol.

Yn olaf, byddai'n anghywyr i mi beidio enwu elfen hanfodol i lwyddiant Yokota Sensei. Yn Prydain, rydym yn siarad yn aml am y 'weddw crefft ymladd', y gwr neu gwraig sydd ddim yn cael gweld ni mor aml a bydden nhw'n hoffi fel bod ni'n teething (fel arfer ar y penwythnos) i seminarau, cystadlaethau, a digwyddiadau eraill. Cafais i'r bleser i gwrdd a gwraig Yokota Sensei a weld y gymorth gadarn mae e'n cael oddi o hi, ac ei teulu, fel bod e'n dilyn ei nodau. Mae'n aml efo gymorth o ein anwyliaid bod ni'n ddarganfod ein botensial llawn, a nid oes unrhyw amheuaeth gennyf bod hi'n bwysig iawn mewn gadael i ni elwa oddi o wybodaeth a ddoethineb Kousaku Yokota. Felly ar ran bawb, dwi'n dweud 'diolch'.

English

As a practitioner of *karatedo* and judo and an academic researcher of martial arts and combat sports, I consider it a great privilege to be asked to write a foreword for this publication. I had the great fortune of meeting Yokota Sensei after reading his earlier works and being impressed with his very laudable goal of promoting the virtues of *budo* around the world. From our initial correspondence to eventually meeting in person, I have come to deeply respect this inspirational man for his knowledge, open mind, and dedication to a worthy cause, and I am proud to support him in achieving this goal. In his usual affable way, he once described himself to me as "semiretired," and yet his dedication to the karate world seems to constitute a full-time job as he manages correspondence, international seminars, blog writing, and publishing.

Yokota Sensei's links to the early internationalization of karate have allowed him to witness firsthand how karate, and the perception of karate, has developed around the world. Subsequently, he has written extensively on the practices, culture, and social effects of *budo* in an attempt to dispel the myths that have developed, particularly in the Western world, around *budo*. I have long believed that karate should evolve with the times so long as it does not lose the fundamental principles and values that make it *budo*; however, the danger of the cultural misappropriation of the traditional Japanese martial arts could lead to a diluting of the practices we hold so dear. I am pleased to have seen the quality and breadth of Kousaku Yokota's work expand and improve in his efforts to prevent this, this latest book representing all his hard work to date.

As martial artists, we often take for granted the practices we participate in and promote, and, in some cases, we cling to incorrect assumptions and ideas. Kousaku Yokota is never afraid to broach difficult or controversial topics to provoke discussion and reflection within the wider martial arts community. This latest work addresses topics encompassing biomechanics, the use of technology, cultural and social developments, and historical and philosophical understanding. You can enjoy chapters such as the one on the infamous karate training method of the "squat kick" and whether, in the light of medical understanding, it is a harmful practice; another on the idea of ceasing *bunkai* training; and a further one identifying the most important element in *budo* karate training. No doubt these are likely to elicit significant reactions from martial arts practitioners, and rightly so.

As an author, Yokota Sensei's writing style is very personable and often makes the reader feel as if he were holding an engaging conversation and not reading words on a page. I encourage martial artists of all experience to take the time to enjoy the content of this book, discuss it, debate it, and even disagree with it if you wish. What matters is that this process will encourage learning and understanding that will benefit future generations.

Finally, it would be remiss of me if I did not mention another essential component to Yokota Sensei's success. In the UK, we often talk of the "martial arts widow," the wife or husband who rarely sees us as we travel (often on weekends) to seminars, competitions, and other events. I had the distinct pleasure of meeting Yokota Sensei's wife and witnessing the unwavering support he receives from her and his family as he pursues his goals. It is often with the support of our loved ones that we discover our full potential, and I have no doubt that she is instrumental in allowing the rest of us to benefit from the knowledge and wisdom of Kousaku Yokota. So, on behalf of all of us, I say, "Thank you."

My sincere thanks to Lucy Parry for providing the translation into Welsh.

Foreword

By Jesse Enkamp

Founder, Karate by Jesse & Seishin International

Renowned International Karate Seminar Organizer & Entrepreneur

Stockholm, Sweden

Karate är en kampkonst fylld med underligheter. Många av dessa kuriositeter härrör från den icke-linjära, och till stor del oplanerade, utvecklingen av Karate - en gammal konst som snabbt var tvungen att anpassa sig till kraven från en modern värld. Okänt för många utövare i dag, var att kritiska delar av Karate förlorades under denna berg-och dalbana av evolution. Nya inslag sattes på plats för att kompensera för de många tekniska, historiska, filosofiska, pedagogiska och lingvistiska inkonsekvenser som bildades. Följaktligen blev Karates ursprungliga essens höljt i mysterium.

Men vad vissa kallar "mysterium", kallar andra "logiska missuppfattningar". Yokota Kousaku Sensei är en av dessa människor. Efter att ha ägnat sitt liv åt att avslöja nycklarna som låser upp Karatens "inte så mystiska" hemligheter, representerar Yokotas arbete ett paradigmskifte i dagens Karate i allmänhet, och Shotokan Karate i synnerhet.

Detta tänkesätt är vad motiverade mig att bjuda in honom som gästinstruktör för min tredje årliga KNX: The Karate Nerd Experience, organiserat förra sommaren. Fram till denna punkt hade jag bara känt Yokota Sensei genom hans skrivelser, och de alltid hade imponerade på mig. Jag kan med nöje säga att han inte svek någon av de passionerade "Karate Nerds" från 20+ länder som deltog i seminariet.

Yokotas introspektiva ord är i nivå med hans fysiska kapacitet, teknisk briljans och graciösa karaktär. På japanska kan man säga att Yokota Sensei förkroppsligar begreppet "shingitai" (心技体) och "bunbu ryodo" (文武両道). Jag skulle gärna förklara dessa två begrepp för dig, men jag har en stark känsla av att Yokota Sensei skulle göra det mycket bättre - genom sina ord och handlingar.

Sammanfattningsvis är vi alla medmänniskor på vägen mot självinsikt och personlig utveckling genom Karate, och vi alla behöver någon att vägleda oss på den här resan. Det är min förhoppning att denna bok kan hjälpa dig med det, genom att ge dig en tankeställare när du navigerar dig igenom Karatens många ”mysterier”. Det finns inga kartor i Karate, men det finns kompasser. Den här boken är en.

Lycka till!

English

Karate is an art filled with curiosities. Many of these curiosities stem from the non-linear and largely unplanned evolution of karate, an ancient art that was quickly forced to adapt to the demands of a modern world. Unbeknownst to many practitioners today, critical elements of the art were lost during this roller coaster of evolution. New elements were put in place to make up for the numerous technical, historical, philosophical, pedagogical and linguistic incoherences that formed. Consequently, karate's original essence became shrouded in mystery.

However, what some people call *mystery*, other people call *logical misconceptions*. Yokota Kousaku Sensei is one of these people. Having dedicated his life to revealing the keys that unlock karate's not-so-mysterious secrets, Yokota's work represents a paradigm shift in the contemporary culture of karate in general and Shotokan karate in particular.

This mind-set is what motivated me to invite him as a guest instructor for my third annual KNX: The Karate Nerd Experience, organized last summer. Up until that point, I had only known Yokota Sensei through his writings, and they had always impressed me. Nonetheless, it's safe to say that he did not disappoint any of the passionate Karate Nerds from over twenty countries that attended the seminar.

Yokota's introspective words are easily paralleled by his physical capacity, technical brilliance, and graceful character. In Japanese, you could say that Yokota Sensei embodies the concepts of *shingitai* (心技体) and *bunburyodo* (文武両道). I would happily explain these two concepts to you, but I have a strong feeling that Yokota Sensei would do it much better (if not through his words, then by his actions).

At the end of the day, we are all human beings on the path of self-discovery and personal fulfilment through karate, and we all need someone to guide us on this journey. It is my sincere hope that this book can help you with that by providing you with food for thought as you navigate your way through the "mysteries" of karate. There are no road maps in karate, but there are compasses. This book is one.

Good luck!

Foreword

By Enoc Duque

Chief Instructor & Director, JKA

Country Representative, ASAI Ecuador

Ecuador

Comencé a practicar el *karatedo* cuando tenía diecisiete años de edad. Me hubiese gustado aprenderlo desde niño, pero me siento feliz de seguir aprendiendo y practicando hasta el día de hoy. He entrenado en la JKA durante unos veinte años y he aprendido mucho de mis maestros y de los maestros japoneses que he tenido durante mi vida. También he aprendido el iaido durante once años y ha sido un complemento muy bueno para el crecimiento de mi karate.

A través de los años, había aprendido la biomecánica del movimiento del karate y la metodología de la JKA, pero, en mi visión del karate, me faltaba algo por seguir descubriendo. En estos años, encontré a un gran maestro que, por su amabilidad y gran conocimiento, me invitó a conocer del estilo Asai Ryu Shotokan *budo*, el cual provenía del gran maestro Tetsuhiko Asai, décimo *dan*, JKA, y fundador del estilo Asai Ryu Shotokan.

Yokota Sensei me invitó a ser parte de su honorable organización, a lo cual accedí muy emocionado. Al ser miembro de Asai Ryu, tuve la oportunidad de conocer personalmente a Yokota Sensei en Brasil, y fue una de las más grandes experiencias de mi vida. Su amabilidad y su espíritu amable me mostraron que la grandeza del karate está en la humildad y en el trabajo duro del entrenamiento diario. Luego, tuve la oportunidad de ver algunos de los exámenes tomados por Yokota Sensei y me quedé asombrado de la diversidad de técnicas. Al día siguiente, asistí al seminario de Yokota Sensei y me quedé muy emocionado por la realidad de las técnicas y lo interesante de sus movimientos.

Yokota Sensei me ha mostrado muchas cosas nuevas y otra visión del karate tradicional. En este tiempo, he aprendido mucho de mi maestro, Yokota Sensei, al cual aprecio mucho por su tiempo, enseñanza y dedicación que me ha dado, y estoy agradecido por pertenecer a esta gran familia.

English

I started practicing *karatedo* when I was seventeen years old. I would like to have learned it since I was a child, but I feel happy to continue learning and practicing even today. I have trained in the JKA for about twenty years and learned a lot from my teachers and from the Japanese teachers that I have had during my life. I have also been learning iaido for eleven years, and this has been a very good complement to the growth of my karate.

Over the years, I had learned the biomechanics of karate movement and the JKA's methodology, but, in my vision of karate, I was missing something to continue discovering. In recent years, I met a great teacher who, due to his kindness and great knowledge, invited me to get to know the style Asai Ryu Shotokan *budo*, which came from the great teacher Tetsuhiko Asai, tenth *dan*, JKA, and founder of the style Asai Ryu Shotokan.

Yokota Sensei invited me to be part of his honorable organization, which I very excitedly agreed to. As a member of Asai Ryu, I had the opportunity to meet Yokota Sensei personally in Brazil, and it was one of the greatest experiences of my life. His kindness and his kind spirit showed me that the greatness of karate is in humility and in the hard work of daily training. Then, I had the opportunity to see some of the exams taken by Yokota Sensei and was astonished by the diversity of techniques. The next day, I attended Yokota Sensei's seminar and was very excited about the reality of the techniques and how interesting his movements were.

Yokota Sensei has shown me many new things and another vision of traditional karate. In this time, I have learned much from my teacher, Yokota Sensei, whom I greatly appreciate for his time, instruction, and dedication that he has given me, and I am grateful to belong to this great family.

Foreword

By Leandre Ricardo Rosa
Yondan, Asai Ryu
President & Ambassador, ASAI Brazil
Brazil

Yokota Kousaku Shihan é uma pessoa admirável. Possui a capacidade de relacionar conhecimentos antigos com assuntos atuais. Assumiu a responsabilidade, compromisso de esclarecer e levantar questionamentos que muitos jamais ousariam. Seu conhecimento prático e teórico de karatê é inquestionável. Digo isso por conhecê-lo pessoalmente, ter treinado, jantado, reunido e conversado por várias ocasiões.

Seu quarto livro, *Karatedo Paradigm Shift*, me parece ser seu convite para sairmos de nossa zona de conforto, abrirmos nossa mente frente ao mundo globalizado onde os veículos de comunicação via internet e redes sociais aproximam cidadãos de todas as nações. Este livro é mais uma de suas contribuições históricas para todos os *karateka* que buscam o aprofundamento no *budo* karate e acompanham a evolução dos tempos.

English

Yokota Kousaku Shihan is an admirable person. He has the ability to relate ancient knowledge to current issues. He took on the responsibility, the commitment to clarify and raise questions that many would never dare to raise. His practical and theoretical knowledge of karate is unquestionable. I say this from knowing him personally, having trained, met, and talked with him on several occasions.

His fourth book, *Karatedo Paradigm Shift*, seems to me to be his invitation for us to get out of our comfort zone and open our minds to the globalized world where the vehicles of communication via the Internet and social networks bring citizens from all nations together. This book is another of his historic contributions to all *karateka* who are seeking depth in *budo* karate and are keeping up with the evolution of the times.

FOREWORD

By Amit Bharat Khatri

Yondan, Asai Ryu

Chief Instructor, AISKF

Ambassador, ASAI India

Mumbai, India

सबसे पले मैं शिान कोसाकू योकोता को उनकी तीनों पुस्तकों - शोतोकान मिथ्स (शोतोकान मिथ्याये), शोतोकान मिस्ट्रीस (शोतोकान के रस्य), शोतोकान ट्रान्सेन्डेन्स (शोतोकान की श्रेष्ठता) के संस्करणों तु ार्दिक अभिनंदन करना चाता ू, जिसने दुनिया भर के उत्सुक कराते चाकों में उत्कृष्ट प्रतिक्रया और सफलता ासिल की ै । और मुझे यकीन ै कि, उन्े अपने चौथे संस्करण में भी इसी तर की बड़ी सफलता प्राप्त ोगी । मुझे बेद खुशी ै कि, उनकी तीनों पुस्तकें ‍ऽशिान कोसाकू योकोताट के स्वस्ताक्षरों सति मेरे पास ै ।

मैने ऐसे कई कराते अभ्यार्थियों को देखा ै, जिन्े अपूर्ण ज्ञान तथा तकनीकी मानकों में गलतियों का सामना करना पड़ रा ै । याँ तक कि उनमें वैज्ञानिक दृष्टीकोण की कमी ै,और वे कराते के इतिास से भी अनजान ै ।

शिान योकोता ने अपनी ऽपुस्तकों, ब्लॉग्स, तथा कराते सेमिनारों की सायता से ऐसे कई अनसुलझे सवालों केा ल किया ै । तथा वे रबार कुछ ऐसे दिलचस्प विषयों को उठाते ै, जिन्े कई बार म सोच भी नी सकते । तथा ऐसे विषयों पर कीं चर्चा भी नी मिलेगी। वे मेशा वैज्ञानिक दृष्टीकोण तथा कराते के इतिास को संलग्न रखते ै , जिसकी सायता से में परंपरागत तथा सी तरीके से कराते सीखने तथा उसे समझने का मौका मिलता ै । और वे अतीत को वर्तमान से जोड़ने का मत्वपूर्ण माध्यम बनते ै । उनके द्वारा अभ्यार्थी अपने रोज के प्रशिक्षण तथा दिनचर्या में अलग नज़रिए तथा सोच की और अग्रसर ोते ै ।

उनकी इस अवधारणा को सीखना और समझना अति मत्वपूर्ण ै, विशेषतः ऐसे युग में जाँ कराते केवल एक खेल के नजरिये से अपनाया तथा विकसित किया जाँ रा ै , और इस कारण नई पीढ़ी मार्शल - आर्ट के दार्शनिक तथा पारंपारिक अवधारणा से लगभग अनजान ै ।

मुझे ऽ शिान योकोता ऽ से प्रशिक्षण का अवसर प्राप्त ुआ जिसकी वज से मेरे प्रशिक्षण का स्तर कई मायनों में बढ़ा। और मैं भाग्यशाली ू कि उनेने अपना ज्ञान , विशेषज्ञता तथा वर्षो का अनुभव मसे बाँटा और में लाभान्वित किया।

मैं ऽशिान योकोताट को सच में ार्दिक धन्यवाद! देना चाता ू, जिनेंने अपना विशेष ज्ञान में उपलब्ध कराया साथ ी मैं प्रकाशक का भी आभारी ू , जिनेने वर्तमान अभ्यार्थियों तथा अगली पीढी के मार्गदर्शन ेतु पुस्तक सामग्री प्रदान किया । साथ ी मैं भविष्य में कई नए तथा दिलचस्प विषयों की भी उम्मीद रखता ू ।

और मैं सभी पाठकों से य कना चाूँगा कि इनकी पुस्तकों को पढ़ने के उपरांत आपके भी कराते के कौशल तथा ज्ञान का स्तर बढ़ेगा । और आप भी मेरी तरऽ माननीय शिान कासाकू योकोताट के अनुयायी तथा समर्थक बन जाएँगे ।

English

First of all, I congratulate the respected Yokota Shihan for his three publications, *Shotokan Myths*, *Shotokan Mysteries*, and *Shotokan Transcendence*, which have received a wonderful response, have been successful, and are impressing karate enthusiasts around the world. I am sure this fourth publication will also achieve the same grand success, and it's to my great pleasure that I have the three previous publications with Yokota Shihan's own autograph.

I have seen many Shotokan karate practitioners facing incomplete and inaccurate technical standards, even lacking a scientific approach and being unaware of the history of *karatedo* training. By means of his books, blogs, and training seminars, Yokota Shihan has covered and solved many issues that karate practitioners generally face during their karate journey. He has raised many interesting karate subjects that readers may not be able to find out about or may not have even thought about.

He has also covered the scientific approach and the history behind karate, which helps us learn and understand the traditional way of *karatedo*. This builds an important bridge connecting the past to the present, which allows practitioners to think with a different perspective in their regular karate training routine. Learning this concept is a must, especially in this era where many have accepted and are developing sport karate, and new generations are unaware of the traditional concept and philosophy of the martial arts.

I got the opportunity to train under Yokota Shihan, and he has explored my karate training in a great way. We are fortunate that Yokota Shihan has shared his wisdom and expertise for our benefit. He has shared the thoughts, opinions, and experiences that he has gained through his many years of study, training, and teaching. I am very thankful to Yokota Shihan for having provided such great knowledge and, of course, to the publisher, too, for having put this imparted knowledge into the form of a book that is available for present practitioners and for the next generation. I expect that many more new topics will be launched soon.

And, to all the dear readers, I am sure that after reading all of these books, you will update your karate skill and knowledge and will be a follower and supporter of Yokota Kousaku Shihan's work (as I am).

Foreword

By Marc Dourieu

French Translator of *Shotokan Myths*

Languedoc-Roussillon, France

Pour ceux d'entre vous qui ne le savent pas, Yokota Shihan est le fondateur d'Asai Shotokan Association International qu'il a créé à la mémoire de son sensei, Tetsuhiko Asai. Il voyage partout dans le monde pour enseigner lors de stages et pour faire la promotion de son organisation, ASAI, et a écrit des articles pour de nombreux magazines de karaté renommés. Il mélange de manière efficace l'héritage qu'il a obtenu de par son affiliation passée à la JKA et la JKS et sa connaissance des concepts et technologies modernes. Grâce à sa vaste connaissance du karaté et des autres arts martiaux, il a une vision unique et rafraîchissante de son art martial de choix et est l'un des enseignants de karaté les plus intéressants du moment.

Yokota Shihan adopte véritablement les technologies modernes et il est l'un des instructeurs les plus actifs sur les réseaux sociaux et sur Internet, que ce soit sur sa page *Facebook*, par l'intermédiaire de son partenariat avec Karate Coaching ou sur son blog sur le site Internet www.asaikarate.com. Il n'a jamais peur d'exposer ses idées et hypothèses en ligne avec ses lecteurs et accueille les avis opposés au sien avec bienvenue. Il fut l'un des premiers enseignants de karaté a utiliser les moyens électroniques tels que Skype afin d'enseigner et d'évaluer les progrès de ses élèves. Ceci est un sujet controversé et n'est pas encore totalement accepté par la communauté du karaté. Dans ce livre, il demande si l'Internet peut être utilisé comme moyen valable afin d'évaluer les pratiquants de karaté.

J'ai eu le plaisir de lire ses trois premiers livres, *Shotokan Myths*, *Shotokan Mysteries* et *Shotokan Transcendence*. Ceux-ci sont une mine d'information pour les passionnés de karaté. Ils contiennent de nombreux articles portant a réflexion sur plusieurs sujets ayant trait au karaté. Bien qu'étant spécialiste du Shotokan, ses connaissances de l'art et ses recherches et façon de penser font que ces livres sont à lire impérativement pour tout karatéka.

Son quatrième livre, *Karatedo Paradigm Shift*, va au-delà des frontières du

Shotokan et étend les recherches pour couvrir des aspects du karaté d'Okinawa et des concepts d'autres styles comme dans les chapitres "What Are Muchimi, Gamaku, and Chinkuchi?" et "What is the Kenpo Hakku?".

Yokota Shihan dédie un certain nombre de chapitres au sujet de l'entraînement et la physiologie, tels que "Is Five-Minute Training Sufficient?", "Are Squat Kicks Medically Harmful?" et "Stop Tube Training". Certains chapitres, tels que "The Relationship between Choku Zuki and the Elbow Position", traitent de l'aspect technique de l'art. Enfin, il présente au lecteur certains thèmes plus philosophiques dans les chapitres "What Is the Most Important Training Point in Budo Karate?" et "Itosu's Ten Precepts of Karate".

Tekki/Naihanchi est bien connu pour être l'un des *kata* les plus importants dans de nombreux styles de karaté d'Okinawa. Il est souvent considéré comme le *kata* référence et est répété constamment, cependant, il semble avoir perdu cette importance pour le karaté Shotokan. Dans ses livres précédents, Yokota Shihan a écrit plusieurs chapitres sur ce *kata* crucial. Dans son nouveau livre, il revoit ce *kata* dans le chapitre "A Deeper Understanding of Tekki (Naihanchi)".

Je suis convaincu que les lecteurs de *Karatedo Paradigm Shift* bénéficieront grandement de la lecture de ce livre. Les recherches de Yokota Shihan et les idées et concepts qu'il y présentent permettront aux lecteurs, quel que soit leur style et niveau, de progresser toujours plus sur leur voie en matière de karaté, tant au niveau physique que psychologique.

English

For those of you who do not know, Yokota Shihan is the founder of Asai Shotokan Association International, which he founded in memory of his late sensei, Tetsuhiko Asai. He travels extensively to seminars throughout the world to promote karate and the ASAI organization and has been a contributor to some of the best-known karate magazines. He effectively blends the karate heritage he gained as a past member of the JKA and the JKS with his understanding of modern concepts and technology. With his extensive experience in karate and other martial arts, he has formed very unique and refreshing views of his chosen martial art and is one of the most interesting karate teachers of our time.

Yokota Shihan truly embraces modern technology and is one of the most active karate instructors on social media and the Internet (be it on his *Facebook* page, through his partnership with Karate Coaching, or via his blog on the www.asaikarate.com website). He is never afraid to discuss his ideas and hypotheses online with his readers and always welcomes opposing views. He was one of the first karate teachers to use online tools such as Skype for teaching or assessing martial arts progress. This is a controversial topic and something not fully accepted by the karate community. In this book, he discusses whether the Internet could be used as a valid method for grading karate students.

I have had the pleasure of reading his first three books, *Shotokan Myths*, *Shotokan Mysteries*, and *Shotokan Transcendence*. These are a mine of information for any karate enthusiast. They contain thought-provoking articles about various karate subjects. Although he is a Shotokan practitioner, his knowledge of the art and his research and thought processes make these books a must-read for all *karateka*.

His fourth book, *Karatedo Paradigm Shift*, goes beyond the boundaries of Shotokan as he expands his research to cover aspects of Okinawan karate and concepts from other styles in chapters such as "What Are Muchimi, Gamaku, and Chinkuchi?" and "What is the Kenpo Hakku?"

Yokota Shihan also dedicates a number of chapters to the subject of training and physiology, such as "Is Five-Minute Training Sufficient?" "Are Squat Kicks Medically Harmful?" and "Stop Tube Training." Some of the chapters, such as "The Relationship between Choku Zuki and the Elbow Position," deal with the technical side of the art. Finally, he introduces the reader to philosophical themes in the chapters "What Is the Most Important Training Point in Budo Karate?" and "Itosu's Ten Precepts of Karate."

It is well known that Tekki/Naihanchi is one of the most important *kata* in many Okinawan karate styles. It is often considered to be the base *kata* and is repeated constantly, yet it has lost its importance in Shotokan. In his earlier books, Yokota Shihan wrote a number of chapters about this critical *kata*. In this new book, he revisits this *kata* in the chapter "A Deeper Understanding of Tekki (Naihanchi)."

I am sure that readers of *Karatedo Paradigm Shift* will benefit greatly from reading this new book. The research carried out by Yokota Shihan and the thoughts and concepts that he introduces will enable readers of all styles and abilities to progress further in their karate journey, both physically and psychologically.

Foreword

By Ali Oskie
Rokudan, Asai Ryu
Member, ASAI Shihankai
Country Representative, ASAI Iran
E. Sharqi, Iran

افتخار دارم که مقدمه ای را در کتاب استاد یوکوتا کووساکی محقق ارزنده ورزشهای رزمی و بنیانگذار سازمان جهانی شوتوکان آسای ریو متنی را به نگارش در آورم استاد یوکوتا کووساکی همواره مباحث جدیدی را در ورزشهای رزمی خصوصا کاراته مطرح نموده است .ایشان در کتاب قبلی اش اسرار و ناگفته هایی را از کاراته شوتوکان تحریر نموده که مورد استقبال عموم اساتید ورزشهای رزمی خصوصا کارته قرار گرفته . این کتاب نیز حاوی مطالب ومباحث جدیدی میباشد که به یقین مورد استقبال اکثر هنر جویان قرار خواهد گرفت .لذا موکدا توصیه مینمایم همه دوستداران و علاقه مندان ورزشهای رزمی خصوصا کاراته این کتاب را مورد مطالعه قرار دهند.

English

It is my honor to write an introduction for Master Yokota Kousaku, who is the founder of Asai Shotokan Association International and a valuable researcher in the field of martial arts. Master Yokota Kousaku has always offered new things to the martial arts. He has written many untold secrets about Shotokan karate, for which he has been given credit by other masters, especially those of karate. This book also has new discussions and topics that will certainly be liked by all who practice the martial arts; therefore, I strongly suggest that all who are interested in the martial arts read this book.

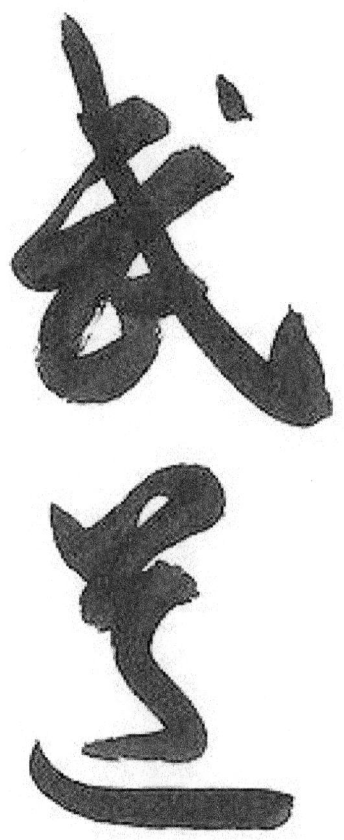

Budo

Preface
初めに

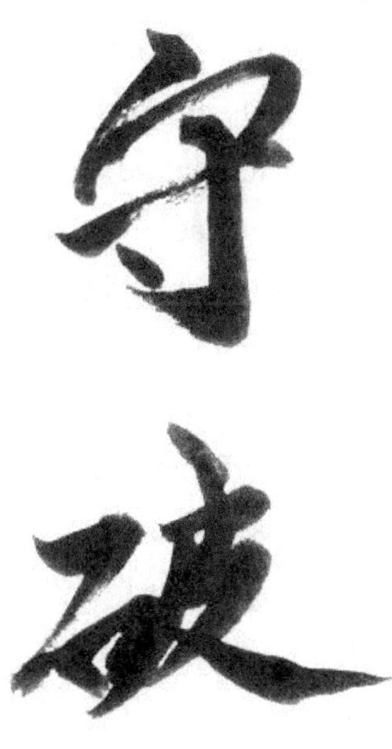

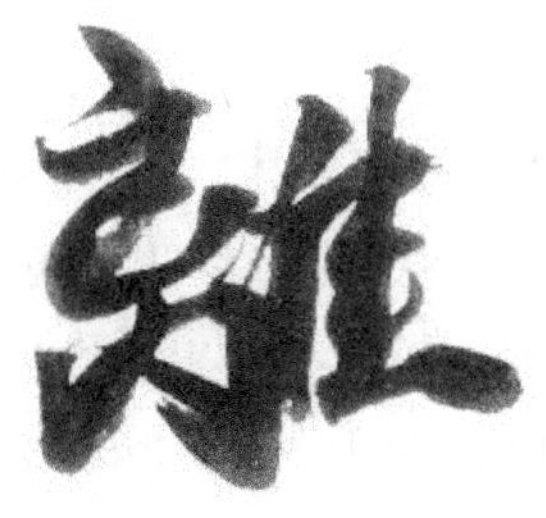

Shuhari

The reader may think the title *Karatedo Paradigm Shift* is a strange one for a karate book. I chose this term as I feel we now seriously need a fundamental change in the way we look at karate. Many *karateka*, including instructors, mistakenly believe that karate is prospering, especially since it was chosen for inclusion in the 2020 Tokyo Olympics. I am aware that there are different ideas about the prosperity of karate, and I respect the seriousness of the instructors and practitioners who are in favor of karate's inclusion in the Olympics. However, I do not discuss this subject directly in this book. Rather, I wish to explore the *budo* side of karate. By doing this, I hope to bring to light some of the aspects that are missing or have been all but forgotten. What is found in this book should be new to most readers.

So, what is this book all about? You will find that its content does not fit into any of the three major categories of typical karate books, which are karate history, how-to guides on karate techniques, and personal karate experiences (often including a journey to Japan). Rather, it focuses on explanations of *karatedo* concepts from a vastly different perspective. Though I am not a medical expert, I try to explain karate movements from a physiological and kinesiological perspective as few others have done before. I also propose some fundamental changes to some of the popular beliefs of modern-day karate training in an effort to return to the original *karatedo*. I am aware that some topics may be controversial and even shocking. My hope is that what you find will be thought provoking, and this is exactly why the title is *Karatedo Paradigm Shift*.

This happens to be my fourth book. In the other three, I focused on Shotokan practitioners as my primary audience given that my karate training of over fifty years has been mainly in the Shotokan style. During the last ten years or so, I have begun to realize that I must go beyond the realm of Shotokan and study and understand the concepts and techniques of other styles of karate and those of other martial arts in order to understand *karatedo* better and more deeply. This is exactly what the famous samurai Musashi Miyamoto told us in his book *Gorin no Sho* (五輪書, 'The Book of Five Rings'). In the process of studying other styles of karate and other martial arts, such as kenjutsu and jujutsu, I began to realize that many of my discoveries regarding techniques, concepts, physiology, and kinesiology apply to all those other styles and arts, as well. This is not surprising as we are all human beings whose bodies are built the same way. Therefore, I am confident that what is found in this book will be beneficial not only to practitioners of Shuri Te styles (Shotokan, Shorin Ryu, Wado Ryu, etc.) but also to practitioners of Naha Te styles (Goju Ryu, Uechi Ryu, etc.) and Tomari Te styles (Ryuei Ryu, etc.).

Karate tradition and instruction demand that we stay within the old ways or the martial art ways (*budo*). But, at the same time, the world around us is going through a rapid fundamental change that is making it smaller and bringing us closer together. So, we karate practitioners live in somewhat of a paradox. On one hand, it is easier for us to receive information, and we are becoming more "educated." But, we must not be blind to the fact that much of this information is superficial. If we wish to climb higher, we need to go much farther than that. It is true that we must keep and respect the customs and traditions of karate. This will not change. However, it is also our generation's responsibility to improve karate and go beyond what our karate ancestors were able to see.

To find a better way, we must dare to take a chance and step outside the box sometimes. When we reach a plateau after having repeated the same training methods thousands of times, we should try some alternatives and try to view things from different perspectives. I am sure you have heard of the concept of *shuhari* (守破離). If you are ready to move on from the *shu* (守) stage or are already in the *ha* (破) or even the *ri* (離) stage, you will truly enjoy this book. I sincerely hope this book contributes to your diligent efforts to improve your *karatedo* and assists you in reaching the next level of your goals.

Contents

Chapter One
第一章

Is Five-Minute Training Sufficient?
五分間の稽古は可能か？

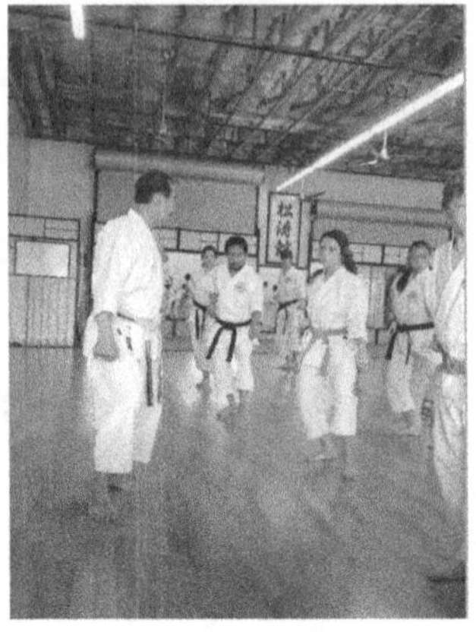

If we were to train in karate for four hours straight, then we would probably say we trained very hard and the training was great. On the other hand, if our workout were only five minutes long, then we would consider this to be too short and a poor workout.

Can a five-minute training session be enough? My answer to this question is "Yes, it can be." In other words, a five-minute session can be a sufficient training period and can actually be better than a session that is much longer than five minutes. Let me explain.

First, we must remember that there are two basic factors to our training that make our workout good or poor. One is certainly quantity, that is, how much time we spend on our workout. This is important, and most people tend to put more emphasis on it than the second factor, which is quality. However, more people should pay attention to quality, which I consider to be more important.

No matter how long or challenging our workout may be, would you not agree that it will be poor and of little benefit if our heart is not in it or if we are suffering from a severe headache or illness? To have an excellent workout, we all agree that the appropriate amount of time and quality must be present.

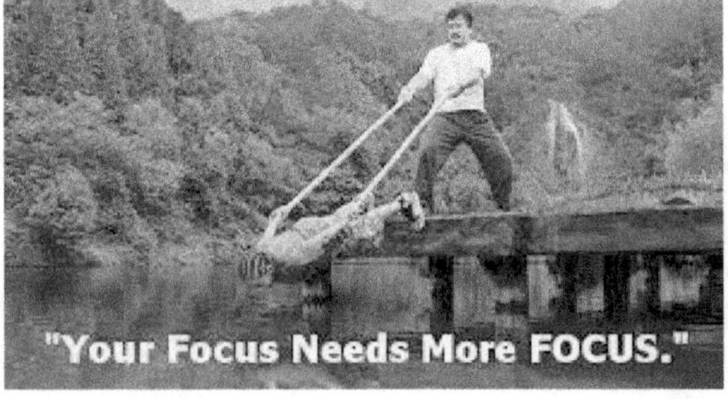

OK, then what is "the appropriate amount of time" for a workout? It will all depend on the practitioner, and there is no one set of answers. A good one-hour workout may be excellent for most beginners and intermediate practitioners. However, one hour is definitely too short for professional instructors and most serious practitioners. On the other hand, this can be too long for children and senior practitioners over seventy years old.

Next we must ask about quality. So, what makes a karate training session good and beneficial? Sweating a lot? Doing a thousand kicks and punches? I hope these are not your answers. I expect the following four elements to exist in all of my training: breathing, focus, accuracy, and *bujutsu*. Let's briefly look at these four elements.

1. Breathing

I have written on this subject in the past, so I will not go very deeply into the technical part of how to breathe correctly here. But, I must emphasize that deep breathing must be exercised in all our training and eventually in our life outside of our training.

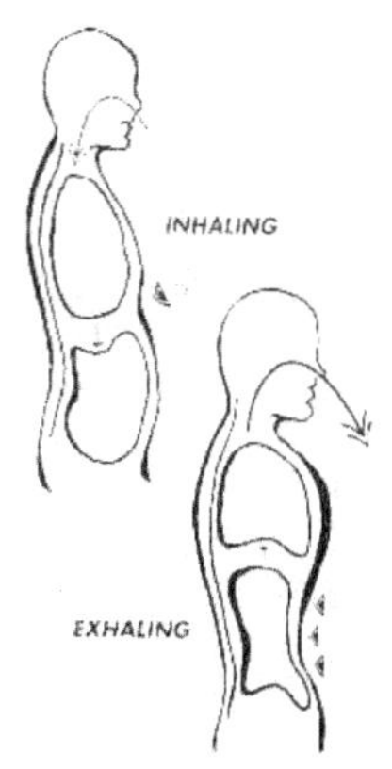

Even though breathing is such a "natural" action, over ninety percent of people are not breathing correctly. In short, their breathing is too shallow or too short. One hint is that you need to use your diaphragm and practice what we call *belly breathing*. Another hint is that you breathe in when you contract and breathe out when you relax or extend your muscles. This sounds counterintuitive, but it is very easy to exercise if you practice a little.

2. Focus

According to *Merriam-Webster's Collegiate Dictionary, Eleventh Edition*, this word is defined as "a state or condition permitting clear perception or understanding." You can do this with your body, such as when you focus your power as you punch; however, we are mainly talking about mental attitude and state here. In other words, you must be thinking that you are practicing karate all throughout the training. You may get tired and slow down physically, but your mind must be as sharp and clear as when you started. If you do not have this mental state, the effects and benefit of the training will be greatly reduced.

3. Accuracy

This is something many people forget or put on the back burner when they get tired. Your kicks become very sloppy when you do a thousand of them per session. Your *kata* (形) becomes noticeably inaccurate after three hours of training. In fact, you will actually get worse the more you practice this way.

This may be shocking for a devoted practitioner, but the concept is not that difficult to understand. If you repeat a wrong technique hundreds or thousands of times, it will become firmly ingrained as your technique. Once a certain physical movement (technique) is learned by your body, it will be extremely difficult to change or modify. I am sure many readers have experienced this and understand what I am talking about.

Trying to keep your techniques correct requires a lot of focus. In addition, a strong commitment to not letting your body dictate your movements is also necessary. Your mind must be in control at all times as you execute the body movements. Once your body acquires the correct techniques, you get into a state in which you can finally deliver correct techniques without thinking.

4. *Bujutsu*

This word refers to the fighting methods that were used by the samurai. In these modern times, there are no longer any samurai, but we have inherited *bujutsu* (武術), which are martial arts such as kenjutsu (剣術, 'sword arts'), sojutsu (槍術, 'spear arts'), jujutsu (柔術, 'grappling arts'), etc. Karate was not introduced into mainland Japan until the twentieth century, but it was developed as *bujutsu* on Okinawa.

If you are a practitioner of sport karate, then this factor may not be of interest to you. On the other hand, if you are a traditional *karateka* (空手家), or if you consider yourself a martial artist, the factor I am touching on here is mandatory and is

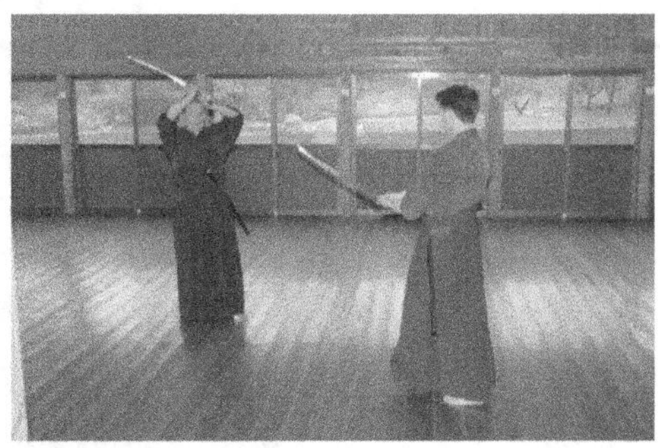

also a key to understanding the answer I provided at the beginning of this chapter.

So, what is the base concept of *bujutsu*? You may have a different answer, but for me, it is life or death. It is similar to the mentality of a soldier who goes onto the battlefield. If you are careless, you get killed. This mentality is also taught to police officers.

You will learn this concept quickly if you are sent to the battlefield, but it is difficult to grasp in our peaceful life. Therefore, it is important that you include this concept in your training so that your techniques can be used in a life-or-death situation. If you are in this type of situation, you will not want your techniques to be sloppy as this may result in your death.

This seriousness separates *bujutsu* from sports. It is true that some people, especially professional athletic devotees, are as serious as *bujutsuka* (武術家), but the objectives are totally different. For a martial artist, it is life or death. For an athlete, it is money, praise, and/or recognition. I am not talking down to athletes or sports practitioners; I am just stating the fact that the level of seriousness must be different. If you claim to be a martial artist, you must have this state of mind.

Conclusion

If you can apply all four factors to your training, then I would say that your training can be very effective, even if it is only five minutes long. You can probably practice a *kata* several times in five minutes. You can also run a *kata* a hundred times in one hour. But, I certainly consider the quality and benefit of running a *kata* a handful of times with full focus of body and mind to easily exceed that of running a *kata* a hundred times without focus or commitment.

Most of us are busy in our daily lives as we have many other duties and responsibilities. It is also true that we all have only twenty-four hours a day. It is easy for us to say, “Hey, I have no time for training today.” But, can you not find just five minutes in your day? If so, put a hundred percent into your five-minute workout and make it count. Now you have no excuse for not training daily.

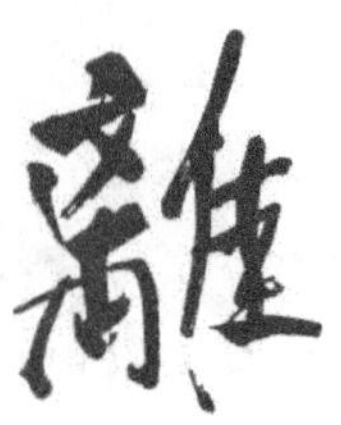

Chapter Two
第二章

Are Big Calluses Necessary in Budo Karate?
空手に拳ダコは必要か？

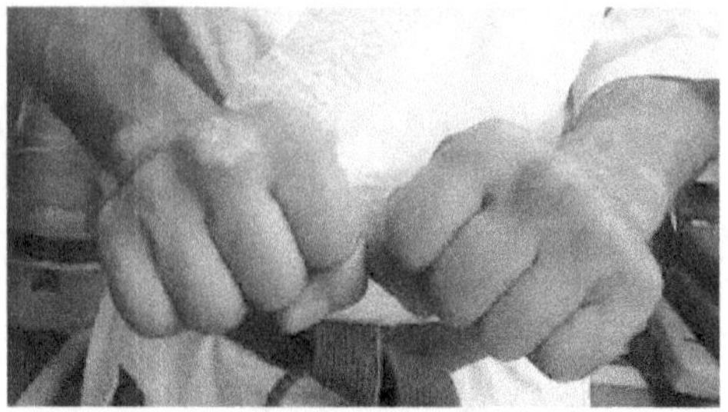

The big knuckles—the correct term is *calluses*—that a *karateka* develops on his hands are called *kendako* (拳ダコ) in Japanese. They are usually developed on the index and middle fingers. Typically, the young *karateka* proudly shows off the bulging and discolored knuckles as proof of his hard training. They are almost like a war medal or a qualification badge. We all know how these knuckles are developed. They become big from pounding thousands of times on a piece of karate training equipment called a *makiwara* (巻藁).

The question I would like to raise here is whether or not these big knuckles are really necessary for a *karateka* to be called an expert. The thoughts I share here are purely my own personal opinions. I do not claim that what I am proposing is correct, but one thing I can say is that I have a very strong opinion about this subject.

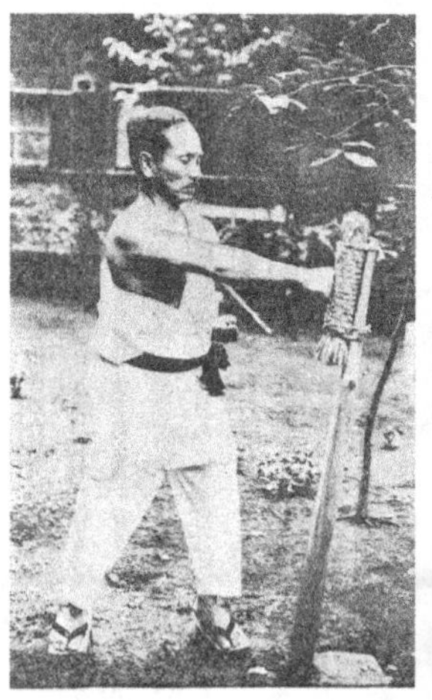

The *makiwara* has become an iconic training tool of karate. It seems that every dojo must have at least one *makiwara* to claim its legitimacy. Most sensei of the dojo I have visited have almost always very enthusiastically shown me their *makiwara*. *Makiwara* come in various heights, thicknesses, and styles, and I have already written about training with a *makiwara* in my book *Shotokan Myths*. If you are interested in this subject, please refer to Chapter 4: "Makiwara" of that book (available in both paperback and electronic format through *Amazon*).

In fact, I must say that *makiwara* training is one of the most popular topics that the *karateka* wishes to discuss. I am a main contributor at Karate Coaching (www.karatecoaching.com), the world's most advanced and comprehensive online karate instruction service provider. The editor of that service has told me that the demonstration clip of my *makiwara* training has received the most attention.

As a conclusion in Chapter 4 of *Shotokan Myths*, I wrote in essence that senior *yudansha* (有段者, 'black belts') need to graduate from *makiwara* training and move on to the next level of training. I almost wrote that *makiwara* training was no longer needed for senior practitioners but decided not to as I was afraid my true meaning would be misunderstood by such a comment.

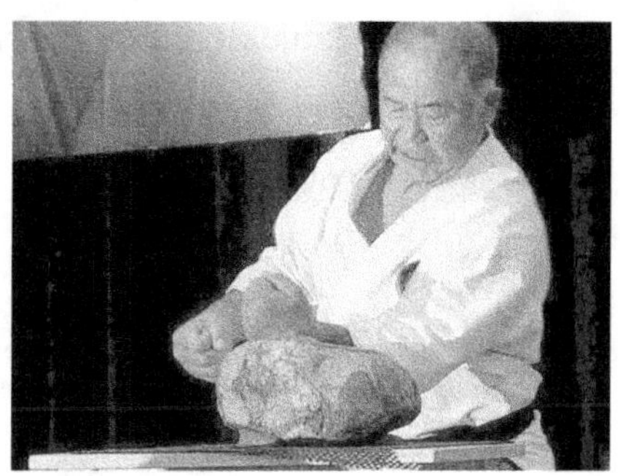

It is true that many senior instructors, including some world-famous ones, are believers in *makiwara* training. These instructors include Gichin Funakoshi (船越義珍, 1868–1957), the founder of Shotokan (松濤館); Masutatsu Oyama (大山倍達, 1923–1994), the founder of Kyokushinkai (極真会); Tetsuhiko Asai (浅井哲彦, 1935–2006), the founder of Asai Ryu (浅井流); and Morio Higaonna (東恩納盛男, 1938– [photo above]), who is a tenth *dan* in Goju Ryu (剛柔流). It is well known that both Master Higaonna and Master Oyama have (or had) huge knuckles. I am not completely against *makiwara* training. These masters are professionals as well as karate experts, so their knuckles are fitting, and there is nothing wrong with that.

That said, however, I still say no to the original question as to whether or not we need big knuckles. I am sure many readers will wonder why I say this. Many of you will probably argue that by having big knuckles, the effectiveness (destructive power) of the practitioner's fists will increase. One *karateka* told me, "Sensei, a fist with big knuckles is like having a .44 Magnum gun. If you have untrained knuckles, you cannot break bricks or a stack of ten tiles. A fist with small knuckles would be like a .22 pistol." Even though I am not sure if the analogy is quite accurate, in essence I agree with what he was trying to tell me.

Even so, I still say we do not need a set of big knuckles in order to be qualified as a senior *karateka*. You do not need more than a .22 pistol to kill an assailant in a standard self-defense situation. Let me explain why I make the claim that we do not need big knuckles.

1. Misplaced Emphasis

The biggest myth regarding huge knuckles is that they are toughened to the point at which they can knock out any opponent. However, I must say that simply having big knuckles does not necessarily translate into a destructive or even scary punch. A .44 Magnum gun does have tremendous firepower, no matter who shoots it. But, you must remember that it is a gun, and a punch is a different story altogether.

In order to have an effective or devastating punch, one must learn how to punch correctly. A big, toughened fist can be a good tool, or at least a scary-looking one, but it must be backed up by good punching technique to make it effective. If your punch is slow or is delivered poorly, then the size and hardness of your fist will not matter. In fact, if you want something for self-protection, it would be more useful to carry a baseball bat or a stick.

If you are a professional *karateka* who can train for four or more hours daily, then it is not a problem to spend fifteen minutes or more of that time punching a *makiwara*. However, I assume that most readers can only train two or three times a week and that each training period is ninety minutes or less. In this situation, I hate to see a practitioner spend fifteen valuable minutes pounding on a *makiwara*. Don't you think spending that time on *kihon* (基本) or *kata* would be more productive for your karate improvement?

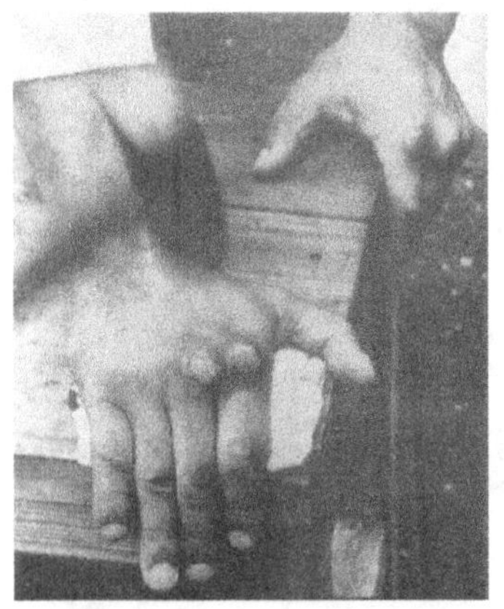

2. Perceived Arrogance and Intimidation

Secondly, I do not think the idea of showing off deformed knuckles is in line with the *karatedo* (空手道) value called *humility*. This is the same concept as not showing off one's black belt in public.

When I would be in business meetings in Japan, I used to hide my hands or position them so that the discolored knuckles would not be visible. It was not because I was embarrassed by my fists or felt ashamed of my karate training. In Japan, people would easily deduce what the condition of my fists meant, and I did not want to intimidate anyone. It may sound as if I'm exaggerating, but it would be like placing a knife on a negotiation table. I do not think the sight of big knuckles brings any pleasure to anyone who is not a *karateka*.

3. Lack of Refinement

The third reason is the most important. As we advance in our skill level of karate, we need to graduate from crude punching and overt techniques to more advanced techniques. These are less visible and are more like piercing or tapping techniques that are mainly aimed at the *kyusho* (急所, 'vital points'), which are the critical parts of the body.

The *kyusho*, such as the eyes, neck, ears, and groin, are typically soft, so toughened fists and hands are not necessary to deliver an effective attack. When striking these targets, the fist, knife hand, fingertips, and wrist are all effective, even if they are not toughened.

In addition, once you learn the one-inch punching technique, you no longer need to smash your fist into an opponent to knock him down. Of course, this is the ultimate technique, but it is not magic, and anyone can learn it.

4. Potential Health Issues

Another reason I discourage people from developing big knuckles is the ill consequences it may bring about. I am afraid deformed knuckles could result in symptoms of arthritis when the practitioner gets old. I do not have any medical expertise or scientific data on this, so I would like to receive reader input if possible.

5. Poor Aesthetics

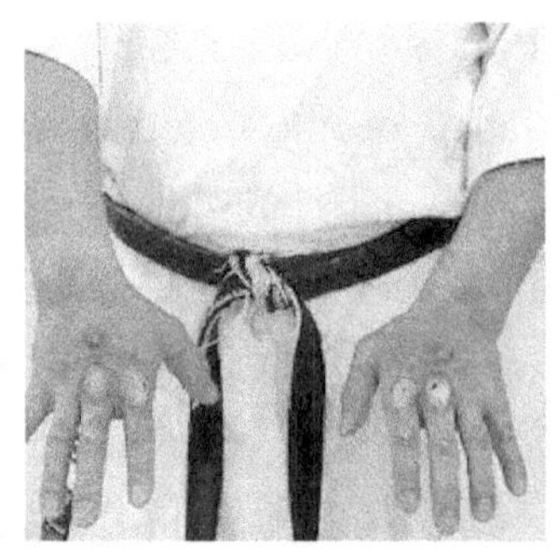

Lastly, I am sort of a romanticist. Frankly, I hate to see our fists deformed and made to look like those of a zombie (see the photo to the right). This is far from beautiful, and I detest it. Earlier I explained that toughened fists are not necessary to deliver an effective karate technique. So, why would you want to deform your fists?

Karate is a gentleman's art, and this is exactly what Funakoshi wanted. For the reasons listed above, it is my strong belief that ugly fists do not fit in with the art of *karatedo*. These are my personal opinions and the feelings I have toward *kendako*.

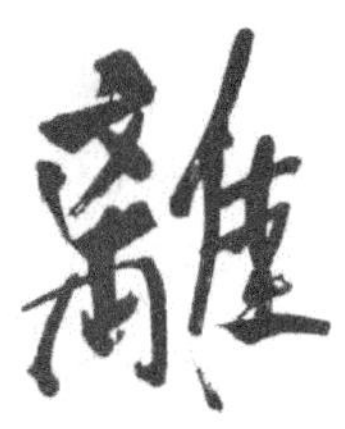

Chapter Three
第三章

What Does "There Is No Gyaku Zuki in Karate" Mean?
「空手に逆突きは無し」とは如何なる意味か？

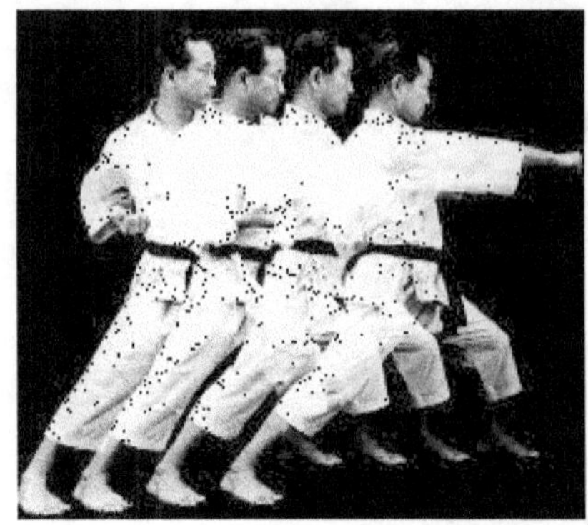

Have you ever heard your sensei say that there is no *gyaku zuki* (逆突き) in karate? I suspect most readers, who I assume are Shotokan practitioners, have not heard this. If you have had some exposure to Okinawan karate styles, you may have heard it, but for Shotokan practitioners, I am sure this statement does not make sense.

I will explain what this puzzling statement means, but first I would like to evaluate how we (or most of us) were taught to execute a *gyaku zuki*. I will try to describe the mechanics of performing *gyaku zuki*, but I find it very difficult to do so, especially in English, as I do not have the necessary skill level in this language. I would hope that my advanced readers (*shodan* and above) know the mechanics so that they can follow my explanation here.

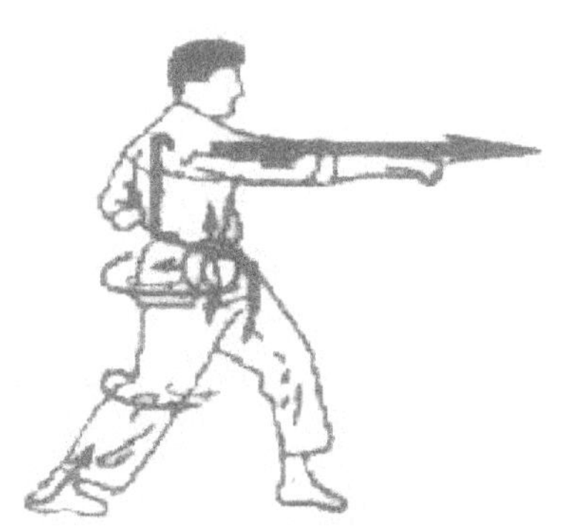

First, think of the punch as it is thrown from a stationary stance, say, *zenkutsu dachi* (前屈立ち). You would most likely perform *gedan barai* (下段払い)—this could be any *uke* (受け, 'block')—from *hanmi* (半身, 'half-facing position') with your front hand forward and your rear hand pulled way back. From this position, you rotate your hips to kick-start your punch. As the hips turn, your rear shoulder moves forward, and your punch shoots out. Your arm ends up tense and in a fully extended position as your hip position ends in *shomen* (正面, 'full-facing position').

I am sure you have practiced this *gyaku zuki* exercise hundreds, or even thousands, of times in the past. When your hips lock into *shomen*, and your *gyaku zuki* also locks in at the same time, you feel the excellent *kime* (極め) and power of this punch.

Let us look at an *ido* (移動, 'shifting' or 'movement') situation. Typically, you would take a step forward as you deliver *gyaku zuki*. Moving backward is harder, but the basic concept is the same. Let's make it an easy situation by starting from the *gyaku zuki* position with our punching arm fully extended and breaking up the forward step into two stages.

The first stage is to pull up the rear foot to meet the front foot in *heisoku dachi* (閉足立ち, 'closed-foot stance'). At this stage, you relax your extended arm a little and may even open your fist into a *tate shuto uke* (縦手刀受け, 'vertical knife-hand block') position. The hips remain in *shomen* with the rear fist still kept at the rear hip.

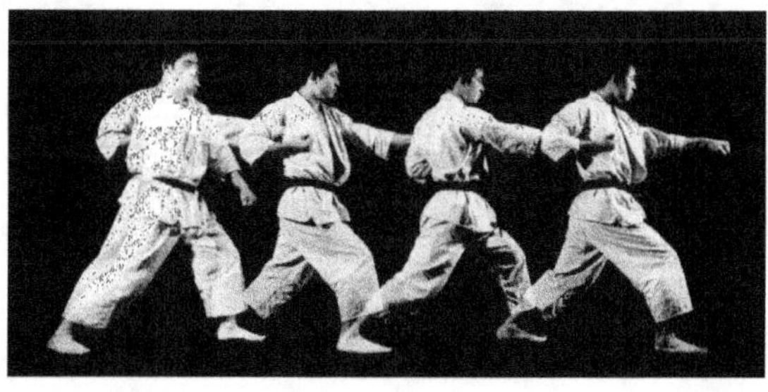

The second stage requires some intricate hip movements. As you move the advancing foot forward, the hip of the advancing side moves forward, but you keep the other hip in position; thus, you are in *hanmi* as you step forward. By the time the advancing foot reaches the target position to assume *zenkutsu dachi*, your rear hip is still behind with the rear fist attached to it. As soon as that final position is assumed, you quickly turn your hips followed by the rear shoulder, which puts you in *shomen*, and the *gyaku zuki* is quickly executed at this point. This final movement is the same as the mechanics that were described for the stationary *gyaku zuki* position earlier.

I am pretty sure that most readers will agree with the explanation given above regarding the mechanics of a *gyaku zuki* performed while shifting or taking a step forward. How about if I tell you that these mechanics are incorrect or, at best, are the worst method when viewed from a *budo* (武道, 'martial arts') perspective? I suspect most of you would not agree or would not understand why I would say such a "crazy" thing. I am aware that now I am obligated to explain myself in a way that you will understand, so I am happy to share the correct mechanics for *gyaku zuki* in *budo* karate.

Unfortunately, the main issue is that the way *gyaku zuki* has been taught to us for all these years is improper, which means that most of us are not aware of the problem. So, you may be asking yourself what problem I am even talking about. Believe it or not, in *budo* karate, *gyaku zuki* must be applied with little to no hip rotation. This statement must come as a surprise to most readers, so we need to continue so you will see what I am talking about.

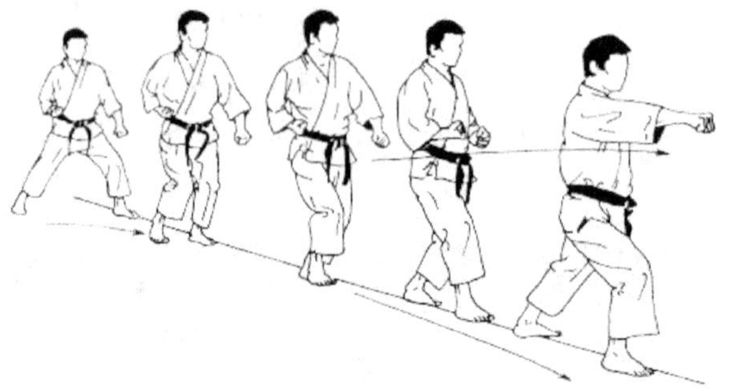

I suspect you were taught not to rotate your hips when executing *oi zuki* (追い突き), and I am sure you will agree that *oi zuki* is thrown without hip rotation. In short, *gyaku zuki* must be thrown in the same manner. In other words, it must be thrown with the hip pushing forward and with very little hip rotation.

I hope the reader can understand this important hip movement that I call *hip pushing*. When you execute *oi zuki* while shifting the body forward, the majority of the power in your punch does not come from your punching arm or shoulder, as you know. The majority of the power comes from body shifting and also from the final push of the hips as you extend your punching arm.

The mechanics of pushing the hips forward cause the pelvis to be tucked under rather than pushed back. By looking at a side view of the pelvis, you will understand that tucking means pushing the bottom part of the pelvis forward. The hip joint (the part where the bones of the pelvis and thigh are connected) is located toward the bottom of the pelvis; thus, to tuck forward, you push the leg part forward as you keep the upper part of the pelvis stationary.

The reason you want to tuck becomes clear once you learn the mechanics of power generation. Having this correct bone structure allows you to generate more power by transmitting the power that was generated by the legs. Having the pelvis leaning forward (the opposite of having it tucked under), however, makes it so that the bone structure of the legs and hip area prevents the power that was generated by the legs from being transmitted to the extended arm, causing it to dissipate. As the mechanics of *gyaku zuki* here are almost identical to those of *oi zuki*, there is no reason to separate these two punches. It is like punching with your left fist or punching with your right fist. This is the reason we say there is no *gyaku zuki*.

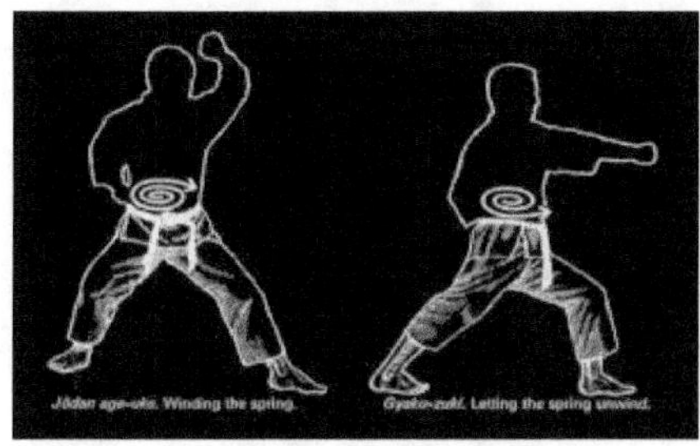

But, you may argue, "Well, how about when you execute an *uke* first and then a *gyaku zuki* counter? We learned to assume a large *hanmi* while performing the *uke* and before executing *gyaku zuki*. Do you claim that this is wrong?" This is a good question. My answer to this is that these mechanics are not wrong, but, at the same time, this should be a last resort. To explain why this is the case, I need to talk about tempo in *kumite* (組手, 'sparring'). In other words, there are several different tempos between the techniques of the attacker and the defender. So, in the event that the attacker steps in with a *jodan* (上段, 'high level') punch, the following would be the different tempos for the defender's block and counter:

1. The most popular technique in Shotokan karate would be *age uke* (挙げ受け, 'rising block') followed by *gyaku zuki*. This technique of using each arm consecutively is a two-count tempo, which happens to be the slowest.
2. A more challenging technique would be *age uke* immediately followed by *uraken uchi* (裏拳打ち, 'backfist') with the same arm. This technique is a one-and-a-half-count tempo, which is faster.
3. A technique that is not as popular but is faster than the preceding two methods would be *age uke* and *gyaku zuki* delivered simultaneously. This technique is a one-count tempo since you deliver the counter as you are executing the block.

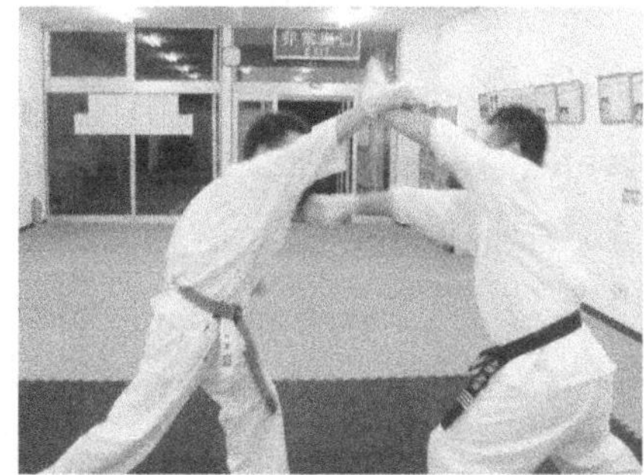

There are other one-count techniques. One example is *jowan osae uke* (上腕抑え受け, 'forearm pressing block') and simultaneous *kentsui uchi* (拳槌打ち, 'hammer-fist strike') using the same arm. Another example can be found in the first move of Bassai Dai (抜塞大).

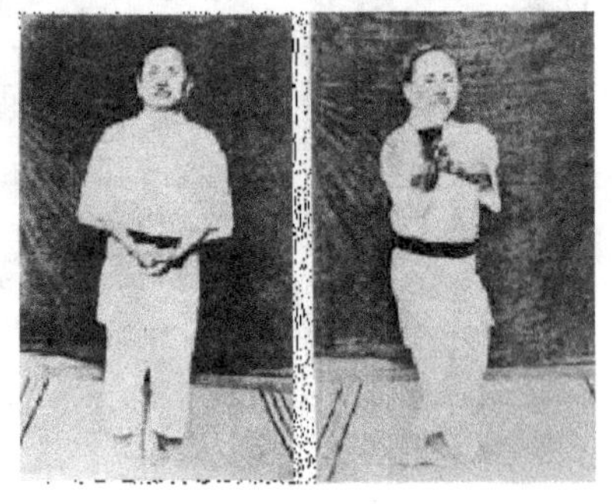

In the *kata*, you were probably taught that the right fist is a *chudan uchi uke* (中段内受け, 'inside middle block') and that the left hand is only a *soete* (添え手, 'accompanying hand') placed against the right forearm. In this technique, your left hand is, in fact, executing *osae uke* (抑え受け, 'pressing block') against the opponent's punching arm (at the wrist or elbow), and your right fist is simultaneously executing *uraken uchi* to the opponent's *jodan*.

There are many other one-count techniques in *kumite*, but I will not go into these here as I would like to explain the concept of *budo gyaku zuki*.

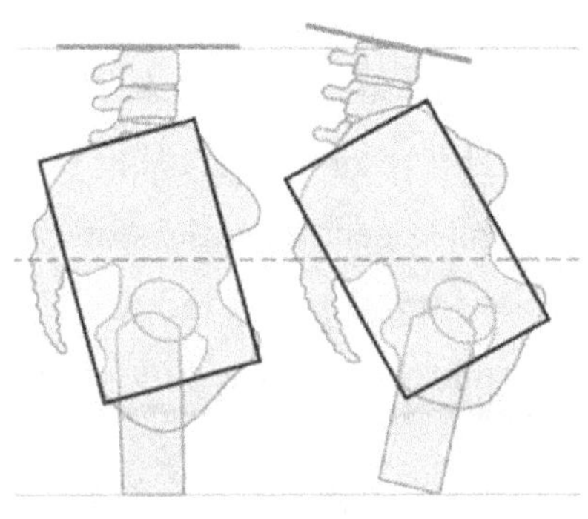

So, let's get back to the one-count technique explained in the third example on the previous page, which is *age uke* and *gyaku zuki* delivered simultaneously. When you execute this technique, it is obvious that you could not rotate your hips much even if you wanted to. What you need to do is tuck in the pelvis as described earlier with the *oi zuki* technique. As you can see, one-count tempo in *kumite* is the fastest of the three options previously described.

Though the first one, *age uke* followed by *gyaku zuki*, is an option, it is the slowest and least desirable of the three. First of all, it takes too much time to rotate your hips to deliver *gyaku zuki*. Secondly, and more importantly, this method generates surprisingly less power in your counterattack. Yes, less power, and I'll explain why.

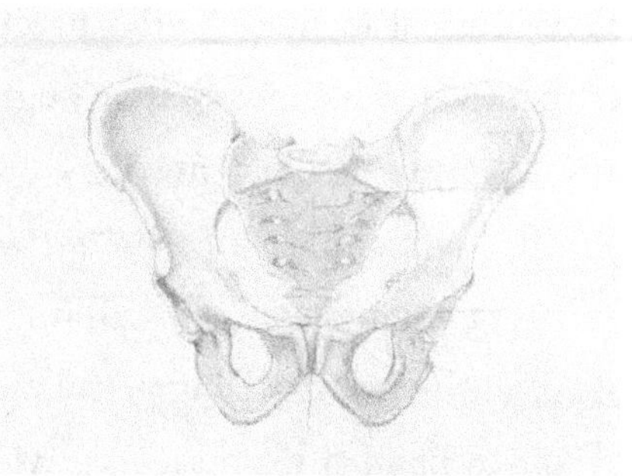

It is a very simple matter of physics. To execute *gyaku zuki* after an *uke*, you must stop shifting your body. Of course, this is why you need to rotate your hips significantly to generate power. If you could execute *gyaku zuki* by shifting your body forward, you could generate much more power than you would with the hip rotation alone.

However, a wise reader will point out, "Yeah, but you are stepping backward, so body shifting will not project the energy forward." You are one hundred percent correct, so you do not want to step backward in *kumite*. Just as with the two-count tempo (*uke* followed by *gyaku zuki*), stepping backward should be the defender's last resort. Unfortunately, in most Shotokan dojo, both beginning and advanced students are taught this least desirable option day in and day out.

In order to generate power with the quickest timing, the defender must step in just like what we find in the first move of Bassai Dai (simultaneous *osae uke* and *uraken uchi*). Why is this not more commonly taught? That is a good question, and this is the very reason I have written this chapter.

In our organization, Asai Shotokan Association International (ASAI), we have kept *sanbon kumite* (三本組手, 'three-attack sparring') but only for the novice who needs to learn the fundamental movements of *kihon kumite* (基本組手, 'basic sparring'). We have dropped *gohon kumite* (五本組手, 'five-attack sparring') altogether as it requires stepping backward five times, which we do not believe to be a good exercise.

As soon as the student advances to eighth *kyu*, we teach him to practice only

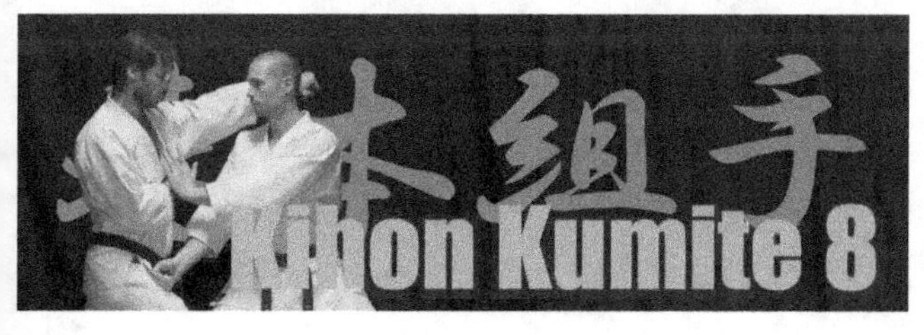

kihon ippon kumite (基本一本組手, 'basic single-attack sparring'). Initially, the student is allowed to step backward as this is the easiest technique after practicing *sanbon kumite*. Eventually, the student is taught to step backward at an angle, then to step sideways, and finally to step forward (yes, toward the attacker).

If you examine all the *kata* we practice, you will see only a few backward-stepping techniques. You will find that most techniques, even in the Heian (平安) *kata*, are forward-stepping techniques. There are also many *morote waza* (諸手技, 'two-handed techniques'), which are very advanced techniques, in our *kata*, including the Heian *kata*. This is also a very interesting subject, but I will not go into it as the subject of this chapter is *gyaku zuki*.

You may be asking, "How about when an opponent grabs your hand? In that case, would you not pull the other fist back with your hip so you can deliver a strong *gyaku zuki*?" Yes, you can do this, but you can also do this without rotating your hips. It is faster and more effective.

Then, you may ask, "Is it wrong to assume *hanmi*?" My answer is that *hanmi* is not just for setting up *gyaku zuki* but for other purposes, as well. One of these is to expose less of your frontal area by turning your body at an angle. Another may be to position yourself to execute *hikite* (引き手) or *nagashi uke* (流し受け).

It is not wrong to execute *gyaku zuki* with a big hip rotation, but it takes too much time and thus is not desirable in a *budo* situation. Executing *gyaku zuki* without the hip rotation may be more difficult to master, but if you can generate the same or more power with less hip movement, then the punch can be delivered much faster. Now, do you not agree that this method is much more desirable and effective?

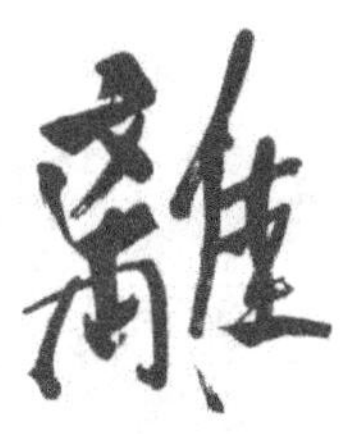

Chapter Four
第四章

Are Squat Kicks Medically Harmful?
スクワットキックは医学的に危険か？

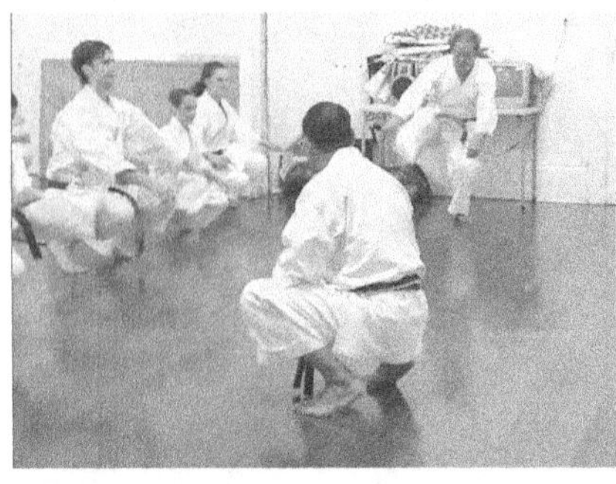

I have posted many video clips of the April 2016 training at Goiânia, Brazil, on my *Facebook* page. One of these clips showed squat kicks. Instead of explaining what these are, I will give you the URL here so you can see the clip for yourself: www.youtube.com/watch?v=MEGW4FMHMpQ.

Some of those who have seen this exercise have criticized it, saying that it is medically harmful to the knees. I expected these negative comments, and this is why I decided to write this chapter to explain why I have done and still do this exercise.

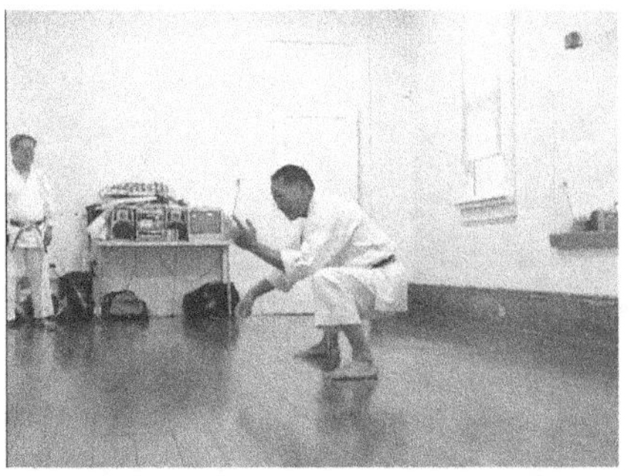

So, you may be asking whether or not their claim is accurate, and my answer is yes and no. The answer can be yes for those practitioners whose legs and lower body are not strong enough or who do not know the correct way of doing this exercise. It can harm their knees if tried repeatedly. On the other hand, for those who know the correct method of execution and have developed a strong lower body, then my answer is a resounding no. Squat kicks will not harm their knees at all.

I emphasize that this exercise is not medically harmful if it is done properly. I guarantee that it will not harm your knees. I think that regularly jogging on a

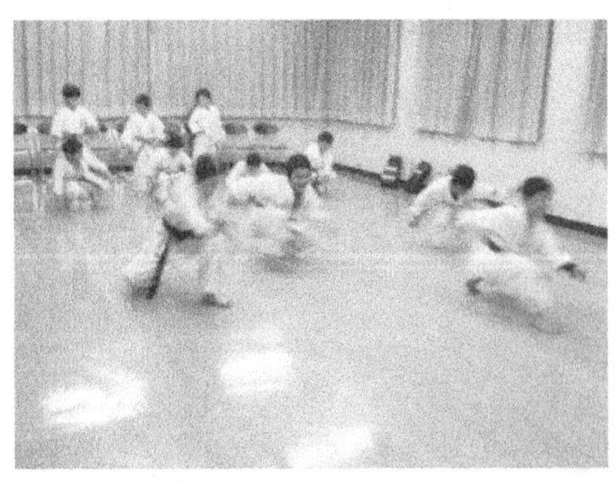

hard paved road would give you more knee problems than this exercise. You may be asking how I can guarantee this. I can because there are at least two people I know who have used this type of kicking exercise for many years and have done so well into their sixties. These two people are Master Asai and I.

Of course, Master Asai had much better form than I, but I, being sixty-nine years old as of July 2016, have included fifty squat kicks in my daily self-training menu for over fifteen years. So, I have done these kicks thousands of times over the last fifteen years and so far have had no problems with my knees or legs. Master Asai told me he had included this exercise in his daily self-training, as well, and, as far as I know, he did not develop any knee or leg problems, either.

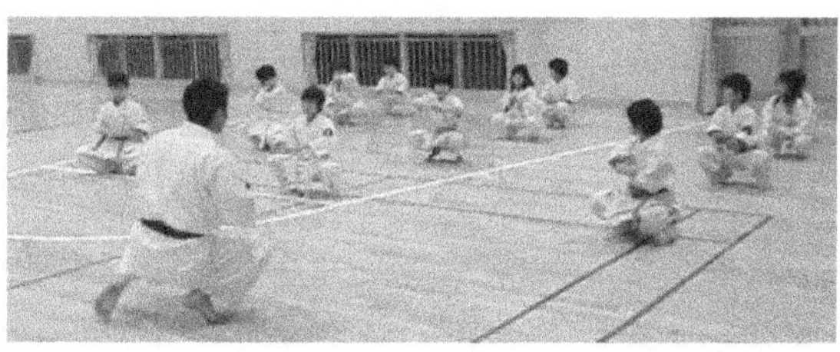

How can we do this exercise without harming our knees? Is it because we are Japanese? Are we the exception? I must say no. Yes, our daily lifestyle of frequent squatting and *seiza* (正座) gives us an advantage because it builds strong legs and a strong lower body. However, intense repetition of this exercise by a regular Japanese student may still result in a knee injury if he is not properly conditioned. We are not medically exempt. We happen to have trained our legs and have learned the correct way to execute this type of kicking. The key point here is not having strong legs but rather knowing how to do the exercise correctly. This is a technique that needs to be learned and acquired.

Asai karate techniques are at the master-class level. They can be compared to the gold-medal techniques of Olympic gymnastics. You can easily imagine that having a high school gymnast do one of the gold-medal techniques could damage his body. But, you cannot say that the gold-medal technique itself is medically harmful an Olympic gymnast. Olympic gymnasts have trained their bodies for just such a technique and, more importantly, have learned the correct way to do the technique.

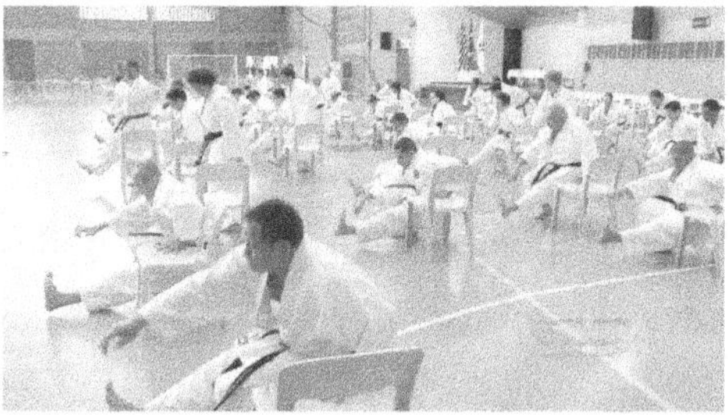

So, at my seminars, I share these Asai Ryu ("gold-medal") techniques with the participants to show how much more they need to train to get up to the Asai karate level. If it sounds as though

I am bragging about Asai karate, this is definitely not my true intention. I am just stating the fact that Asai karate is an advanced form of Shotokan karate, and you can see this (though you may not be thoroughly convinced) in the complexity and difficulty of the techniques found in Asai *kata* such as Joko (常行), Kakuyoku (鶴翼), Hachimon (八門), Suishu (水手), Seiryu (青龍), Rakuyo (落葉), Fushu (風手), Kashu (火手), or Roshu (浪手), to name a few.

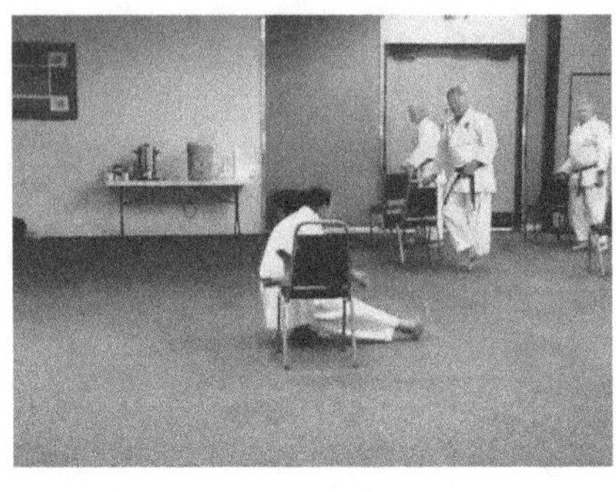

So, how am I able to execute this challenging kick that is claimed to be medically harmful by some? I could try to write several key points of the technique here. Initially, I thought I would do that but decided not to because I realized that one cannot learn a high-level technique by just reading an explanation. My explanation may even give you the wrong impression or idea. If you saw the video showing the squat kicks with your own eyes, you know how they are performed. But, if you did not see the technique, then understanding it from a written description will be impossible.

Having said that, I am not hiding the "secret" of this technique. In fact, I want to show and share more. This is exactly why I am spending the time right now to write this chapter instead of ignoring the criticism, which would have been much easier to do. What I recommend is that you find an opportunity to participate in one of my seminars. See my technique and try it with me. You can ask questions and discover how to do it correctly.

It is like learning to ride a bike. You have to get on the bike and fall off several times before you learn how to ride it. It is also like learning how to swim. You need to jump into the water to learn. You cannot learn how to swim by reading a how-to-swim article.

The fact is that the squat kick we did in the video is far from being a gold-medal technique or any sort of Olympic-level technique. I consider it to be an intermediate-level technique that any senior-ranking karate practitioner should be

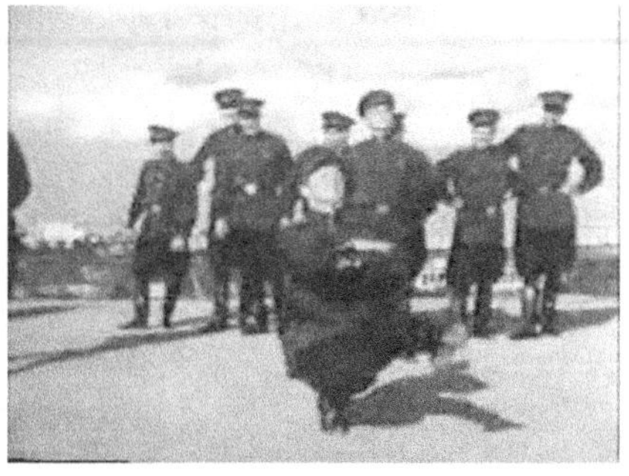

able to do (with the exception of those who suffer from knee problems, of course). If you do not believe my statement, I would like you to watch this video of Russian soldiers doing the famous Cossack dance: www.youtube.com/watch?v=gqEtq34dSUo.

This type of exercise is found not only in Russia but also in Ukrainian folk dance: www.youtube.com/watch?v=t9Gpm62kqO0.

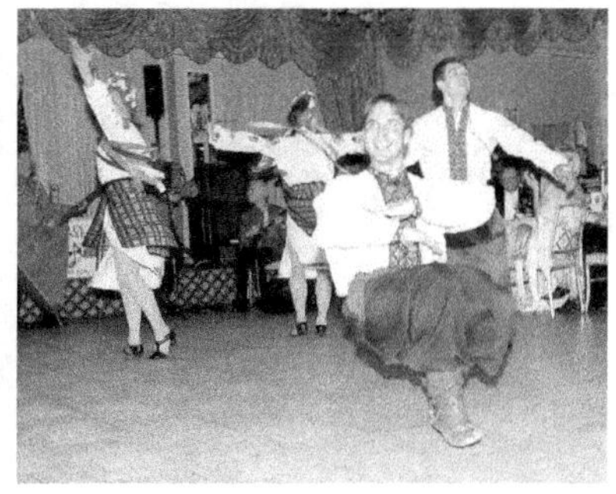

If this were bad for their knees, then the Russian army and the Ukrainian people would never allow them to engage in such a dance. What they are doing here cannot be medically harmful. If these soldiers and dancers can do this, then why not martial artists?

To prepare for this exercise, we do many other exercises, including bunny hops, the duck walk, jumping squats, one-legged squats, and kicks from a kneeling position. In order to master this technique, all *karateka* must strengthen their lower body first.

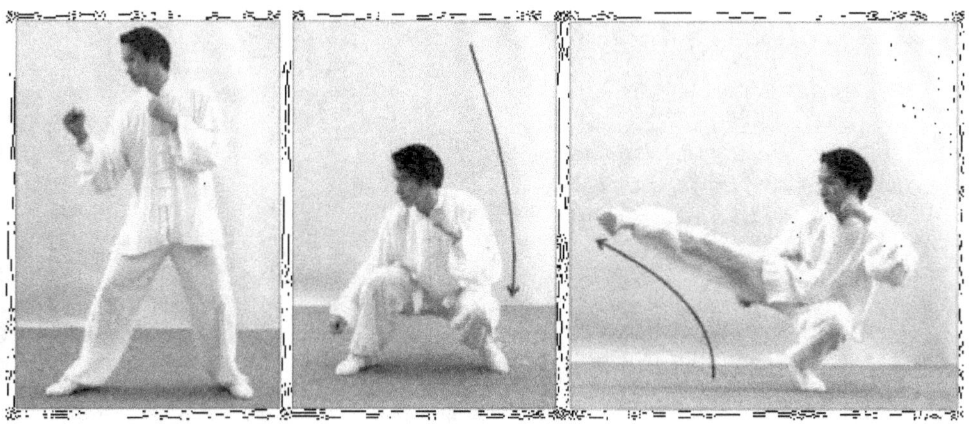

I ask everyone to train harder so that instead of criticizing a difficult exercise, you can learn to do it, too. Isn't it better to improve your karate level than to stay at the same level?

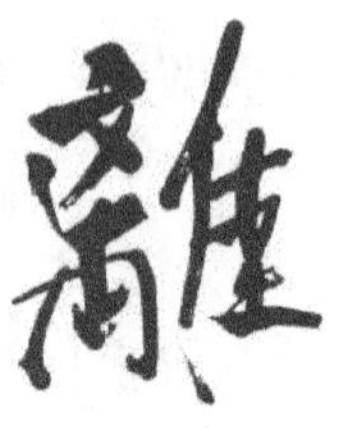

Chapter Five
第五章

Speed Is Unnecessary in Budo Karate
武道空手にスピードは不必要だ

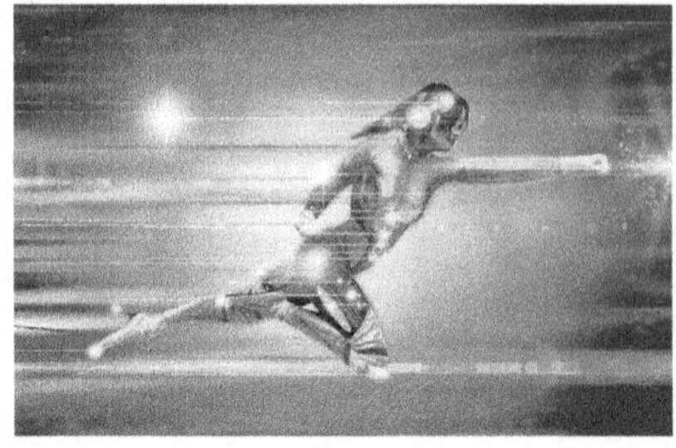

Yes, the title of this chapter is "Speed Is Unnecessary in Budo Karate." I am aware that this title will cause some controversy. Some people will consider my claim to be ridiculous or utter nonsense as no sensible person would believe that speed is not necessary in karate.

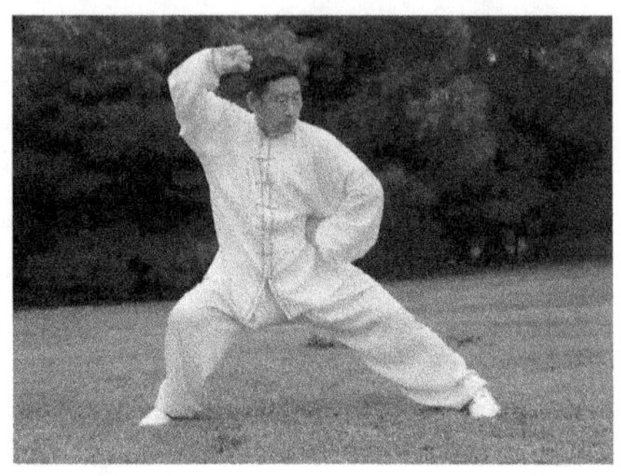

Am I saying we need to move slowly as in tai chi (formerly *tai chi chuan* or *tàijíquán* [太極拳])? No, I am not saying this. However, there is truth to this method of training if one considers tai chi to be a martial art. Without going too far into why the movements of tai chi are performed so slowly, although this is an interesting subject, I would like to explain that speed is not the most important aspect, nor is it even of secondary importance, in karate. I can just see the look of surprise on many readers' faces.

Before I give my explanation, I must clarify that the karate I am referring to is strictly *budo* karate, not sport karate. Many people do not understand this distinction or realize that there is a big difference between these two kinds of karate. Sport karate, though this explanation may be unnecessary, is *kyogi* (競技, 'contest' or 'tournament') karate. It is similar to a hundred-meter dash, where the competitors line up on the same line, start at the same gunshot, and run the same distance. In these two sports, speed is very important. The faster you can execute *gyaku zuki*, *oi zuki*, *mae geri*, etc., the better chance you have to score a point.

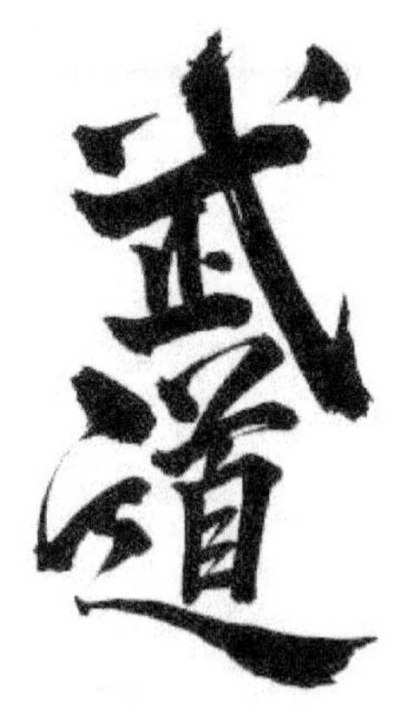

Budo karate, on the other hand, is more like a street fight (or other similar scenario). In *budo* karate, we practice with the mentality that there is not a set distance between us and the opponent or opponents. In a street fight, there is no "*Hajime*!" (始め, 'begin') command. Here, the first punch, shove, kick, etc., can happen at any time. You need to be ready, which means that you need to take the following actions before the fight even begins:

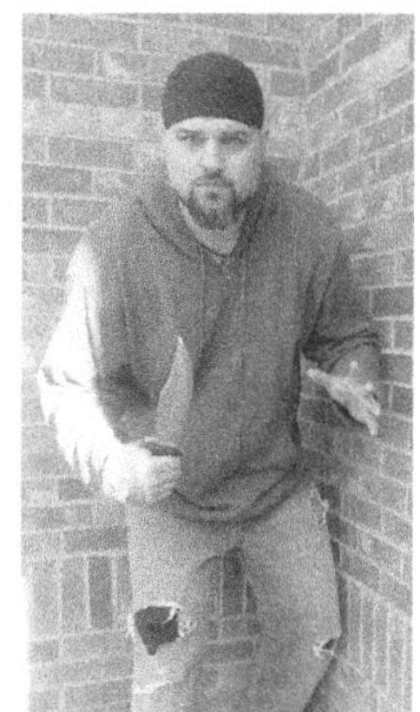

1. Know if there is only one opponent or multiple opponents, and know exactly where they are.
2. Determine if the opponent is armed or unarmed. If he is armed, find out exactly what weapon(s) he has to the best of your ability. Whether the opponent has a knife or a gun can very easily change the outcome of the fight. You need to know this as it will affect the next point: distance.
3. Assume and control the distance that is most favorable to you before the first attack is thrown (whether by you or the opponent).
4. Keep your mind clear and calm so that you can make the right decisions regarding your next moves. You need to decide if you want to avoid the fight or if you need to engage. If you engage, you need to decide if you will throw the first strike or if you will tactically force the opponent to strike first. If you want to avoid the fight, then you need to choose between running away or talking it out, for instance. Of course, there are many other options, but the process is the same. You need to be able to make the right decision in a very short period of time.

Before the actual fight starts, you need to take these steps, and maybe more, to prepare. To survive in street combat, I am sure you will agree that preparation and control of the situation are the most important points.

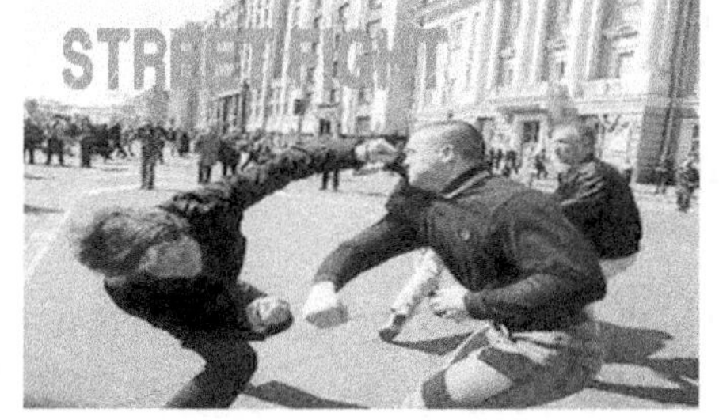

Most readers, I expect, will now understand why I say that speed is not the most

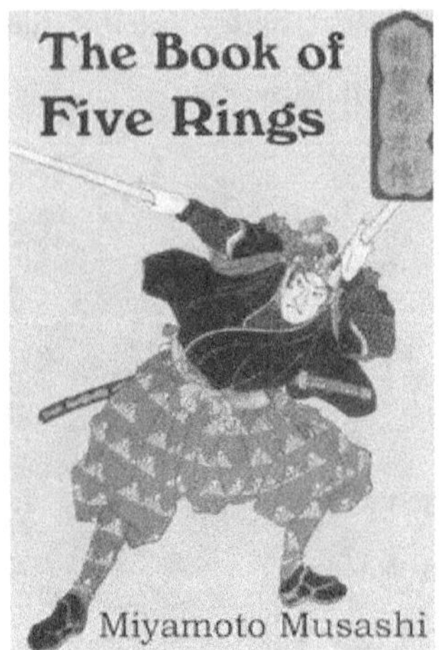

critical requirement in *budo* karate. However, you may still have some reservations about speed's not being a major necessity in *budo* karate. Believe it or not, I am not the only person who says this. In fact, a very famous samurai, Musashi Miyamoto (宮本武蔵, c. 1584–1645), wrote the following in the fourth volume (entitled "Kaze no Maki" [風の巻, 'The Wind Volume']) of his book *Gorin no Sho* (五輪書, 'The Book of Five Rings'):

> 兵法のはやきと云所、実の道に非ず。はやきと云事は、物毎の拍子の間にあはざるによって、はやきおそきと云う心也。
>
> Relying on speed in the way of the samurai is not the real way of swordsmanship. The true meaning of fast action is this: it must be understood that the heart or mind setting of fast and slow is only fast when the action purposely misses the expected tempo of the opponent.

I have included Miyamoto's original quote here as I want to share what he said about speed and tempo and how they should be taken into consideration. The English translation provided is my own direct translation, so I apologize for the potentially poor work.

I know that his statement is deep and possibly mysterious, so let me explain in my own words. In essence, Miyamoto is saying that seeking speed in *budo* is not the right way. Being fast doesn't necessarily mean speed. Rather, it is the ability to beat the opponent's tempo (*hyoshi* [(拍子]).

Even after reading Miyamoto's words, some may still not be totally convinced that speed isn't a key factor. OK, let me give you a simple example of how a slower person can win against an opponent with a very fast punch. Now, what I am giving you is a hypothetical situation with exaggerated figures to clarify this point.

Say your speed is only half that of the opponent. (I am aware that this is not realistic, but we are assuming this just as an example.) If you and your opponent punch at the same time from the same distance, the opponent will be able to punch you first since your punch has traveled only halfway. There are a few other factors, but we will ignore them for the purposes of this example. This means you will lose (provided you do not block, dodge, etc.).

However, suppose the opponent uses his rear fist and swings it as with a round punch (as you might see in a boxing match). You, on the other hand, use your front fist to throw a straight punch that we know as *kizami zuki* (刻み突き). Say, just for the sake of argument, that the distance of the opponent's fist is three times greater than that of your front fist. Once again, there are other factors, and my example is not very scientifically accurate, but I am using this only to illustrate a fairly common situation. Your front fist will reach your opponent's face before his widely swung round punch hits yours, despite the fact that his punch is twice the speed of yours.

The above situation is based on the assumption that you and your opponent start punching at the same time, but this is not realistic, either. Let's bring out a few other examples that are more realistic.

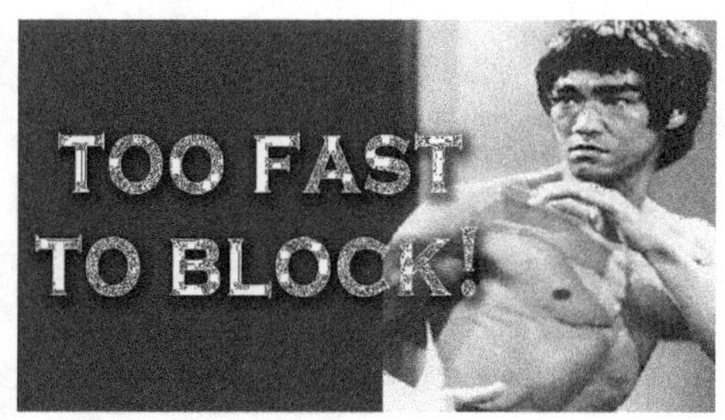

One case is that you start your punch much sooner than your opponent. In this scenario, you can punch him before he punches you, despite the fact that your punch is much slower. Another case is that your punch is so fast that the opponent cannot block or dodge, much like the fast punches that Bruce Lee (李小龍, 1940–1973) showed off in his movies (though those scenes were most likely mechanically sped up).

However, as a *karateka*, you may remember this *kun* (訓) from Funakoshi: "*Karate ni sente nashi*" (空手に先手無し, 'There is no first attack in karate'). So, you may choose not to throw the first strike. In this case,

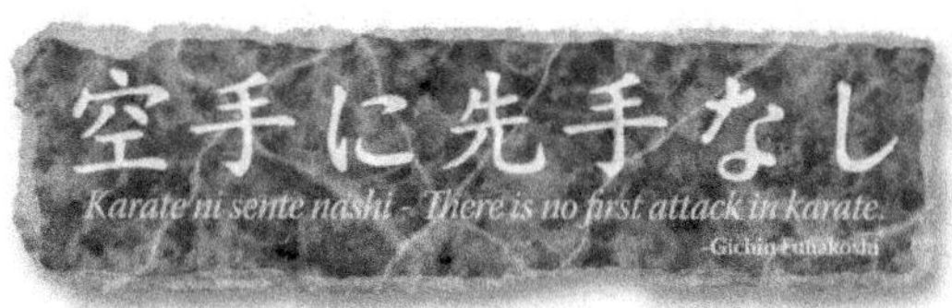

you can still have the upper hand by using *go no sen* (後の先). In other words, you let the opponent throw the first attack, and you either block or dodge it by using *taisabaki* (体捌き). Here again, you do not need to be extremely fast. You can outpace the opponent by having better timing and being able to read the opponent's moves and intentions.

I am not going to bring up other scenarios because there are numerous possible situations in a street fight. The point I am trying to make here is that all you need to have in your karate techniques is normal or standard speed. What I am trying to say is that you do not need to spend all your effort on making your punch or kick faster. I am certainly not saying that slower is better. Speed always helps, but there are other elements of karate that are far more important.

This goes for the power of the techniques, too. I am not going to get too deep into this subject; I will just say that the regular speed that one has is good enough and that the same goes for power. We all have enough power to knock down an opponent. In other words, you do not need to lift weights to make yourself stronger as this will not help your karate. In fact, it may actually slow your techniques down.

OK, let's get back to the subject of speed. Let me share the major problem I have frequently seen among practitioners in the seminars I have given around the world. Believe it or not, many of them are stopping or reducing the speed they are capable of. In other words, they can be faster, maybe much faster, if they want to.

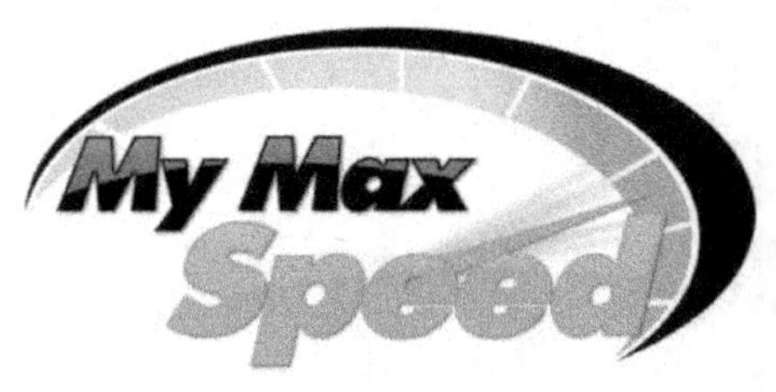

You may say that this is exactly the reason you are doing exercises to increase speed, such as tube training. Did you know that you can increase speed simply by working on the fundamentals of proper punching and kicking? Correct techniques increase not only power but also speed. For instance, keeping your elbow close to your body when you punch and raising your knee to its proper position when you kick will naturally increase speed. Do you not agree that this is a much smarter and more productive training method to increase your speed and power?

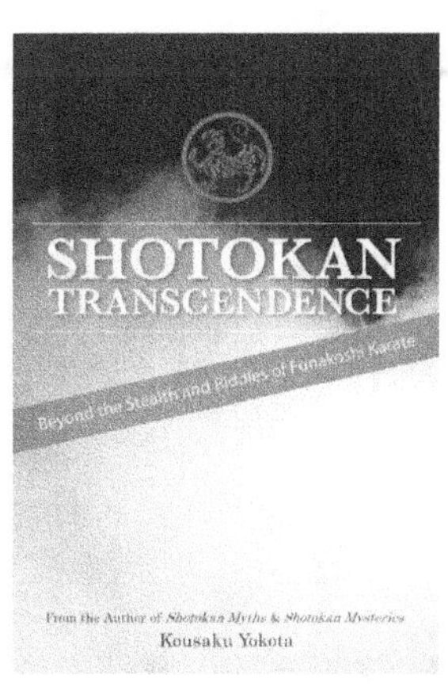

Yes, these exercises may help you, but there is a faster and easier solution. I will not go into the details here; I will simply say that all you have to do is learn how to relax. Those who have speed also have the problem of having too much tension or mistimed tension. I know it is not easy to relax when you are fighting. How do we do this? I wrote about it in Chapter 10: "Why Is Relaxing Our Muscles So Difficult?" of my book *Shotokan Transcendence* (available in both paperback and electronic format through *Amazon*).

Once they have fixed being overly tense, I believe almost all karate practitioners will have the necessary speed for combat. For *budo* karate, what they need to practice first is their mind-set, which includes *zanshin* (残心, 'remaining mind'), *heijoshin* (平常心, 'calm mind'), and *toshi* (闘志, 'fighting spirit'). But, this is a long process, and it must be done daily. I have written about this subject in this book, as well, in Chapter 15: "What Is the Most Important Training Point in Budo Karate?"

Conclusion

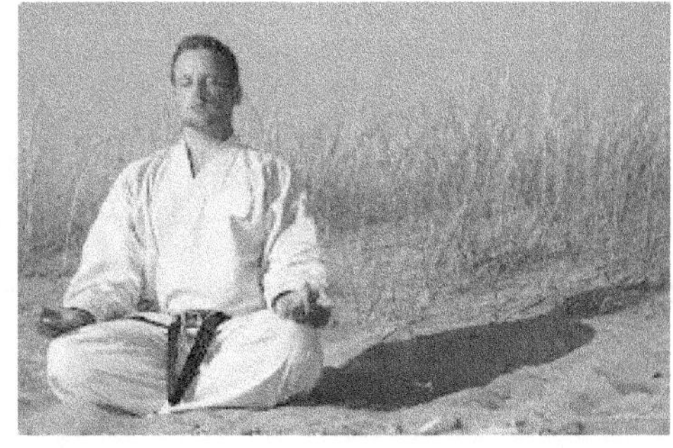

I have presented my case here that speed is not the ultimate objective in *budo* karate. I used the sensational phrase "Speed Is Unnecessary" in the title of this chapter to grab your attention. I wanted to write this chapter as there seems to be too much emphasis on speed and power in karate techniques.

The martial arts, including karate, have very complex and sophisticated physical maneuvers. In fact, they hold the most complex and challenging categories

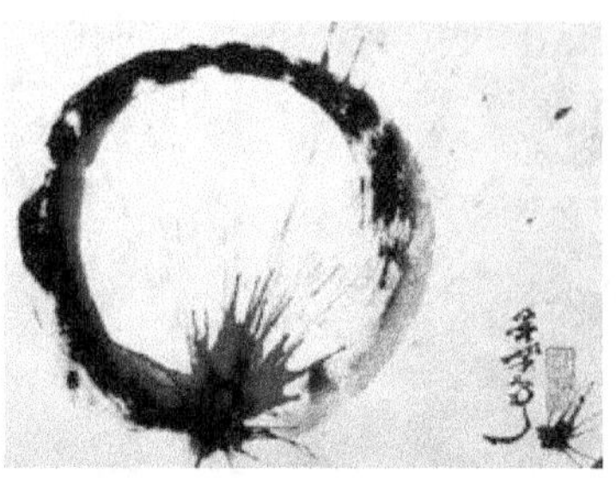

of all athletic events as they require the highest level of physical, mental, and spiritual concentration and mastery. I am not saying this just because I love karate. If you study their methodology and kinesiology, you will understand this.

I am proposing that you spend your training time wisely and correctly if you are training in *budo* karate. I am also proposing that you choose to spend more time learning how to relax rather than trying to speed up your techniques. Most of all, the mental and spiritual aspects are just as, if not more, important in actual hand-to-hand combat. We tend to spend all our time and attention on the physical workout, but what we must really do is spend more time on and give more attention to these invisible aspects.

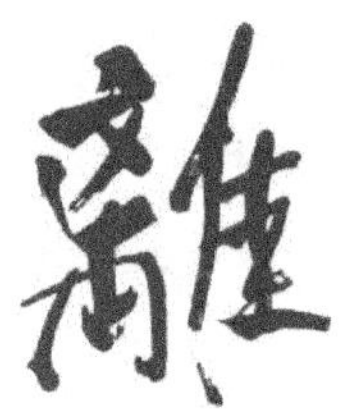

Chapter Six
第六章

Stop Tube Training
チューブトレーニングは止めよう

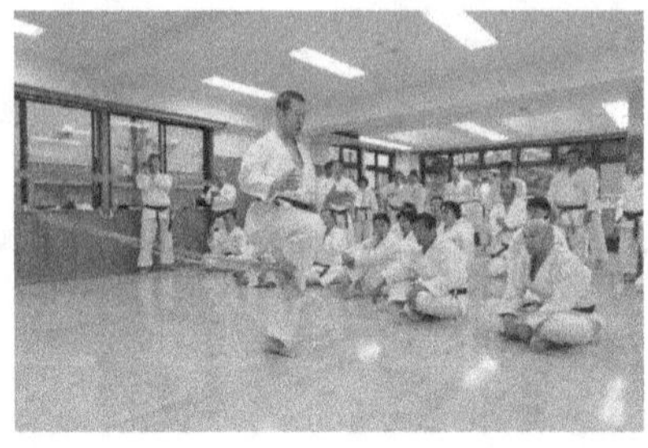

Karate training with the use of tubes is becoming more popular. I remember using them when I was training in Philadelphia in the mid seventies. Then, in the early eighties, I moved back to Japan and trained at the Hyogo Prefecture Headquarters Dojo (兵庫県本部道場) of the Japan Karate Association (日本空手協会 [JKA]) in Kobe, where tubes were also included in the regular training menu, which was held every Saturday for five hours.

At that time, we did not have any commercially manufactured tubes available. We used busted bicycle tire tubes, and they were great because they were free. Of course, a single tire tube was not long enough, so we would tie two tubes together for training in punching and would use three or four tubes for training in kicking and forward body shifting. I thought this was great and enjoyed the training.

When I started to teach karate in California, I brought this custom to my new dojo; however, I dropped this training method about twenty years ago. I know that my statement can be controversial. I am used to this, so I would just like to explain why I made this decision in this chapter as it may, in fact, help you in your training. I am also open to hearing the opinions of sports scientists and/or kinesiology experts.

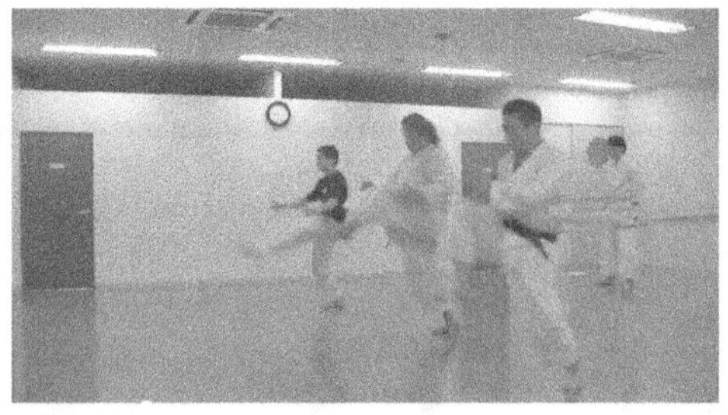

Did I drop tube training because I became too old to pull them? No, that was not it. Then, did I become too lazy to do it? That was not the case either, of course. Then, what was the reason?

During my years of training, I have picked up many cross-training exercises, such as tube training, running up hills, bunny-hopping down hills, etc. In the nineties, I began to seriously evaluate whether or not these were actually any good, not only for strengthening my body but also for improving my karate. Though I did keep some, I dropped the rest, in-

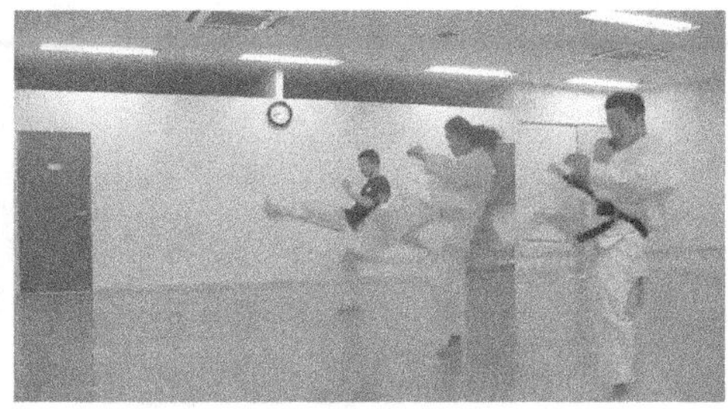

cluding running and tube training. I will not discuss running here because we are focusing on tube training.

Before I evaluated tube training, I asked myself what it was for. Did I want to develop strong punches and kicks? My answer was no. I wanted to focus on increasing speed, not so much on developing power.

In the past, I had not paid too much attention to my punches after tube training. My arms were tired when I would use this type of training for punching, and so were my legs when I would use it for kicking. I was happy with this and had not checked to see if my punches and kicks were actually any faster. I naïvely believed that they would be faster since my arms and legs had gotten tired.

This may be the biggest myth and miscalculation shared by many other karate practitioners. We go to a dojo to sweat and get tired. How many of us are really checking on quality of performance and improvement of skills? For many, it seems that their degree of satisfaction is determined not by how much they improve but by how much they sweat or get tired. If this is our sole purpose, then we can achieve this goal much better and much more easily by lifting weights at a gym.

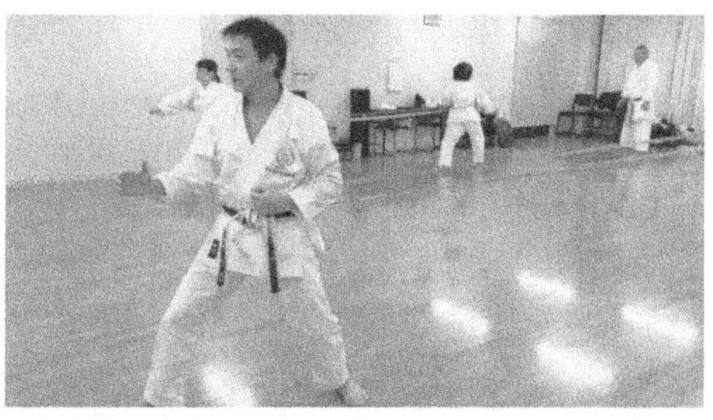

I am sure we all want to believe we are improving our karate techniques as we repeatedly go to our dojo and train. But, just going to the dojo every week will not guarantee the improvement of our karate skills. If we want to improve our skill level, then we must pay more attention to what we are doing and carefully evaluate whether or not it is beneficial to this end. You will be surprised, and maybe disappointed, to find that many of the things we do are not beneficial and are even counterproductive. In fact, some may even degrade your technique if you are not careful.

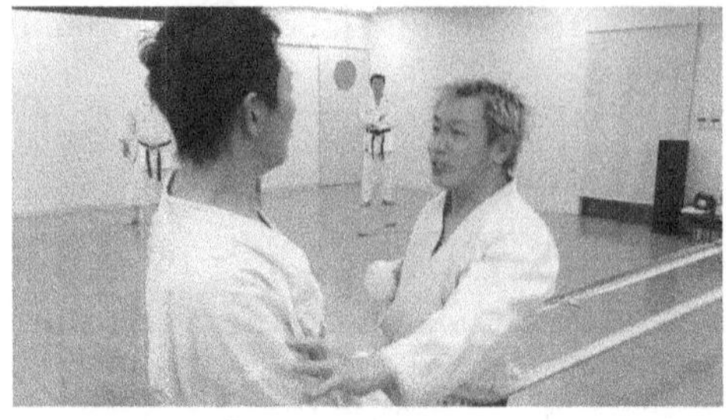

I am afraid tube training can be one of these. Why do I say this? Let's look at the gears of an automobile. When a car first starts moving forward, it requires a lot of power because of the law of inertia. In other words, when a mass is at rest, it takes a lot of energy to move it, but once it has started to move, it takes less energy to keep it moving.

I am sure you know that this is Newton's first law of motion. So, this law, of course, applies to automobiles. If you only drive cars that have an automatic transmission, you may not feel this. People like me, who like to drive cars with a manual transmission, know that you need to start in first gear. From then on, you shift upward into second gear, third gear, etc., as the speed of the car increases.

You can also experience this when your car has a problem and stops running. If you try to push-start it, you will find that it takes much more energy at first to move the car even one inch. Once it starts to move a little, though, it is much easier, and you can push it with much less energy.

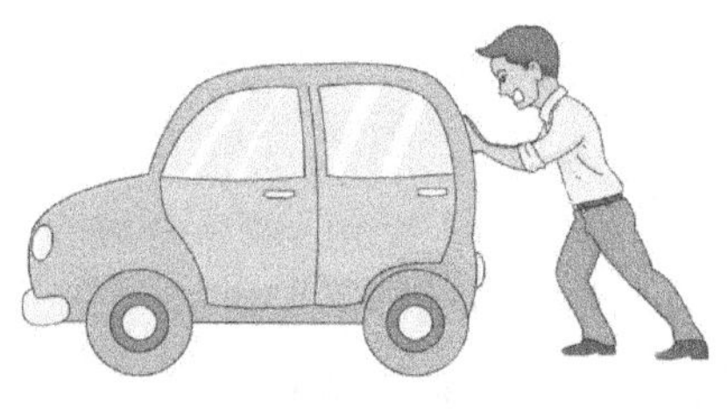

I am sure you can follow what I have been trying to explain up to this point. Let us continue with the case of the automobile. What happens if you keep it in first gear and continue to press down on the gas pedal? The engine will make a hell of a noise, that's for sure, but what about the speed? Well, it will increase, but will you be able to get it up to 60 mph (roughly 96 km/h)? Maybe, but it will be a trying and noisy task, and it sure won't be good on the engine. If you want to accelerate to 60 mph, you gradually shift up to fourth or fifth gear. Then, it is an easy task.

You can experiment with this on your ten-speed bike. Try to speed up to 12 or 18 mph (roughly 20 to 30 km/h) while staying in first gear (the lowest gear). You will probably have to stand up and pedal mighty hard to get up to that speed. If you

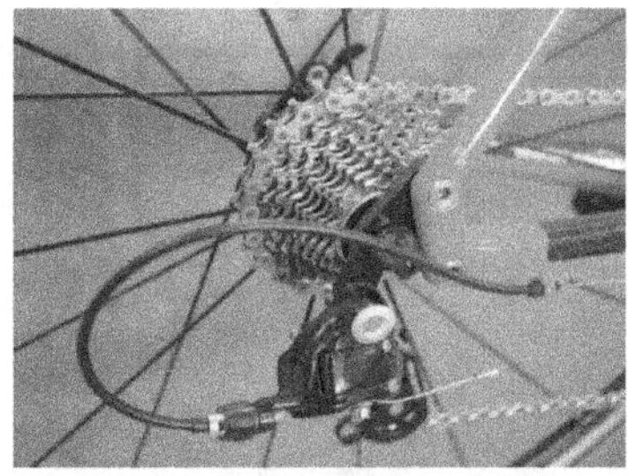

have strong legs, you will certainly get there, but will you be able to maintain that speed for thirty minutes, or even for ten minutes? Most will not be able to do this.

OK, enough of this example as you clearly know what I am talking about. So, you may be asking, "What is the relationship between this and tube training?" Well, that is exactly where I am heading.

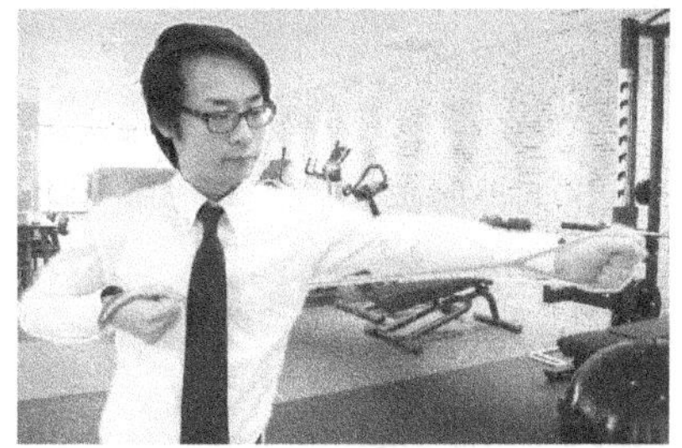

Now let us look at tubes. Most tubes, such as the ones I used to use, are made of rubber. The length and thickness of the tube do not matter. You will agree that it is easy to pull—that is, it does not require much energy—initially, but it gets harder (takes more energy) the farther you pull it. So, what does this mean? The farther you move, the more the speed of your punch or kick decreases, so you need to expend more energy in order to expand it or stretch it farther.

So, I used to believe this exercise of expending more energy, even if it did not increase the speed of my punch, was good. In fact, we used to do a series of ten or twenty "hard" punches with the tube—these were barely moving forward toward the very end of their travel since the tube was fully stretched at that point—and then drop the tube and immediately throw air punches. The air punches thrown right after I dropped the tube were great. I felt I could punch much faster and much more easily. This is natural and self-evident and is nothing to be surprised at. It happens to everyone. This is the law of inertia.

It is like shooting an arrow. You let go of the fully stretched bow, and the arrow shoots out. The tube was stopping my fist from moving forward. It was acting like a brake, so without the brake, my fist would fly forward. If you have tried tube training before, I am sure you have experienced this sensation. Well, this is the very reason this training is still popular and is practiced by many karate practitioners.

Well, then what is wrong with this?

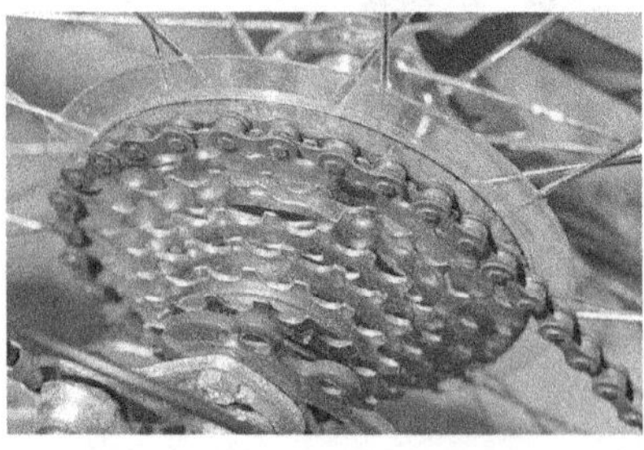

Do you remember the bike-riding example? Using this analogy, this would be the same as if you started in tenth gear and then downshifted as your speed increased. Is this how you would ride a bike? Say you went up a hill and got to the point where your bike was almost stopped. Would you shift all the way down to first gear to head back down the hill? I do not know of any cyclist who would train in this manner to increase short-distance speed ability.

It is true that soccer players and sprinters also train with tubes. Are they practicing incorrectly? Yes, if they tie them down or if the person who holds the other end is immobile. Look at the photos below, which show tube training by soccer players and sprinters.

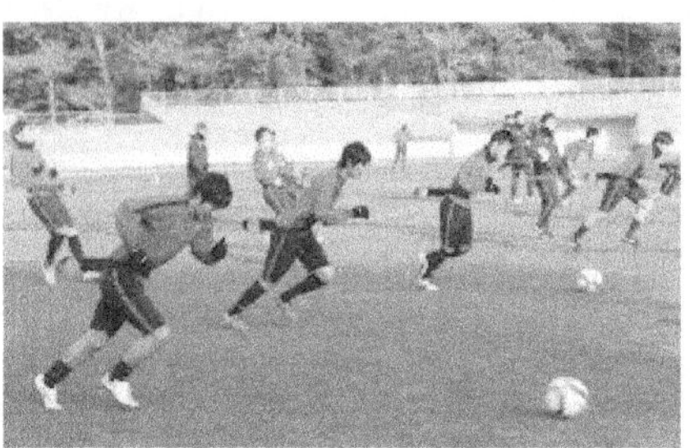

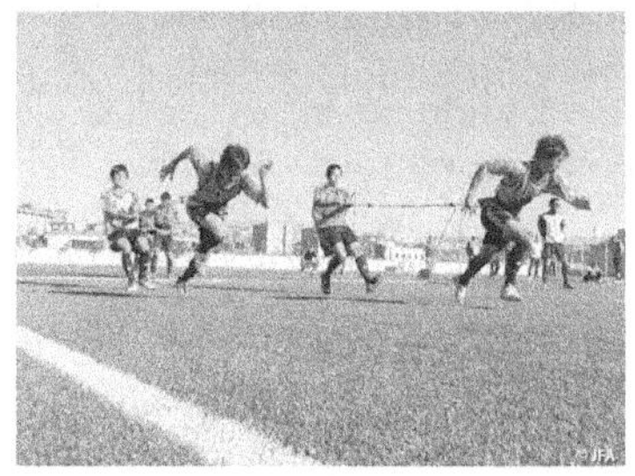

One thing you will notice is that the people who are holding the end of the tubes are moving with the runners. This is important. By doing this, the runners are not using their first gear (the gear used to initiate movement) but are working on the other gears. They can vary the gears by changing how fast their helpers move with them.

If the helpers allow the runners to run close to their top speed, then they are, of course, running in fifth gear (to use the car analogy). If the helpers are fixed, then the runners will soon have to stop when the tubes are fully extended. They will be pushing their feet against the ground, trying to move forward, but will hardly

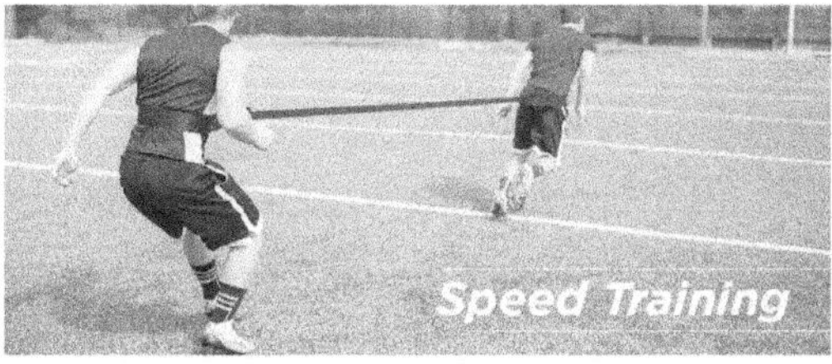

move. They will be working hard in first gear.

So, if you want to practice the initial move only, this training may be good, but you can accomplish the same thing by doing power squats with a heavy weight. I could be wrong, but I do not think too many sprinters do many power squats.

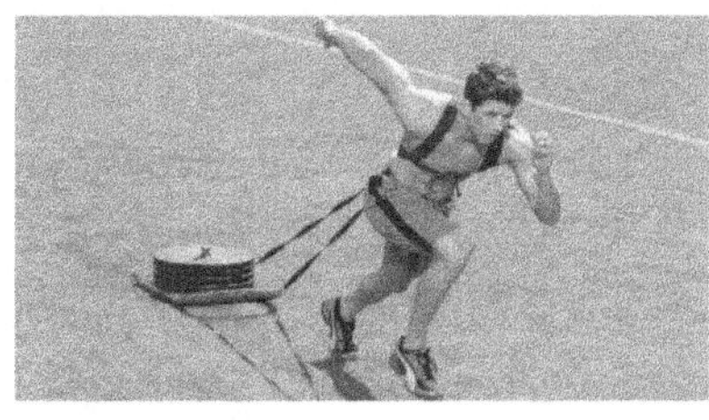

Regardless, karate kicks and punches have a physiological mechanism that is different from the muscle works of this type of training. Let us take *choku zuki* (直突き, 'straight punch') as an example. If you wish to execute a fast punch, your punching arm must be completely relaxed until your fist reaches the target (with your arm almost fully extended). It is critical that you have a very quick start or an explosive initiation of the arm, which means that the fist needs to be relaxed while it is traveling toward the target.

So, you need to have the most energy at the moment of initiation. As you extend your arm, it is more important to relax it than to tense it. At the moment of impact, you tense your entire arm for less than a tenth of a second (*kime*) to deliver the energy to the target. The effect of the punch will be a snap similar to the impact made by a whip. If the tension at the moment of impact is long, say, more than a second, it will become a pushing punch.

Let us summarize the mechanics of punching again.

Choku Zuki

1. The initial movement requires the most energy as it must break the inertia of a dead stop.
2. During travel, the arm should remain relaxed.
3. At the point of impact, full tension should be applied for a minimal amount

of time, and very little energy is required.

Tube Punch

1. The initial movement receives the least amount of resistance.
2. During travel, the tube gives gradually more resistance.
3. At the final point extension, the tube gives the greatest amount of resistance, requiring the greatest expense of energy.

When you compare the mechanics of these two scenarios, what do you find? Are they not almost the exact opposite of each other? In other words, tube training does not imitate the sequence of energy generation that is needed for *choku zuki*.

What we need is a device that gives us the most resistance initially, much less resistance as we extend our arm, and very little to no resistance at the point of full extension. Unfortunately, we do not have a device, as far as I know, that can provide such a workload.

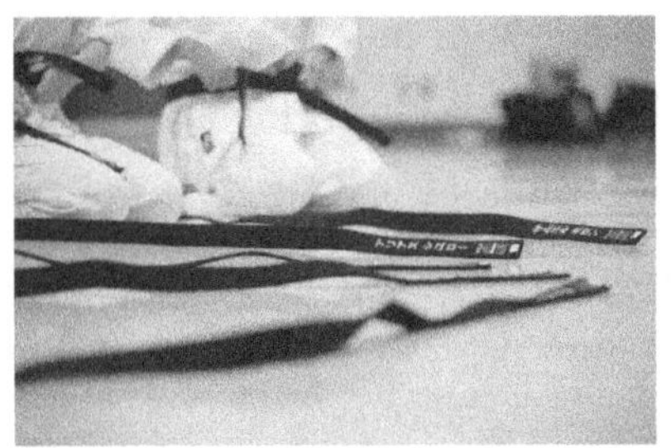

So, what can we do? If you happen to have a training partner or are in a class situation, you can team up to do the following. Instead of a tube, use a karate belt. Let us assume we will be practicing *gyaku zuki* while standing in *zenkutsu dachi*. You will train with the belt in almost the same way you would train with a tube.

Preparation

You hold your punching hand, whether left or right, at your waist as your partner puts the belt around the bend of your elbow. Your partner then holds the ends of the belt, steps back, assumes *zenkutsu dachi* or *kokutsu dachi* (後屈立ち), and pulls the belt until it's stretched tightly.

You could also hold the belt in your punching hand, but placing it around the elbow is much better because you want to keep your fist fairly relaxed during this type of training. If you hold the belt, then you will be tensing the muscles of your hand during the initial period of resistance, which is not advisable.

As you know, when done from a stationary stance, the power of *gyaku zuki* comes from the hip rotation. Thus, this should be the first movement, and the arm should not move. This is where your partner needs to apply the most resistance.

So, you have the training belt around your elbow. Before you try to rotate your hips, I suggest that you grab your own belt at your side. You will receive a lot of resistance, so much, in fact, that you will hardly be able to move at all and will tend to use your arm muscles rather than just your hips to move the technique forward. So, by grabbing your own belt, you will fix your punching arm to your hip, so to speak.

If your belt is not securely tightened, it may not work well. If this is the case, place your hand over your hip so that your arm can have a connection to your hip that is better than just holding your fist next to it.

Now the preparation is done. Next is the first step of the actual training.

Step 1

Your partner should make sure the belt is fully extended so that there is no play in it. You begin to rotate your hips, and, at that very moment, your partner gives maximum resistance, meaning your hips will not be able to turn easily. You really must maximize rotational power by using the muscles of your leg and hip regions.

As I warned earlier, you must not use the muscles of your arm or shoulder area to assist the rotation. It must be done by the hips alone, which is why you keep your hand on your hip. This step lasts one or two seconds.

Step 2

Your partner now reduces resistance down to sixty or eighty percent so that you can rotate your hips. During this process, you do not move your arm. Rather, you hold your arm still until your hips are facing straight ahead (*shomen*).

Step 3

At this moment, you stop rotating your hips and begin extending your arm to execute the punch. Your partner must reduce resistance considerably, maybe down to ten percent or less, because the power was being generated by the hip rotation.

In fact, we do not depend on the arm muscles for speed. It is better for the arm to be relaxed as it travels forward. This is why there should only be minimal resistance applied to it at this point. At the same time, your partner should not remove resistance completely or let go of the ends of the belt.

Step 4

When your arm is fully extended, the belt should slide to the shoulder or armpit area. At this point, your partner can drop all resistance.

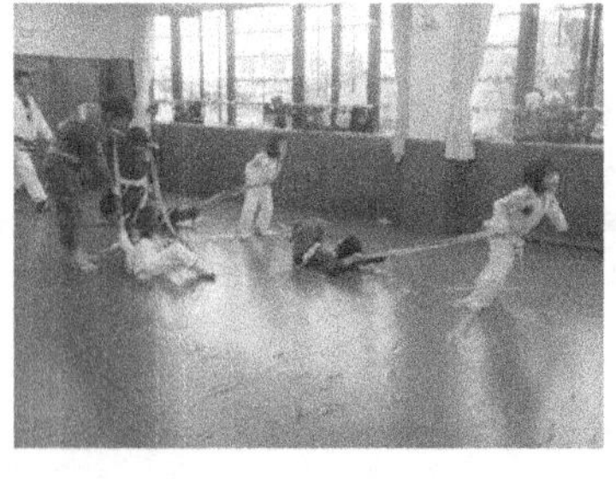

In the case of *oi zuki*, I do not recommend that the belt be wrapped at the elbow or even held in the hand. Why? Because with *oi zuki*, you do not punch or move your arm until the last moment. First, you need to step forward without moving your punching arm. OK, so can you use a belt to do resistance training for this punch? Yes, you can.

Preparation

For *oi zuki*, the belt is used to pull your hips back. I suggest that you keep your own belt on and find another belt to put through your belt in the back. Your partner holds the ends of this belt and assumes the same position as in *gyaku zuki* training. The process is the same. You assume *zenkutsu dachi* and get ready to step forward and execute *oi zuki*.

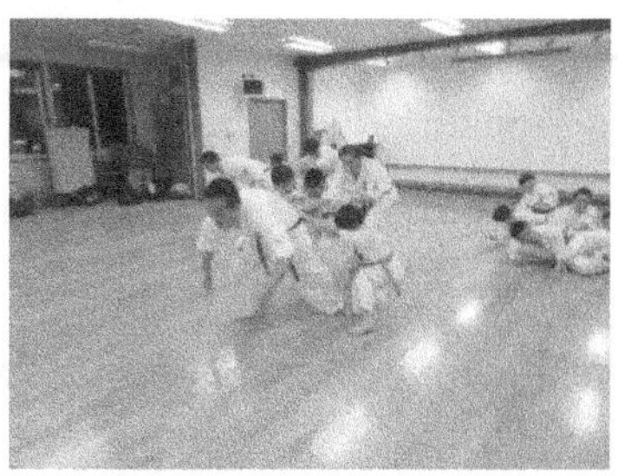

Step 1

Your partner applies maximum resistance when you initiate forward movement. In other words, this is when you lift your rear foot up to move forward. At this time, you must try not to kick off against the floor with your rear foot to gain power. Rather, you must try to shift your hips forward by bending your front knee.

Also, try not to lean or swing your head and/or upper torso area forward to generate power. Naturally, this happens, but try to avoid it. Using only the shifting of the hips is the hardest thing to master, but you will learn this by receiving resistance to your hips.

This part is easy for your partner, who should be sure to pull hard enough so that you will barely be able to move forward. Hold this for one to five seconds, depending on how hard you want to make this step.

Step 2

This next step requires more coordination by your partner. After the first step, your partner decreases resistance, but more gradually than in the case of *gyaku zuki*. Resistance should be decreased to fifty to eighty percent, depending on your ability. With this release, you can begin to move forward.

Step 3

As your foot passes your supporting leg, your partner moves forward with you and maintains the same resistance. This requirement is challenging because what often happens is that your partner decreases resistance too much in the process. During this step, you get ready for the punch but must keep your upper body, including your arms, totally relaxed.

Step 4

The final step is the last ten percent of the movement, when the forward foot touches the ground, which is a critical time for you as you must coordinate your punch with the last step. The important thing is that the punch be withheld until the last moment. The *oi zuki* should be delivered as the foot touches the floor but not too long afterward as the forward-moving inertia of the body will have stopped, at which point it is too late to deliver an effective punch.

This can be done with kicks, but I will not go into the details here. If you understand the concept from the punching examples above, you can figure out how to apply this to your training for kicking exercises.

I have dropped this method from my own personal training mainly for one simple reason: I do not have a partner to do it with. But, even if I had one, he would have to know the exact resistance levels (and body shifting if necessary), which is extremely difficult. In addition, I have also concluded that the speed that karate techniques require for short-distance movements is quite different from the running speed of sprinters and soccer players.

Even though it is still true that we have to rely on our muscles to make these movements, I have found that it is better to increase speed by being more relaxed than by being more tense. You receive resistance with any of these training methods, whether by tube or by belt; thus, your muscles are forced to tense up more in order to move.

Of course, if you tense the correct muscles, then you will have faster, and possibly stronger, technique. Unfortunately, when a body receives resistance, it tends to activate too many different muscles. A good example of this is that of a weight lifter, who will tense his face as he lifts something heavy. Tensing the muscles in the face technically does not help the lift, but the weight lifter believes it does.

This is what happens in karate, as well. An example is found in how many people swing their arm down as they execute *mae geri* (前蹴り). In karate, if it is *budo* karate, you must minimize body movement so that you do not telegraph to your enemy.

Here is another one. Many practitioners believe that in order to generate a faster punch, you must pull back the other fist. In *budo* karate, you must be able to use the different parts of the body separately and independently without having them rely on each other. Many times, contrary to your intentions, these extra movements not only prevent you from maximizing your speed but also actually reduce your speed. I refer to this as pushing on the brake pedal and the accelerator at the same time.

In conclusion, I consider my time better spent doing stretches to keep my muscles limber and elastic. I also consider meditation and breathing exercises to be better as they keep me relaxed and focused so that I can operate only the necessary muscles while the others are relaxed and ready for my command.

As I have mentioned many times before, in an orchestra, a good conductor must have well-disciplined musicians. What happens when instruments start playing when they're not called for during a concert? I guarantee that you will not have beautiful music. You may be an excellent conductor, but have you disciplined your muscles to play only when you want them to?

I have also found that extremely slow movements with focused control are beneficial to the development of fast body movements. This sounds like a contradiction, but it is not. Believe it or not, if you can control your body movements perfectly in extremely slow motion, you will be capable of moving those parts very quickly.

This is exactly what tai chi practitioners are able to achieve. The oldest style

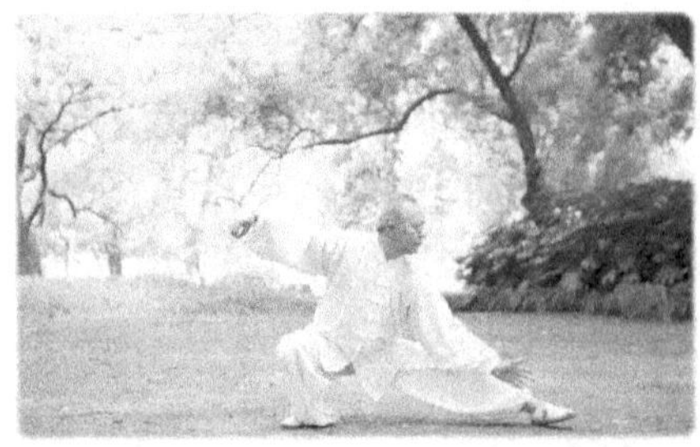

of tai chi, Chen Family Tai Chi Chuan (*Chén jiā tàijíquán* [陳家太極拳]), has some fast and powerful hip-vibration movements in its *kata.* However, the more modern and popular Yang Family Tai Chi Chuan (*Yáng shì tàijíquán* [楊氏太極拳]) has only slow movements, which may be an excellent exercise method for senior citizens, but applying this to the martial arts, though not impossible, can be a difficult challenge.

So, my stance on cross-training is that it can be beneficial if it is the right kind and is also done correctly. On the other hand, if a particular exercise is not compatible with what you are trying to achieve or is done improperly, then it can actually harm you, just as any other physical exercise can. In fact, it may also hinder the improvement of your karate skills.

I would also like to add that some methods are more beneficial to karate training than others. We need to be wise and educated enough to select the ones that will result in genuine benefit and will be worth our valuable time.

I normally do not write chapters on how to do techniques or exercises. There are many other, more capable writers who specialize in this. I prefer to write about technical concepts, philosophy, physiomechanical matters, kinesiology, etc. In addition, I find it extremely difficult to adequately explain the different body movements with my poor English. However, as far as I knew, no one had written about belt training (as opposed to tube training) and its mechanics, so I decided to write this how-to chapter in order to explain the exact steps and movements needed to do this exercise correctly.

If you happen to have a partner and are looking for a new way to speed up your *gyaku zuki* and *oi zuki*, why not try this exercise for a few weeks and see if it helps. If it works, please report back to me and let me know the outcome of your new training.

I would also like to hear from any *karateka* who train with tubes regularly. I would like to know if this chapter made any sense or if you are opposed to my claims. I think a healthy and constructive discussion is always good for karate.

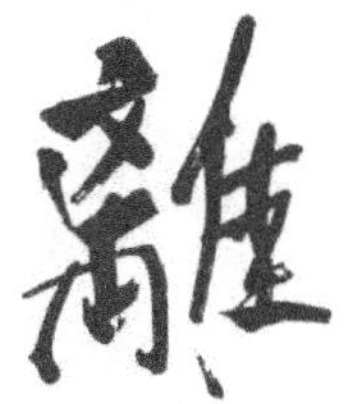

Chapter Seven
第七章

Do Not Teach Bunkai
分解稽古は教えるな

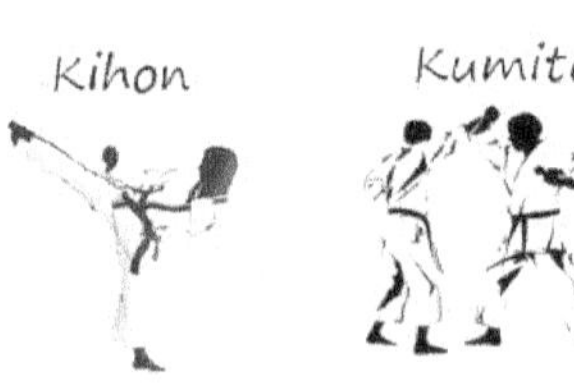

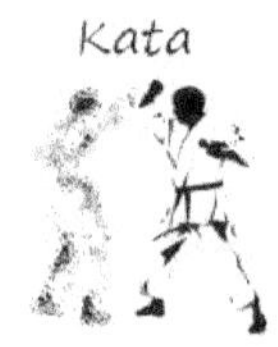

I know that I am touching on another controversial subject. I am sure the title of this chapter has already raised the eyebrows of some, or maybe many, readers. I am aware of the risk of being misunderstood, but I felt I needed to speak out as *bunkai* (分解) training is becoming more and more popular. Let me make it clear that I consider *bunkai* training to be important. In fact, it is a must. Karate without *bunkai* is just a karate dance.

Then, why have I written this chapter? Let me explain. I have a strong fear that many practitioners, mostly beginners and intermediate students but also advanced practitioners, may be wasting time and training in *bunkai* incorrectly. I am aware that my statement may be confusing. I hope you will read the entire chapter so that you will understand why I have written it.

So, I am proposing stopping *bunkai* training. Let me explain why I propose such a "crazy" idea. As I stated above, I do not consider *bunkai* to be an unimportant or unnecessary element of karate. Why am I proposing to stop *bunkai* training, then? There are three main reasons.

One reason is that training in *bunkai* for beginners not only produces no benefits but also has a negative effect on their karate development. Let me explain why. A beginner needs to practice the *kihon* movements in as perfect a manner as possible. This is the important process of learning and internalizing the techniques. This means a beginner must concentrate on repeating a particular physical movement in the correct way and following the same course without any modifications as much as possible. If this person gets into *bunkai* training sessions repeatedly, he will need to change the course of the movement frequently to accommodate imaginary fighting situations.

Then, you may be asking, "If that is the case, is *kumite* such as *sanbon kumite* and *gohon kumite* bad for beginners?" This is a good question. Personally, I think it is better to keep white belts (tenth to eighth *kyu*) away from *kihon kumite* for the same reason I stated above. However, many beginners want to experience training in "fighting," so it is probably difficult to keep them motivated without getting them involved in *kihon kumite* training.

On the other hand, I must add that *kihon kumite* is less harmful than *bunkai.* It is simply that *bunkai* situations are far more complex and present far more variables. In *sanbon kumite* or *gohon kumite* for beginners, the situations are limited to *jodan* and *chudan oi zuki*. Though the opponents will be different (tall, short, fast, slow, strong, weak, etc.), the punches are basically the same, and the blocking techniques are also specified (e.g., *jodan age uke* [上段挙げ受け], *chudan soto uke* [中段外受け], *gedan barai*, etc.) and used in the same way. Therefore, despite some variables, the beginner can concentrate on repeating the same techniques in a very similar manner in each situation. So, you can easily guess that this is the very reason *jiyu kumite* (自由組手, 'free sparring') should never be introduced to beginners.

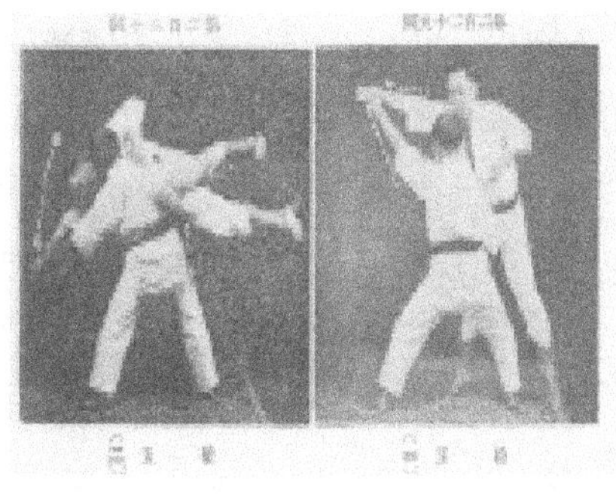

The second reason is a little more complex and less obvious. To say it in a very short statement, *bunkai* is limitless, so it would be impossible to cover each and every situation in *bunkai* training, even if you did it every day. So, what happens is that a certain sensei or organization will decide on just a few *bunkai* ideas, and, sadly, in many cases, they choose only one.

For instance, I was visiting the dojo of a major organization during my visit to Japan this year (2016). During the training, they practiced Heian Nidan (平安二段), and the sensei told the students, "The second movement is for catching the opponent's forearm when he punches. We used to do this technique as a combination of a block (*nagashi uke*) and a counter (*ura zuki*), but now this is considered wrong." Frankly, I was shocked at this statement. It was shocking to me to hear that a certain *bunkai* idea was "wrong" just because it was not written in a textbook or approved by an organization. Most of the students there were very young (high school kids, in fact), so they would believe the sensei's statement without any doubt or questioning.

As I stated earlier, *bunkai* is limitless, so teaching one or even a few different ideas as being the only correct *bunkai* is certainly wrong. Besides, those "correct" *bunkai* ideas will most likely not help the students in a real fight anyway. In fact, they may put them at a disadvantage.

For instance, no street fighter is going to throw a straight punch like the *choku zuki* used in karate. He's certainly not going to throw a punch from the hip. He will most likely stand in a boxing-style stance and throw a hook punch (similar to our *mawashi uchi*) to your face. But, he could aim his attack at the ribs or throw a kick to the groin. In a street fight, you really never know what the other guy(s) will do. In this situation, *age uke*, *soto uke*, and *gedan barai* will most likely not work.

Thirdly, and maybe most importantly, some of the techniques you find in the Heian *kata* are, in fact, too complex and advanced. It would be almost impossible for beginners to learn how to execute them.

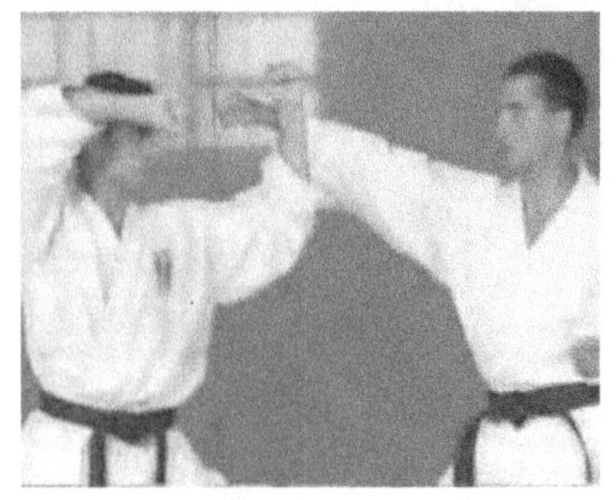

For instance, as shown in the photo to the left, the very first move in Heian Nidan is taught as a *jodan uchi uke* (上段内受け) with the front arm. The rear arm held at the forehead is just supposed to be a *kamae* (構え). The teachers had to teach this *bunkai* as the advanced (more realistic) *bunkai* was too hard (even for advanced students).

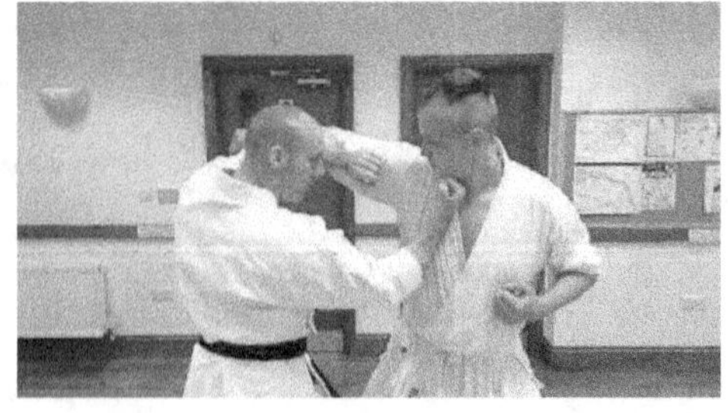

The original *bunkai* that was taught on Okinawa was a *jodan age zuki* (上段挙げ突き) with the front fist and a simultaneous *jodan age uke* with the rear forearm (photo right). Until you get used to this, it is quite challenging to do *morote waza* using the rear arm as the *uke*. If you do not believe me, just try it when you do *ippon kumite* in your next class. For beginners, it is almost impossible as their level of technique and *kumite* experience is far too low to accommodate such a *bunkai*.

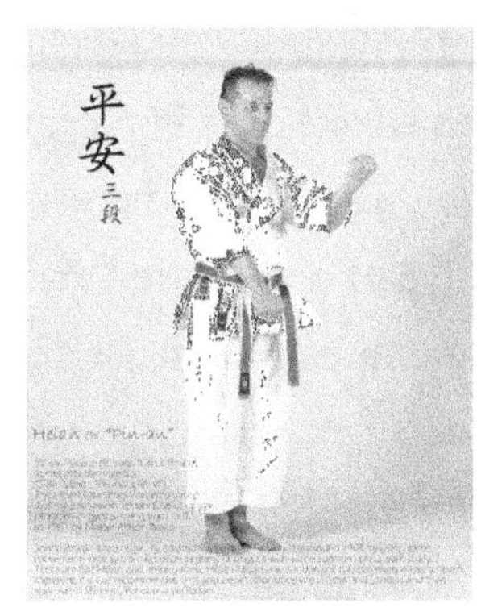

Another example is the second move in Heian Sandan (平安三段), which is shown in the photo to the right. This is commonly taught as a double block (a combination of *chudan uchi uke* and *gedan barai*) against a double punch aimed at *chudan* and *gedan* or against a simultaneous *mae geri* and *chudan gyaku zuki* (photo left). Even though any *bunkai* that works is a "good" *bunkai*, in this case, the attack itself is unrealistic. And besides, how do you explain the *heisoku dachi*?

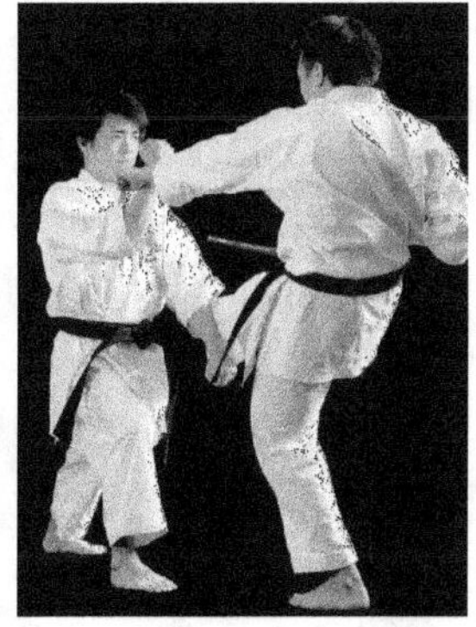

The commonly taught *bunkai* explained above is much easier than the more realistic application, which is that you execute the *chudan uchi uke* against the opponent's *chudan zuki*. Then, you step in, grab the opponent's hand or sleeve with the same hand you used to execute *chudan uchi uke*, and bring it down to throw the opponent off-balance as you simultaneously throw *chudan* or *jodan uraken uchi* with your other fist (photo right).

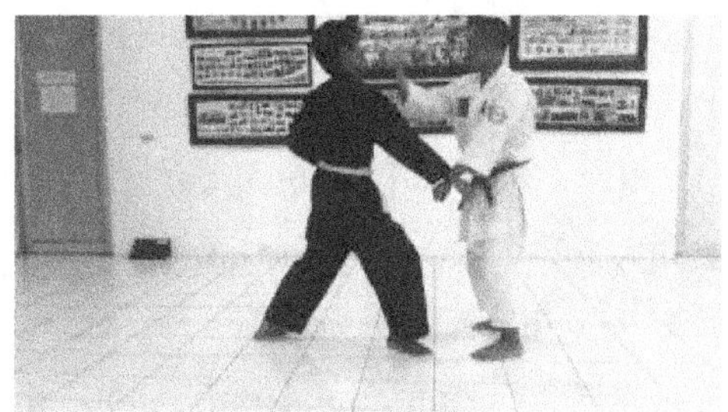

Another situation is that the opponent throws *mae geri* instead of *chudan zuki*. In this case, you use your front arm to execute *gedan barai* against the *mae geri* and still simultaneously throw *chudan* or *jodan uraken uchi* with your other fist (as in the previous example).

In this better *bunkai*, getting into *heisoku dachi* also makes more sense. You step forward into *heisoku dachi* because you are pulling the opponent toward you as you are executing *deai waza* (出合い技) with a right-side *uraken* attack.

There are many other realistic *bunkai*, but it would be impossible to list them all. An important point to remember is that the fact that a given technique is labeled as an *uke* does not mean it is always a block.

This makes more sense but is much more difficult to execute from the perspective of both timing and distance. So, what happens here is that instructors find it too difficult to teach beginners how to do the realistic *bunkai*; thus, they have to downgrade to an easier but less realistic *bunkai*. Their students can do the easy *bunkai*, but most of the time it does not make good sense or is not workable. So, why should we waste our time and theirs on such a *bunkai*?

What beginners and intermediate students need to do is practice *kihon* to learn the basic techniques and become very familiar with them. They also need to get a lot of experience in *kihon ippon kumite* so that they can learn correct timing and the proper distance between the attacker and the defender. Eventually, when they become a brown belt, they should get more experience by practicing *jiyu ippon kumite* (自由一本組手, 'semifree sparring'). They should focus on *kihon* and *kihon kumite* and not so much on *bunkai*.

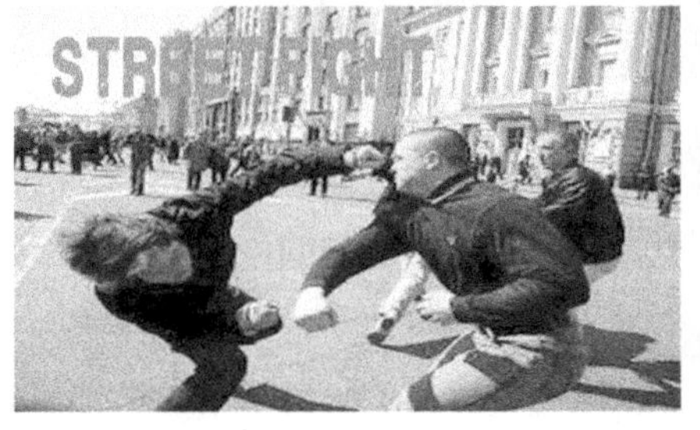

We practice karate for self-defense purposes. In other words, we are training so that we can defend ourselves if we get into a street fight. I mentioned above that beginners and intermediate students must practice *kihon* and *kihon kumite*. Ironically, I must tell you that all the hard training you do in *kihon ippon kumite* or *jiyu ippon kumite* will not help you in a real street fight. In fact, *jiyu kumite* will not help you much in these situations, either, though many may disagree with this statement.

If you do not believe this, I am happy to explain. There are so many things that are totally different between a street fight and a dojo *kumite* situation. Here I present three major reasons our *jiyu kumite* will not help much in a street fight.

1. The distance used in *jiyu kumite* in Shotokan karate (and, in fact, in all traditional karate) is much too great. In a street fight, you will face the op-

ponent from only three feet (one meter) away or less.

2. The timing is totally different. You may have multiple opponents, too. You must develop true *zanshin* to be able to cope with the unexpected timing of an attack, yet this *zanshin* cannot be learned from our *jiyu kumite*.
3. Grappling may precede or follow the first punch, and most have not been taught these grappling and ground techniques.

Then, what do we need to do if we want to be ready for a street fight? I suggest two things. Even though there are many others that would help, these two are the minimum one needs to do.

1. Practice different *kata*, concentrating as much as possible and believing you are fighting against many opponents.
2. Learn the *bunkai* for these *kata*, especially if you are not sure of the meaning of every move in the *kata* you practice.

Now, you may have been surprised to hear this. You may be saying, "What do you mean by this? I thought you were telling us not to practice *bunkai*. Now you are saying we need to learn *bunkai*? I am confused." I understand if you are confused. Let me explain.

What I am proposing is this. We need to perfect each of our techniques in the *kata*, but we need to know the basic idea of the application. If we execute *age uke*, we need to be able to do the technique correctly so that we can block an attack. Of course, we also need to know that *age uke* could be used as an attack or a counter-attack. We cannot limit our mind to only one or two applications. At the same time, I am strongly cautioning that we cannot think of or train for all the applications as they are literally infinite.

So, instead of spending so much time on *bunkai* training, I am claiming it is better for most practitioners to spend their time on *kihon* and *kata*. For beginners, I even recommend not teaching any *bunkai*. I say this because this very knowledge may damage their ability to learn the basic techniques. In other words, it may be better for beginners (referring to students up to sixth or even fifth kyu with less than two years of training) not to know the *bunkai*. This may be a shocking statement, but I sincerely believe this.

The very reason I am opposed to teaching *bunkai* to beginners is that they may alter the techniques to "fit" a certain *bunkai*. Then, why do I say this is not good? This is an extremely important point, so I hope the reader will pay a lot of attention to it. In the past, I have written much regarding the importance of passing through the stage of learning a technique before we move on to the stage of using that technique. I will not repeat the full explanation here, but you can read more about this in Chapter 5: "The Reasons Why We Must Preserve Our Kata" (specifically, pages 56–58) of my book *Shotokan Transcendence*.

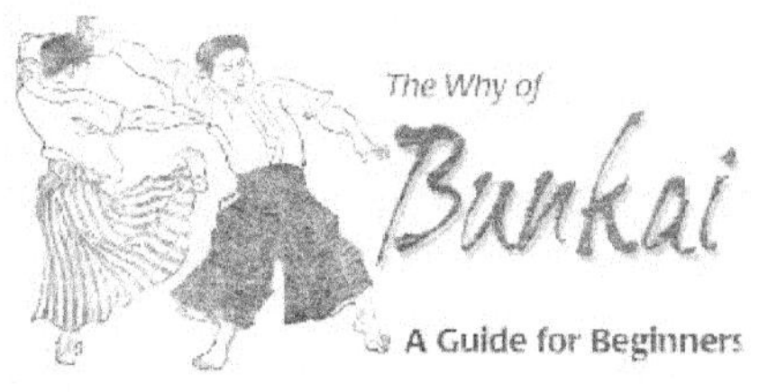

The essence is that the beginner should repeat the correct body movement without worrying about how it should be used. Let me illustrate one example of why knowing *bunkai* may have a negative impact. I am sure you remember when your sensei told you to make your arm movement large when you were a white belt learning, say, *soto uke*. A white belt does not understand *karada no shinshuku* (身体の伸縮, 'expansion and contraction of the body'), so you need to tell him to make his body movements large (almost to an exaggerated degree). This is very important for any beginner or intermediate student. If he does not learn this, what will happen? His movements will tend to be very small and jerky, which may not work well in *kumite*.

So, what is wrong with that? First of all, it will be difficult for him to generate and manage power. This type of student's movements look very jerky, which I am sure you have seen before. His technique is a small movement, so it cannot be adapted as well to the various situations that arise in *kumite* and street fighting; thus, his technique will not work. Once he learns this movement, and it has become natural to him, it will be very difficult, though not impossible, for him to change later on.

A good example of the difficulty encountered when trying to change one's techniques can be found in those practitioners who switch styles. A black belt in Shito Ryu (糸東流) or Wado Ryu (和道流) will have a very difficult time adjusting to many of the techniques of Shotokan, and the reverse is also true. If you (a Shotokan practitioner) have tried other styles, I am sure you have experienced this.

So, it is best to teach the correct technique to a white belt without any distractions. This is like drawing on a blank sheet of paper. Our body is not so much like a pencil, which is easy to erase, but more like a pen or a paintbrush, so it is difficult to make changes after the fact.

Finally, you may have the ultimate question: if there are an infinite number of *bunkai* possibilities, how can we practice all of them? Certainly, we cannot practice each and every option, but I will give you a similar situation. Even though this is not a perfect analogy, it will give you an idea of the concept.

Think of how you would teach a baby to walk. There are many different conditions (almost an infinite number) in which one will have to walk. You do not put the baby in all these conditions in order to teach him how to walk. You find a flat, open space and teach the baby how to walk there (*kihon*). You require him to walk repeatedly in the same room or hallway (*kata*). Once he learns how to walk in the easiest (that is, the flattest and safest) conditions, you take him out to a park where the ground is uneven and where there are many obstacles for further training (*kumite*). After walking up and down the uneven surfaces, climbing up and down the stairs, etc., the child learns how to walk on almost any kind of surface and in virtually all conditions.

Well, this is a very simplified example, but the learning process is the same. You can compare this to any other physical skill, such as swimming, surfing, cycling, skating, skiing, etc. What makes karate and self-defense skills more challenging is that they involve one or more opponents. Learning how to kick a ball is one thing, but being able to play in a soccer game is quite another. Playing well in a ball game, of course, is much more challenging. Regardless of the physical skills,

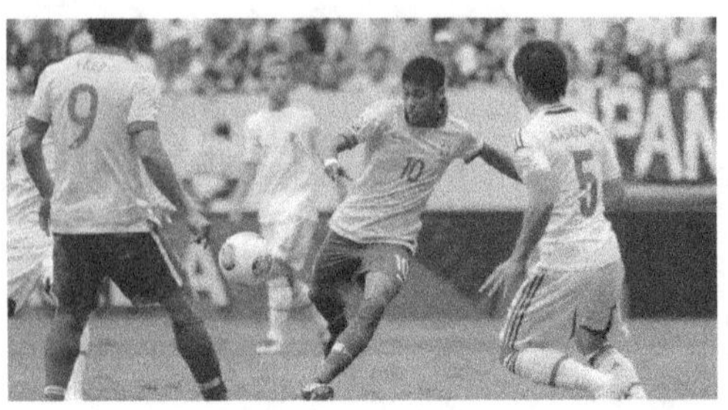

the basic concept is the same. You need to master the basic techniques (*kihon*) first.

Then, what would be an analogy to *bunkai* in a ball game? It may be a unique situation in which a player needs to perform in a certain way. This training may be important for a soccer player; however, you do not want to teach these situations, say, to a child or even an adult who has just started learning how to play soccer. If you are a soccer coach, you want to make sure the players know how to correctly kick the ball in a straight line before you teach them how to kick an inside shot, chip shot, outside shot, bending shot, etc. Teaching specific challenging shots and tricky dodging techniques comes much later.

I hope you now understand why I do not recommend *bunkai* training for beginners and intermediate students. I also hope you see more value in teaching *kihon kumite* and *kata* to these students. You want to reserve *bunkai* training for your more advanced students.

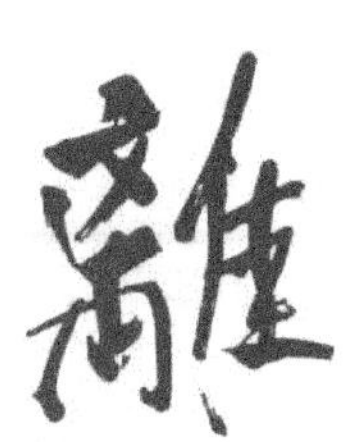

Chapter Eight
第八章

Are Internet Dan Examinations Valid?
インターネット段位審査とは

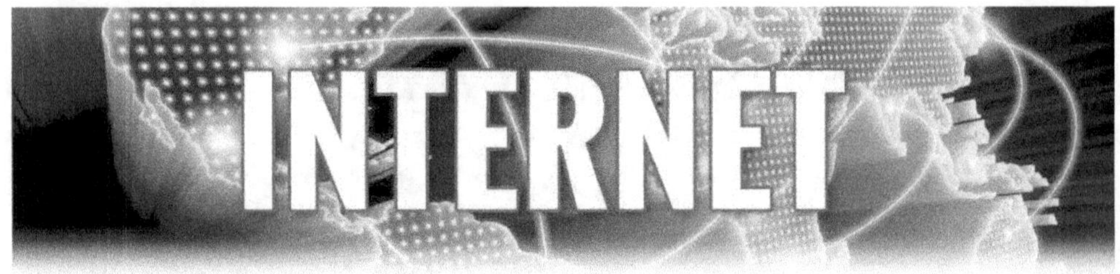

The subject of online or Internet *dan* examinations is a very controversial one. When I made the announcement a few years ago that our organization, ASAI, would provide this as an option, I received a lot of feedback. Much of the feedback was positive, but some was negative. At that time, my friends and colleagues approached me and advised me to stay away from this subject. One even warned me that supporting this method would affect my credibility. I knew that all those who had advised me against this were sincere and worried about my reputation. I appreciated their concern for me but had to respond with the statement that I believed in this method and felt very strongly that it was about time someone came out and educated the public (despite the fact that my statement may have sounded a little arrogant).

It is my sincere hope, from the bottom of my heart, that this method will gain the respect and acceptance it deserves in the near future. I am aware that many practitioners of all ranks and levels of seniority are against it or are at least skeptical of it. Let me emphasize that I am not writing this to convince anyone. All I am trying to do is simply present all the facts and share my analysis with the reader. I believe one can only judge a given subject appropriately after having obtained all the facts, including not only the advantages and benefits but also the limitations and shortcomings. After completing this process, it is up to the skeptics whether or not they wish to change their mind.

First, we must look at distance learning and online education in general to understand what they really are. Many readers may have already heard about this, but the term *distance learning* meant something completely different during most of the twentieth century. For students during those years, this referred to learning subjects through textbooks and sending homework and examinations to a teacher via regular mail.

Now *distance learning* is another name for online or Internet education. Online education has made many advancements and created many opportunities as an unconventional learning process. When first marketed, it was geared toward the working adult who wanted a college degree but didn't have the time to attend a brick-and-mortar location. In the 1990s, the dot-com boom gave schools the necessary tools for a more Internet-based teaching module. In 1993, Jones International University, founded by Glenn Jones, became the first web-based university.

The text-based teaching module had involved the use of slides for instruction and presentations. But, online education has since graduated to being a fully flexible environment that has implemented streaming media, webcam access, and even blackboards and Flash presentations. Nowadays, online education is regarded as a credible way to learn and study in order to obtain a higher education. It is very common now for almost all universities and colleges to offer some form of online course.

Online education in general is no longer a new fad or something foreign. I do not need to try to convince you of this as there are numerous statistics and reports to support my claim. Below is one example, a graph showing the growth of U.S. online higher education students for the period between 2009 and 2014.

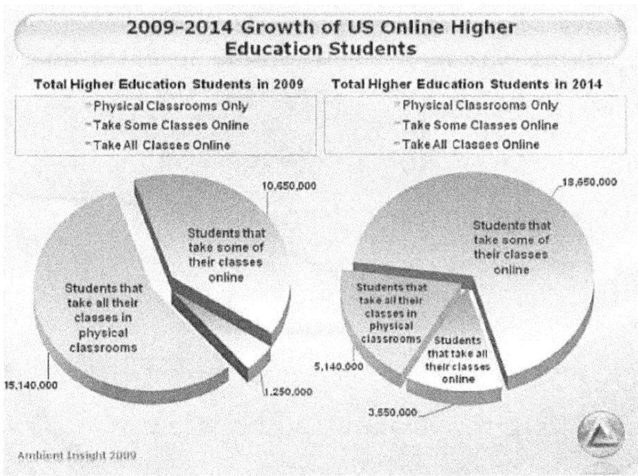

It is very obvious from the graph that online education became even more pervasive during that five-year period. However, the education mentioned here is static, meaning that the students typically sit and learn the subjects just by listening to their instructors. The physical movements required are minimal or nonexistent. Even the instructors, other than giving a presentation or writing something on the whiteboard, hardly move, either.

It is very true that online education in arts involving movement is still new and is almost unheard of in the martial arts, including karate. But, this is changing very quickly just as it has in many other industries. This is why I have written this chapter to share the changes that are already occurring.

Next, we need to touch lightly on the history of the Internet as doing so will show you that I am no stranger to the Internet world. Shall we start?

The World Wide Web (abbreviated as *WWW*) was introduced in 1989; however, pundits in the industry claim that the start of the Internet for the general public was in 1991, when domains became publicly available. Interestingly, I found my first software industry job in 1992 at a subsidiary of Xerox that developed the Internet language called *Smalltalk*. I was hired as a sales executive to market their software development tool to the Asia-Pacific region. During the five years of my tenure at this company, besides selling their software tool, I was involved in the establishment of the very first online university in England. I recall it was around 1993 or 1994, so this was more than twenty years ago.

At that time, no one was sure if it would be accepted by the public, and we thought it would take many decades for it to eventually be accepted and then become popular. Of course, we were totally wrong as it took less than twenty years to become almost a standard offering. As you may know, you will now have a very difficult time finding an institution among the accredited universities that does not offer some kind of online course.

After that job, my professional career progressed as the Internet industry boomed with the dot-com bubble until I lost my last job in 2009. During those years, online business experienced a revolution as many new business models appeared, such as online book stores (*Amazon*), search engines (*Google*), social networks (*Facebook*), auctions (*eBay*), videos (*YouTube*), and many others that you are already familiar with. The history of the Internet is really a fascinating thing, and I sort of grew with it. If you wish to learn more about it, you can find a brief history of the Internet at the following page on *Wikipedia*: www.wikipedia.org/wiki/History_of_the_Internet.

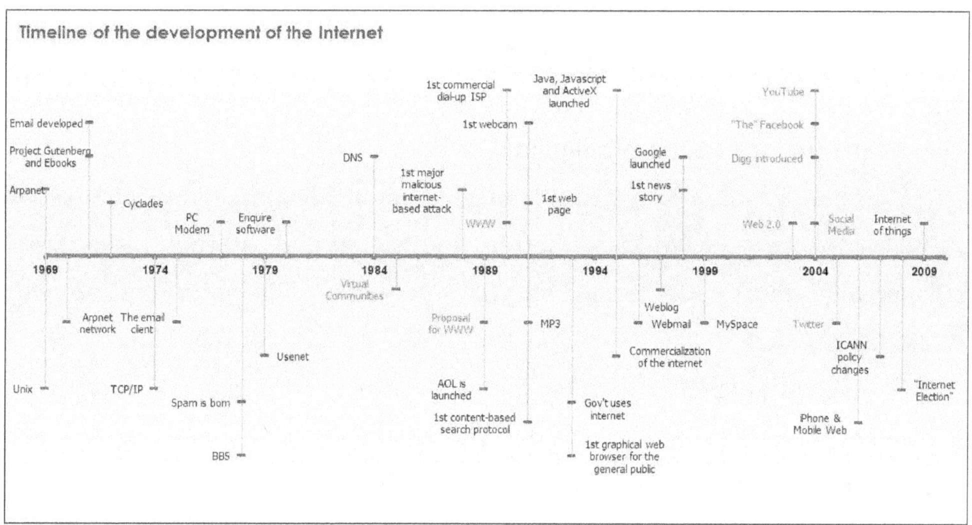

Throughout those years, I was not a full-time karate instructor. I believed my livelihood should not depend on my karate income, and this was my way of keeping my karate teaching pure. After passing the age of sixty, I was forced to "retire" from my high-tech job, which enabled me to take on full-time karate instructor status. By no means am I complaining. In fact, I feel that I have now come back home to my passion.

Anyway, I wish to mention that my experience with the Internet did not stop with my retirement from my high-tech job. My involvement is found in three different areas of karate teaching that are related to the Internet. The first area is that I already have some actual experience with giving a few "online" exams. The second is Online Dojo, which is my virtual dojo program. The third is a three-year partnership that I had with the online karate teaching company Karate Coaching.

Let me cover these three areas in chronological order.

The first experience was a recorded examination that I carried out in 2005 for some members in Mexico after receiving permission from Master Asai. In fact, he was the one who told me that we should do this for our members who live remotely and are too poor to make the long trip to an examination site.

Even though I was already familiar with videoconferencing, I must admit that it was not very easy to evaluate the practitioners' performances via DVD. However, a big advantage of the DVD method is that I could view the performances repeatedly until I was totally satisfied. I believe there were eight of them, all of whom I passed, and I believe I did the right thing.

After that, I examined two more practitioners in 2006, both of whom lived in East Coast states (New York and Florida). I failed one and passed the other. I will talk about this more in depth later, but it was very easy to determine the ones who were not up to par.

The second experience with the Internet started in 2010, when I started a virtual karate program called *Online Dojo*. This program consists of a group of karate lessons that are offered via an online videoconferencing tool. Currently (2016), I have four students: one in the U.S., two in Latin America, and one in Asia. For your information, I am not taking any more online students because I travel too much to allocate time for such a program.

Through this actual teaching and coaching experience over the last several years, I believe I have learned a great deal about the benefits and the limitations of this teaching method and the online videoconferencing tool that it employs.

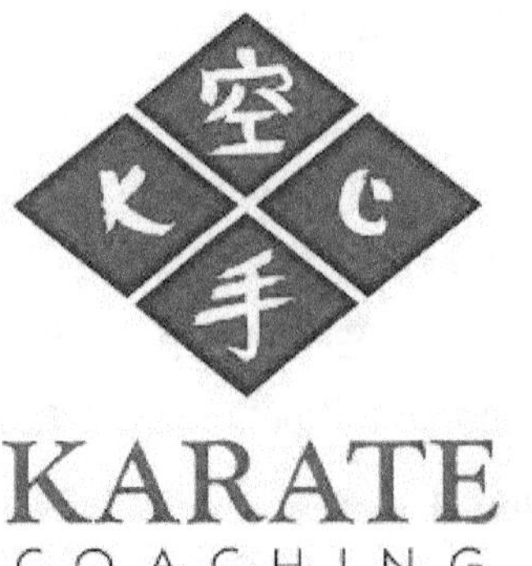

The third experience with Internet programs is my involvement with Karate Coaching, the largest and most reputable online karate instruction service provider. This company had been in operation since 2008 when I joined them in 2012. I knew the owner of the company because he also runs another enterprise called *Tôkon*, which is a karate uniform manufacturer. When I was invited to join the team, I immediately accepted the invitation.

As I mentioned earlier, I had already started an online teaching service, but the method I was using could only reach out to a few individuals. Through the Karate Coaching medium, I realized that I could reach out to thousands of people.

Interestingly, in this format, I am the one who is filmed and viewed by the students. I have found this to be a good complement to my Online Dojo project, but I have also found that video recording can be almost cruel as it records all the flaws and mistakes one makes.

I have made it clear that I am not an amateur in the area of the Internet or the online karate experience. Now we need to look at the program we offer.

Our online examination is not the standard examination method for our members. We encourage all our members to participate in the in-person examinations. We reserve the online examination only for those practitioners who find it economically impossible to participate in an in-person examination.

The online examination method is available only for the *dan* ranks of *shodan* through *godan*. Those who apply for *rokudan* or above must have an in-person examination.

In addition, the online examination method cannot be used more than once. For instance, if a student takes a *shodan* examination online, then he cannot take another online examination. He must take an in-person examination for his *nidan* diploma. We believe there will be sufficient time to prepare for his next examination in terms of both karate skills and financial requirements.

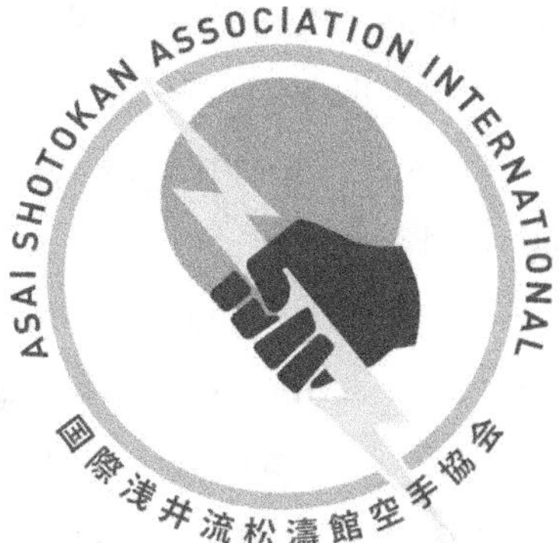

I am proud to say that ASAI has some of the most challenging exam requirements of all Shotokan organizations. Our syllabus is not static; we are constantly refining it. If you are interested in our exam syllabus, please feel free to write to us at administration@asaikarate.com, and we will be happy to share the most current version with you.

I was a lifetime member of the largest Shotokan organization in Japan for nearly forty years. Maybe this organization feels that its syllabus is permanently set. I do not recall any improvements or major changes to it during my forty-year tenure. If this lack of recollection comes from my poor memory, I apologize, but I do not think this is the case. But, as the main topic of this chapter is not the content of that organization's exam syllabus, I will not go into the details of that here.

Back to our syllabus, what I began to say with pride was that ours is one of the best exam syllabi one can find. Anyone who passes an exam using this syllabus should be proud. For an online exam, the syllabus becomes more challenging because there are some additional requirements. There are two different online methods, and I will describe what the additional requirements are along with a general explanation of each method below.

1. The Real-Time Online Method

By using an Internet videoconferencing tool (e.g., Skype), the examinee can perform his exam requirements in front of an examiner via camera. By the way, I am not limiting this to Skype as the only conferencing tool. There are other Internet videoconferencing tools, such as those provided through *Google+* and *Facebook*, but Skype has so far been the main conferencing tool that I have used. Whichever one works the best should be considered and used.

There are a couple of requirements. One is that both the examinee (sender) and the examiner (receiver) must have high-speed Internet capability. The other, which is not necessarily a must but is highly desirable, is a large screen (twenty-nine inches or larger), especially on the examiner's side so that he can adequately view the performance.

For those who use this exam method, the content of the syllabus itself is the same as, or very similar to, the in-person exam. One additional requirement is the repetition of some, if not all, of the *kihon*, *kata*, and *kumite* performances. In other words, the examinee will be asked to repeat some or all of the syllabus once or more if necessary. For instance, he will be asked to run a given *kata* not only facing the front (as he would in an in-person exam) but also facing other directions, such as the back or the sides. This is a necessary requirement as the examiners only have a two-dimensional, and thus limited, view. A typical in-person *shodan* exam takes about one hour. The time requirement for a Skype exam may be as much as ninety minutes or more.

Another requirement is that only one examinee is allowed at a time, even if more than one person is taking the same exam. In an in-person examination, I have witnessed as many as five or six students lined up at one time. I have always been opposed to this process as it is almost impossible for any examiner, even if he holds a senior rank and is very experienced, to review each examinee's performance with sufficient attention to make a sound judgment.

2. The Video-Recording Method

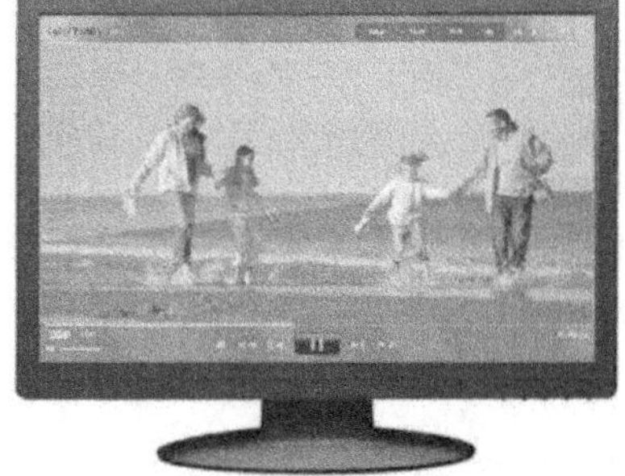

I suspect this method is the one that will receive the most concerns and objections. I am aware of this and agree that it has many limitations, which I will discuss later. Having said that, I still consider this to be a viable and valid option.

Let me explain. We must recognize that there are many countries where high-speed Internet services are still not available or, if they are available, are too expensive. For some practitioners, an open space that is large enough to hold an exam may not be available, regardless of the availability of high-speed Internet service. I personally much prefer to conduct a real-time exam with a videoconferencing tool, but for some people, this is just not possible. For these people, the video-recording method may be the only option.

The syllabus for this method becomes most demanding as the examiner and examinee cannot have two-way communication. The examinee will be asked to perform the *kihon*, *kata*, and *kumite* requirements in at least two directions. In addition, he will be asked to perform more *kata* to demonstrate his ability. For instance, in an in-person *shodan* exam, the requirement is to run either two or three *kata*. For the video-recording method, the examinee may be asked to run all of the Heian *kata*, Tekki Shodan, and one *tokui kata* (得意形), such as Bassai Dai, Kanku Dai (観空大), Enpi (燕飛), Jion (慈恩), and Jutte (十手), etc. For the Heian series, the requirement is *gyaku kata* (逆形, 'reverse form'), which is the mirror image of the *kata* (i.e., starting the *kata* to your right).

On top of this, the examiner may ask the examinee to submit a written essay before or after the exam. For an in-person *dan* exam, the essay requirement starts at *yondan*. For the video-recording method, it may start at *shodan*, depending on the applicant's karate background and/or exam performance.

Now you have seen that the syllabus for the online exam is not a piece of cake for many practitioners. In fact, some practitioners will feel that the syllabus is too difficult, but that is exactly the intention, to discourage examinees who want an easy exam.

If the syllabus is acceptable, then what would be the next concern? I suspect it would be the qualifications of the examiners. Can the exam be performed at a satisfactory level by just any examiner? We do not believe so. In our organization, there are four levels for the examiner license, starting from D Class and going all the way up to A Class.

To receive a D-Class license, the applicant must be a *sandan* or above. With a D-Class license, the examiner can grade his students up to *shodan*. The rank requirement goes up as the degree of the license advances. The *dan* requirement to receive an A-Class license is *rokudan* or above.

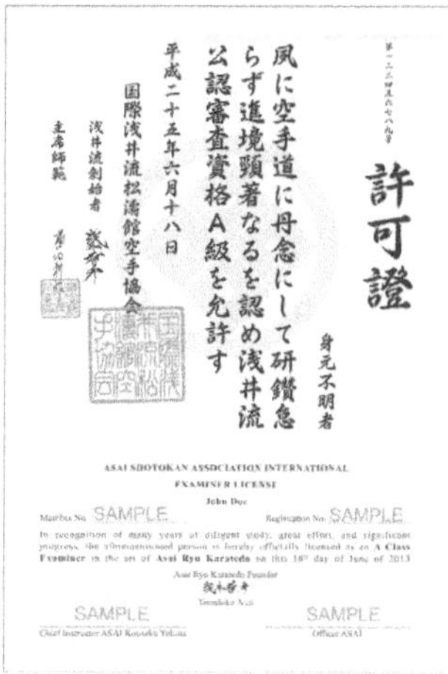

These requirements are for in-person examinations. To qualify to conduct an online exam, the candidate must have an A-Class license and must have received the authorization of the *shihankai* (師範会), a group of senior instructors who are *rokudan* or above. Currently, we have seven *shihankai* members around the world: one in Japan, two in the U.S., two in Europe, one in the Middle East, and one in South America.

The *shihankai* checks out the applicant's experience and ability to determine if he is qualified to conduct an online examination. If approved, the board provides advice and suggestions to the applicant before granting the special license and will not grant it unless the applicant is fully qualified at a very senior level. As of the close of 2016, I am the only qualified online *dan* examiner. The other *shihankai* members also have the option to become online *dan* examiners by undergoing the examination process (verbal Q&A) and a background check of their experience with online instruction.

We have now discussed the strict qualification process for approving examiners for the online exam. Additionally, the *dan* syllabus will be shared and reviewed at the end of this chapter, and I expect that reviewing this information will dispel any notion that this is an easy exam.

I am well aware that the online examination method is not perfect and that it has some limitations. Thus, it is definitely not a replacement for the standard in-person examination, but even though there are several inherent limitations, most of these can be managed and kept to a minimum. Let me describe these limitations and also share with you how we can manage them.

Technical Limitations

There are two major technical limitations. One is the Internet itself, and the other is the difficulty of watching a student on a computer monitor.

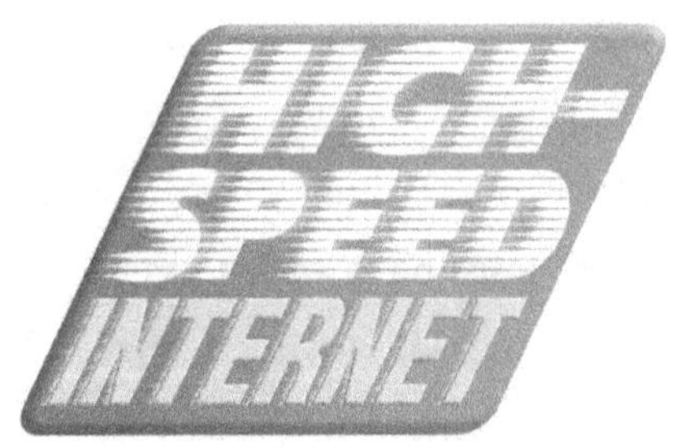

The Internet limitation has to do with the flow of data that is needed for online video communication. When the connection is poor or the speed is low, the video freezes up very frequently, which is literally a show stopper. This is common as the examinee moves quickly, which requires a lot of bandwidth.

In my case, I resolved this initially by getting a better modem, which increased my download speed from three to six megabits per second (Mbps). In 2015, I started a new fiber-optic service with AT&T that provides an amazing speed of forty-five Mbps. At least on my end, there should be no problem with the bandwidth. On the other hand, there can be a problem on the examinee's end if he does not have high-speed Internet service as a fast connection is required on both ends.

It is unfortunate that there are many countries in the third world where a high-speed Internet connection is either not available at all or offered at an extremely high cost. However, technology is advancing almost daily, and I am convinced that this limitation will disappear within the foreseeable future.

The other technical limitation is the issue of viewing the examinee on a small screen. Once again, the problem resides on both sides, that of the sender and the receiver. This problem is not as much a technical issue as it is a financial one as one has to spend some money to purchase a larger monitor. However, once again, with the rapid increase of technology, the prices of these types of monitors are going down. A twenty-nine-inch monitor is only a few hundred dollars these days, which is very affordable.

This problem is more pronounced on the examiner's side. It is not necessary for the examinee to have a huge monitor as he does not normally need to see any moving objects. He typically just needs to listen to what the examiner orders. Even if the examiner needs to show a movement, when such an action is called for, a regular computer screen is good enough to see and understand.

Financial Hardship

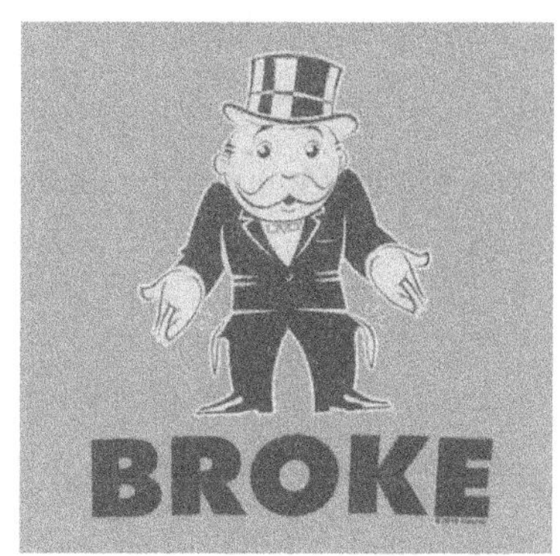

It is true that the fees for the online examination are higher than the fees for the in-person examination. And, if you are interested, you can contact ASAI for specific information regarding our online exam fees. But, you may be wondering if these higher fees are justifiable. I definitely believe they are. In fact, for many examinees, taking an online exam is a bargain. I can emphatically tell you that the savings for the examinee are unbelievably huge.

For instance, if a *shodan* candidate wishes to take an in-person exam, he has two choices. One is to travel to the city of an examiner, and the other is to invite an examiner to his own city. We are talking about practitioners from remote regions such as South Africa, Latin America, Asia, etc. Just imagine the cost of airfare, lodging, meals, and other expenses. It could easily add up to a thousand dollars or possibly even more for the examinee to take a weekend trip.

The cost is even higher if he invites an examiner to his city. Typically, an examiner will not make the trip to give an examination for just one person, so this will usually be combined with a weekend seminar of some sort. This means that the examinee or the host must bear the expense of the weekend event in addition to the examiner's (possibly international) airfare, lodging, meals, and other expenses. So, for a lone practitioner or a small dojo in a remote country who has almost no opportunity to participate in a local exam event, the online exam is certainly a life-, time-, and money-saving option.

How about for the examiner? Are the higher exam fees too much for him to ask? I do not think so. Just imagine the amount of extra time the examiner has to spend on an online exam. Even if he can spend less time by not traveling, he should get paid more for his expertise as judging an examinee's level of karate skill under the more challenging conditions presented by online tools really requires more experience and a unique ability. Judging and evaluating a performance on a screen also requires much closer attention. For these reasons, the fees for the online exam are more than justifiable.

Lack of Physical Presence

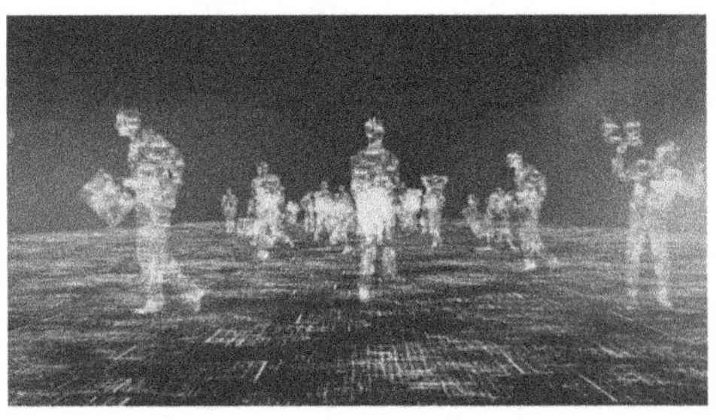

This limitation is real and true. The examinee cannot shake hands with the examiner, and the examiner has a two-dimensional rather than a three-dimensional view. However, for the examination itself, I have already discussed how this can be overcome by compensating with added syllabus requirements. In the twenty-first century, with so many advanced communication tools, not being physically present is no longer a show stopper or even a significant handicap.

Lack of Formality

What makes anything formal? The examiner wears his *karategi* (空手着, 'karate uniform'), and the examinee is required to wear his, as well. If the exam is taken in the living room of a residence, does this make the event informal and inappropriate? I don't think so at all. Does it really have to be held at a dojo or a gym? When you consider that our karate training can be done in our house, then why not the exam, as well?

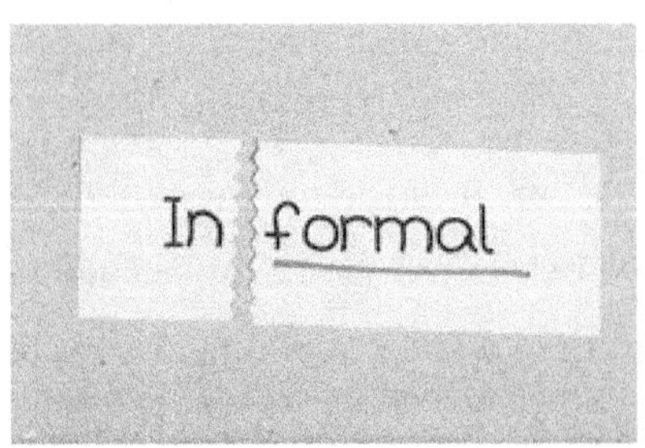

How about the formality of the event itself? I have seen more than one in-person exam where the examiner was wearing a T-shirt and casual attire instead of his *karategi*. If the requirements for being formal include ambience, then I feel examiners should wear their *karategi*. If a line-up ritual (*seiza* [正座], *mokuso* [黙想], etc.) is required, this can be done sitting in front of a computer and included in the event.

So, the fact that the examiner and examinee are hundreds or thousands of miles apart does not automatically make the exam informal. The level of formality totally depends on how the event is conducted. It can easily be made very formal by running it just as we would for an in-person exam.

Lack of Pressure

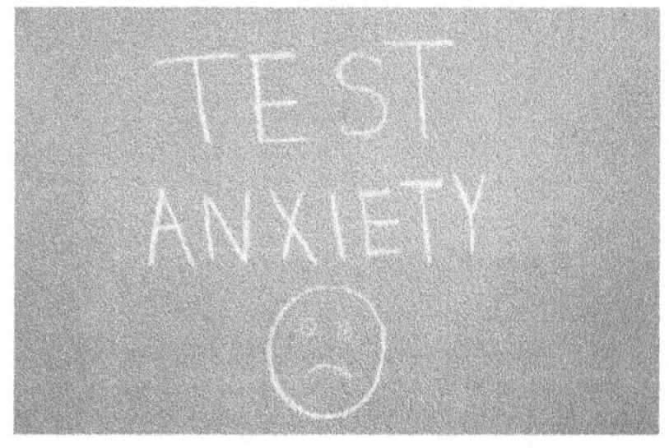

This may be partially true as the exam is very private and exclusive. In an exam held in a dojo situation, the examinee may have many of his *senpai* and *kohai* watching him. So, if you think this pressure should be an exam requirement, then it is true that an online exam can be "easier." However, if you consider the main reason for taking an exam, you will realize that it is to judge the examinee's karate skill. Is it fair that in an in-person exam, the examinee performs very poorly because he gets stage fright? A shy person is always at a disadvantage, and I do not consider that fair.

Some may say that with the video-recording method, the examinee can reshoot the video if he makes a mistake or is not satisfied with his performance. This is true, but, once again, we must consider the objective of the exam, which is to determine the person's skill level. As an examiner, I consider the performance shown in a recorded video to be the examinee's best performance. Therefore, if the examinee shows any flaws or mistakes, these will be viewed *very* negatively. Also, you must consider it to be a disadvantage that the video-recording method allows the examinee's performance to be viewed repeatedly and scrutinized very closely. You just can't hide your mistakes there.

Unethical Editing

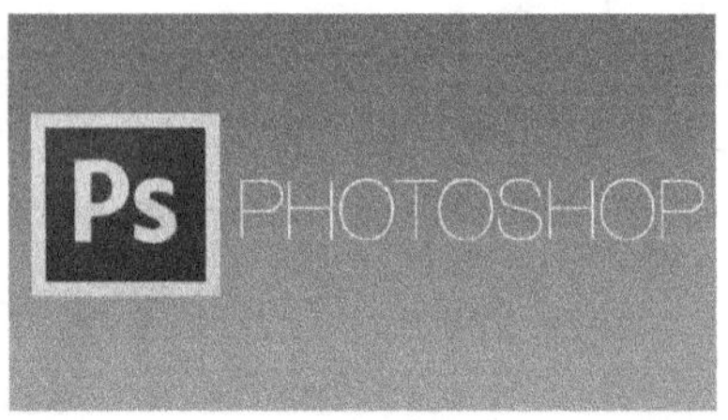

I understand that some examinees can be technically skilled at video recording and may be able to speed up their performance. It is true that there is no indication on the screen if such an effect has been implemented. If the speed is increased by ten percent or so, then I may not be able to detect it. If it is increased by more than twenty or thirty percent, then the examinee's performance will look very unnatural, and it will be very easy to detect foul play.

If such a thing were found, the examinee would be immediately disqualified, of course, but I doubt anyone would be stupid enough to risk such a thing by doing this. Even if the examinee were to risk this and increase the speed by, say, ten percent, what good would that do? Speed itself cannot correct or improve a technique. This works only if the technique is correct to begin with. If a technique is poor at a slow speed, then making it faster will not make it any better. If there is a mistake, then it will still be mistake, even at a higher speed. So, in the end, I do not worry about this possible infraction.

Identity Fraud

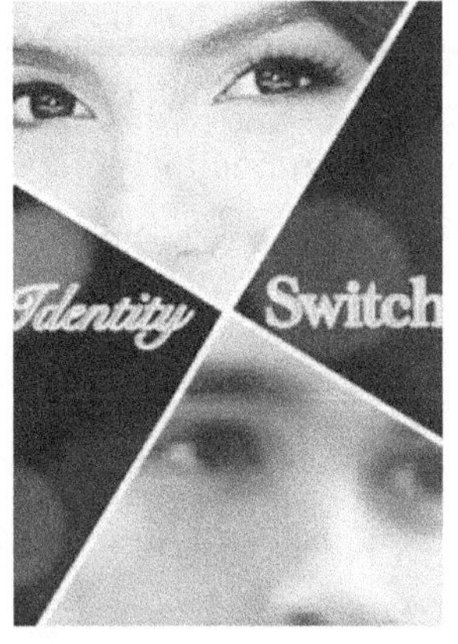

This refers to when the examinee does not perform the exam syllabus himself. Instead, he has someone else who is supposed to be better perform in his place. This is like having a stuntman in a movie.

I hope no one is stupid enough to do something like this, but it is indeed possible. So, we ask the examinee to submit a photo of himself with his exam application forms. When he passes his exam, we post the photos so that everyone can see. If the name does not match the face in the photo, then someone will inform us of this strange discrepancy.

Even if someone were to successfully pull this off in an online exam, he would have to take his next exam in person since the online exam is limited to one time only. So, an identity switch is not really feasible or desirable.

What else? One person on *Faceboo*k wrote that an online exam was disrespectful to Master Funakoshi and Master Asai. He was even worried that Master Asai would roll over in his grave.

It would be wonderful if Master Asai would appear in my dreams, even if he were unhappy. But, I do not think that would be the case. As I explained earlier, it was Master Asai's idea to hold a recorded examination in 2005. As many of you may already know, Master Asai was a very innovative person. He created not only many new *kata* but also many new *kihon* and *kumite* systems. He even invented *kata* and *kumite* for practitioners in wheelchairs. Online instruction and examination were part of his agenda and were approved by him.

How about Master Funakoshi? I believe he was as innovative and creative as Master Asai in his own way. He did not create any new *kata*, but he did change the names of the *kata* as well as many techniques within them. He adapted the judo (柔道) uniform to create the karate uniform. The *dan* ranking system, along with other ideas from judo, was also adopted by him. He not only changed but also invented some key aspects, such as the new stance *kokutsu dachi* and the famous *Niju Kun*.

I have written about these subjects in the past, so you can find information on this in the other books I have written. If he were alive today, and if he understood what the Internet can do, I am totally confident that he would not only approve this examination method but also congratulate me for starting it.

Conclusion

So, after having read all these facts, what do you think now? I hope you have at least learned the full scope of the program and understood my analysis of the feasibility of this examination method. Of course, it is up to you to decide if this option is a good thing for karate practitioners in remote areas and, consequently, if it is beneficial for karate in general.

As I stated at the beginning, I have not written this to convince anyone. I can only say that the world is getting smaller because of the Internet. In addition, business structures are rapidly changing from brick-and-mortar to virtual locations. Just look at the book business as a good example. We no longer see big bookstores in shopping centers. Once-famous stores such as Barnes & Noble, B. Dalton, and Borders, to name a few, are now gone. Almost everyone buys from *Amazon* these days.

Change must come to karate, and I believe it is changing gradually. I am proud that ASAI is the first organization to provide this option. We will continue to provide this service to those members who need it to get their rightful ranks recognized. I am confident that one day in the not-too-distant future the online examination method will be granted citizenship in the karate world.

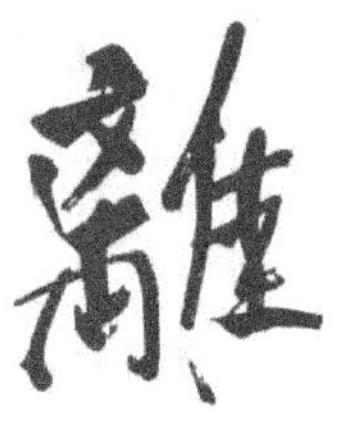

Chapter Nine
第九章

A Deeper Understanding of Tekki (Naihanchi)
鉄騎形(ナイハンチ)をより深く理解するには

鉄騎初段

Tekki Shodan

Tekki (鉄騎) used to be a fundamental *kata* for Shuri Te (首里手) karate, from which Shotokan evolved. Until Funakoshi changed its name, it was called *Naihanchi* (ナイハンチ), *Naifanchi* (ナイファンチ), or *Naifanchin* (ナイファンチン). Although it is interesting to discuss the names of this *kata*, we will not do that in this chapter.

What I want to say about this *kata* is that, unfortunately, it is no longer receiving the proper attention, and students are no longer receiving sufficient training in it in most Shotokan schools. In many dojo, Tekki Shodan is only considered to be a required *kata* to advance from fourth *kyu* to third *kyu*, that is, a *kata* that you learn before brown belt, when you begin to learn the "real" *kata*. This trend is very unfortunate, and even damaging, because it means a huge loss for Shotokan karate in general.

My hope is that this chapter will provide the missing information that will make the reader realize the important essence that is built into this unique *kata*. I hope this realization will result in more appreciation for Tekki and more motivation to practice it more frequently and with more respect.

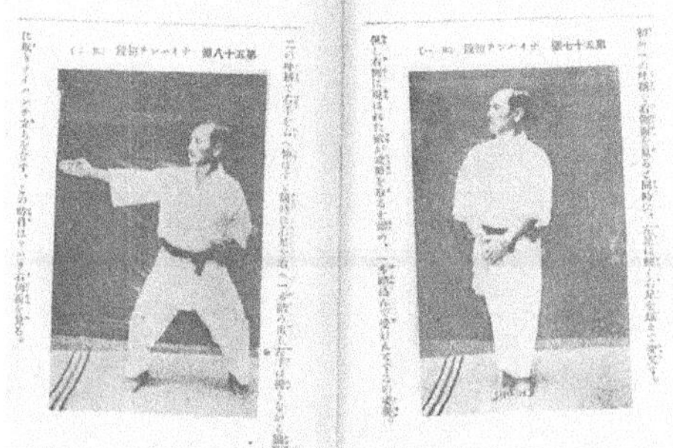

Before I continue, I wish to ask the instructors and senior practitioners out there a quick question. Why is the left foot moved in front of the right foot in the first step of Tekki Shodan as demonstrated by Funakoshi in the photo to the left, which comes from *Karate Do Kyohan* (空手道教範 [Kobunsha, 1935])? Why not move it behind? Is there any significance to this movement, or is it an irrelevant or worthless point? Please think about this as I will cover it in Key Point 1.

Tekki is unique because other than *heisoku dachi* and *kosa dachi* (交差立ち), the only stance it uses is *kiba dachi* (騎馬立ち). In addition to its use of *kiba da-*

chi, this *kata*'s body shifting is done only to the sides, which is one more thing that makes it unique and mysterious. I will talk about this in Key Point 2.

Of course, *kiba dachi* is a perfect stance to train your legs, but there is one other hidden objective in this stance, and I will address this in Key Point 3.

There is one more interesting point, which is that there are three Tekki: Tekki Shodan (鉄騎初段), Tekki Nidan (鉄騎二段), and Tekki Sandan (鉄騎三段). All three of these start to the right side. You will remember that you start to the left in all of the Heian *kata*. I will not go into this topic in this chapter; I will leave it as homework for those who are curious and interested and will share my hypothesis somewhere else in the future.

Key Point 1

The *kamae* of Tekki Shodan is *heisoku dachi*. Interestingly, the *kamae* of the next *kata* you learn, Bassai Dai, is also *heisoku dachi*. In Tekki, you learn to shift your body sideways, while in Bassai Dai, you learn to step forward. I see the wisdom in this and am truly impressed with the deep understanding of the Okinawan master who developed the *kata* syllabus.

The student learns to shift sideways first because it is easier to show him how to shift his body weight between his left and right foot. In other words, in the *kamae* of *heisoku dachi*, your body weight is distributed evenly between the left and right foot.

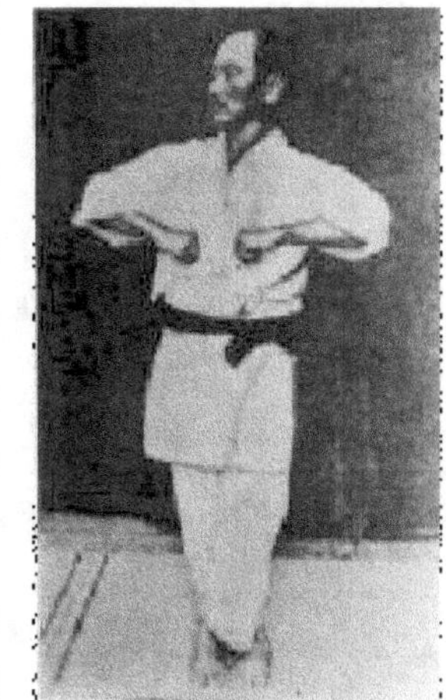

In the first movement, you cross your legs in *kosa dachi*. The photo to the right shows this movement in Tekki Nidan. The same mechanics are taught in both Tekki Shodan and Tekki Nidan. The only difference is that the latter starts from *shizentai* (自然体), which is a more natural stance than *heisoku dachi*.

What happens on the first step is that the weight on your left leg becomes zero as you lift it to step over, and the weight on your right leg becomes one hundred percent. Of course, in *kosa dachi*, a small amount of weight (maybe ten percent or so) is applied to the left leg, but in the next instant, this leg receives one hundred percent of the weight as the right leg is lifted up high for *fumikomi* (踏み込み). Then, you end in *kiba dachi* (back to fifty-fifty).

This change in weight distribution from fifty-fifty to zero-one hundred (or ten-ninety) to one hundred-zero and finally back to fifty-fifty is the biggest lesson in Tekki. Every time you step to the side and move through *kosa dachi* into *kiba dachi*, you learn how to shift your body quickly and strongly. The Okinawan masters believed that once the student had learned how to move sideways, he could start learning how to shift his body forward. I agree with them completely.

The value of this technique has been lost in Shotokan, as far as I can see, and it is not taught this way anymore. Thus, many students fail to learn this key point. They mistakenly believe Tekki is a strange and unimportant *kata* they go through before they become brown belts so that they can tackle more important *kata* such as Bassai Dai. This is a great shame, and I wish many people would study this amazing *kata* again and discover its true value.

Let's go back to my first question. Why do we move the left foot in front of the right foot instead of moving it behind? Take a close look at Funakoshi's left foot in the two photos shown on the previous pages (from Tekki Shodan and Tekki Nidan). You can see that his entire foot is planted firmly on the ground. This is critical. If only the ball of your left foot touches the ground, as in *kosa dachi*, then you will have to put your heel down before you can shift all of your body weight to the left foot, which is an extra movement.

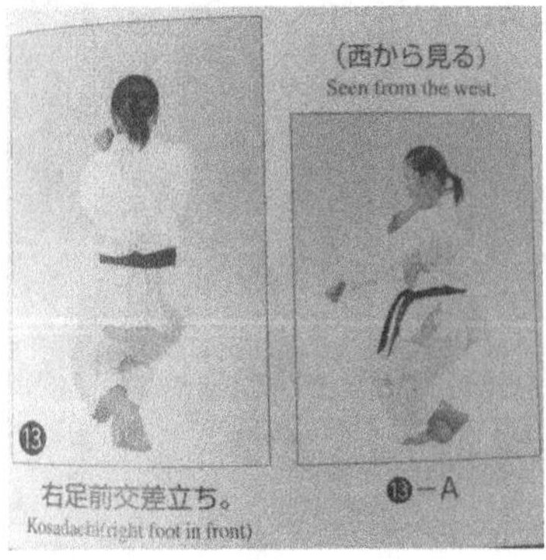

Is very much time lost in this movement? No, it is only a split second, but it is still significant if you are trying to develop a quick weight-shifting process, which is one of the key objectives of Tekki training. So, if you move your left foot behind your right foot, your feet will look like the illustration on the previous page. If you force your left foot to be totally flat on the ground, you will lose your balance or need to shift toward the rear. This is only natural as your leg is attached to the back side of your foot. You have much more space in front, so you can easily cross over and put the entire foot on the ground.

Then, what's wrong with moving the left foot behind the right foot and just shifting backward as a result? This is not wrong as this step can be used effectively if you are going to throw *ushiro geri* (後ろ蹴り) or *yoko geri kekomi* (横蹴り蹴込み) with your right foot. From *kiba dachi*, you shift and turn your back to the opponent as you move your left foot behind your right foot. If I remember correctly, Bruce Lee used this movement (stepping behind and throwing *yoko geri*) in one of his movies. I also remember that many *kumite* competitors adopted *kiba dachi* in the seventies because of his dramatic acting.

Regardless, the use of this stepping motion is limited; therefore, the fundamental concept of *kata* is to move forward. This concept is also adopted in Tekki by stepping in front of the other leg.

Key Point 2

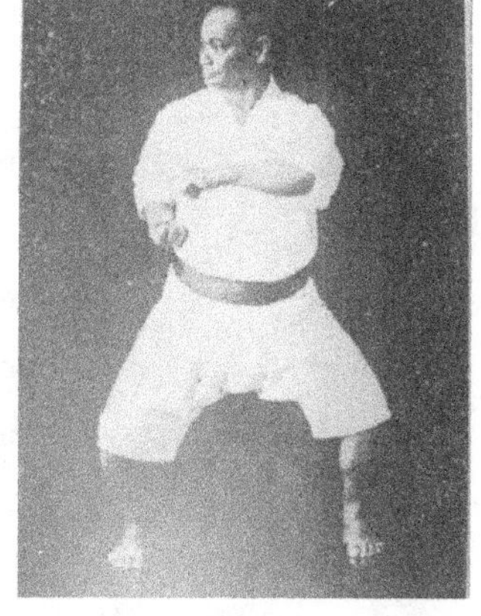

There are two good reasons Tekki is based only on sideways movement from *kiba dachi*. The first one is obvious and very well known: *kiba dachi* is an excellent stance for training and strengthening the legs. The second one has been a mystery and has to do with why the movement is exclusively sideways.

I have heard a few ideas. One was that this *kata* was created to fight with one's back against a wall. Another was that it was for learning to fight in a narrow corridor or on a boat. I will talk about *bunkai* later, so I will not go into this now.

Let me present my understanding of this unique *kata*. I have already mentioned the uniqueness of its body shifting. Before the Heian series was invented in the late nineteenth century, Tekki was the very first *kata* in the syllabus, and the Okinawan masters used it to teach beginners how to shift their body sideways before teaching them to shift forward. Why shift sideways first? Because it is physically easier to shift in that direction.

I know many people do not see this point as they feel more comfortable moving forward than they do moving sideways. But, I ask you to do the following experiment. Stand up straight in *heisoku dachi*. Your arms can be held at your sides, or you can hold onto your belt as you are experimenting only with body shifting. Now lean forward. You have several muscle groups in your feet and calves that prevent you from falling. After you have felt your physical reaction to this, try leaning sideways from the same *heisoku dachi*. You will find that it is a lot harder to prevent yourself from falling sideways.

Believe it or not, the ninja (忍者) of medieval Japan found this method useful for running and actually trained running sideways. Regardless, by "falling" to the side, a beginner on Okinawa learned a quick body-shifting method. Once he learned the sideways method taught in Tekki, he moved on to Bassai Dai, in which he learned another quick body-shifting method by "falling" forward. This idea is analogous to the hidden energy of the water that is held in a dam. I must say this old-time curriculum of learning fast body shifting is so wise and amazing. I covered the details of this concept in Chapter 9: "Unstable Balance" of my book *Shotokan Mysteries*.

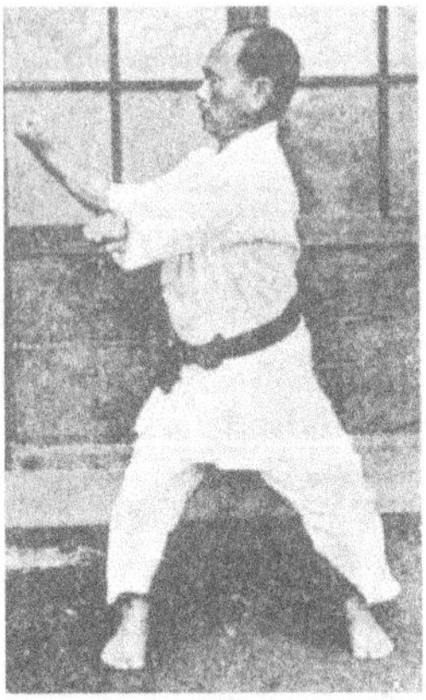

In fact, there is another reason for *kiba dachi*, which is not emphasized in most dojo. *Kiba dachi* is classified as one of the outward-tension stances. However, by moving sideways, one learns how to tense the inner muscles of the upper legs. This, again, helps with fast body shifting.

I must add one more point on the training purposes of Tekki Shodan. As you can see in the photo to the left, Master Funakoshi is beautifully demonstrating the flexibility of his hip joints. The student must learn to rotate his upper body 180 degrees in these particular combinations without deforming his *kiba dachi.* Unless his hips and midsection are flexible, he will find it extremely difficult to rotate his upper body as shown in the photo. This is an excellent example of a solid, immovable stance with flexible upper-body movements.

Key Point 3

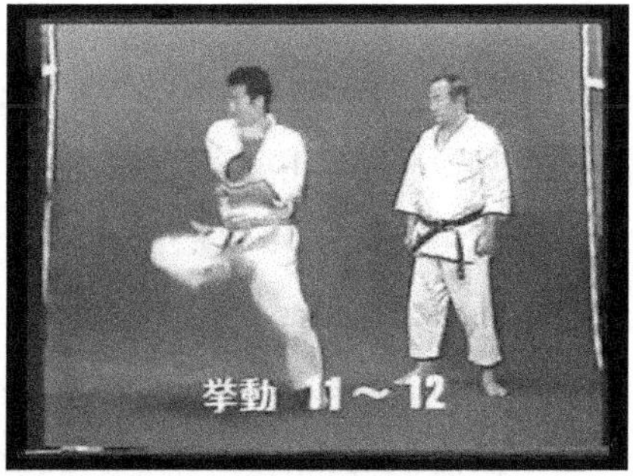

The last key point is the most challenging to understand and has never been explained before. It is the concept of the invisible leg, and in this, I see the true wisdom of the Okinawan master who created this *kata.*

I will explain, but first take a look at the photo to the right, which shows Masatoshi Nakayama (中山正敏, 1913–1987) giving instruction in Tekki, using his assistant, Yoshiharu Osaka (大坂可治, 1947–), who is executing *nami gaeshi* (波返し). As you can see, he is not standing straight up on his left leg as he executes this technique. He remains in *kiba dachi* except that his right leg is executing *nami gaeshi.* In other words, if he keeps his right leg in the air, he will fall to his right side. Of course, he will bring his right foot down quickly and continue to the next technique.

I suspect many students might have been instructed by their sensei to do the exact same thing when they learned this *kata.* In the video, Nakayama Sensei is saying, "Don't lean to your left. Execute your *nami gaeshi* very quickly and put your right foot down before you fall so that you can keep your upper body in the same position." To do this, you have to remain in this position for a split second while you execute the *nami gaeshi* technique.

So, look at the photo again. If you only looked at his upper body, you might think Osaka Sensei was in a stable *kiba dachi.* In other words, for a split second, he was standing as though he had an invisible right leg under his right hip. You could almost draw an invisible leg there. To be able to do this, you have to learn to use your internal muscles, which I will not explain here as it is a very involved concept.

But, now you must be asking why you have to learn this. Some sensei probably told you that you need to learn how to execute *nami gaeshi* quickly. This sounds like a no-brainer. No one has explained that there is a hidden objective in this particular technique. Mind you, the technique I am referring to is not *nami gaeshi* but the invisible-leg technique.

OK, so I said this was to develop your internal muscles, but for what purpose? Believe it or not, this is to develop the balance that is necessary to provide strong support for *zenkutsu dachi* and kicks. Let me explain further. When I say, "*zenkutsu dachi*," I do not mean a static *zenkutsu dachi* with both feet on the ground. I am talking about the *zenkutsu dachi* you assume when attacking forward.

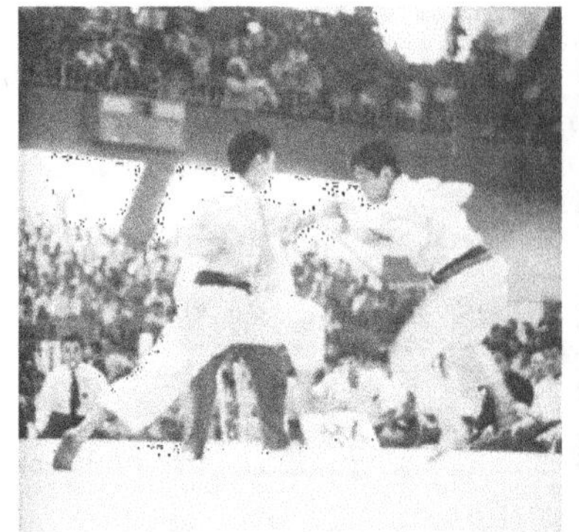

Take a look at the photo to the right. This is a famous photo taken at one of the matches of the 1961 JKA All Japan Championship in Tokyo, Japan. The opponent on the left is Takayuki Mikami (三上孝之, 1933–), who now holds the rank of ninth *dan* and resides in New Orleans, Louisiana, U.S.A. The one who is doing *taisabaki* in midair is the late Tetsuhiko Asai, tenth *dan* and founder of the Japan Karate Shoto Federation (日本空手松濤連盟 [JKS]). Asai Sensei won this match and went on to win the championship that year, but this is not the topic at hand. What I want to call your attention to is Mikami Sensei's stance. Look at the extension of his left leg; he looks as if he were flying through the air. I am not saying Mikami Sensei developed this great extension ability by just practicing Tekki. What I am saying is that this invisible-leg technique in Tekki can help practitioners if they wish to develop a strong extension ability.

Astute readers will quickly realize why this ability is also used with kicking techniques. You have probably figured out that this ability is not for aiding the kick itself but rather for strengthening the supporting leg, which will give you the necessary forward reach. A rifle has an advantage over a pistol because it has more range. The same can be said of a kick that has more reach. A high kick is fine in a short-distance fight, but you need reach if the opponent is far away. The photo to the right shows a well-extended *mae geri*, but this can be applied to all kicks.

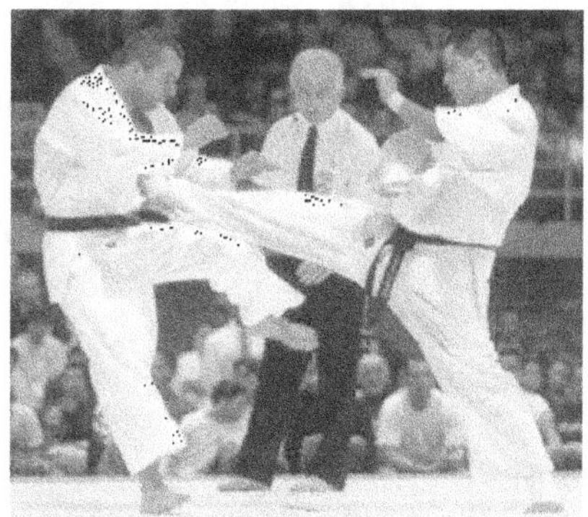

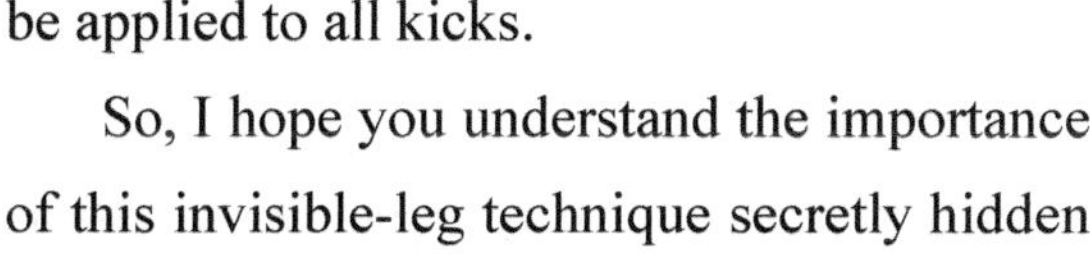

So, I hope you understand the importance of this invisible-leg technique secretly hidden within the *nami gaeshi* that is practiced in Tekki. Now you may be curious about the internal muscles and their training methods. Maybe someday I will spend some time addressing this interesting and important subject. For now, I suggest you practice Tekki, and I hope that you do so with a different vision. If you like *kumite,* it is worth your time to improve the invisible-leg technique as it will make your *tsuki* (突き, 'punching') and *keri* (蹴り, 'kicking') attacks much more effective and threatening to your opponents.

The last thing I want to include in this chapter is *bunkai*. Here, I only wish to provide you with the basic concepts you need to build your understanding.

We have already established that there are several levels of interpretation and application, which are called *bunkai*. If the application works, then that *bunkai* can be considered applicable or realistic. If it does not work, then it means either the application is incorrect or your technique is poor.

There are two fundamental concepts we must know about Tekki *bunkai*. Unfortunately, these concepts are not well known, and some incorrect interpretations have become widespread and generally accepted.

1. Short-distance Techniques

Tekki *kata* teaches many short-distance fighting techniques, such as *tsukami uke* (掴み受け), *kagi zuki* (鉤突き), *ashi uke* (足受け or 脚受け), knee kicks using *nami gaeshi*, *enpi uchi* (猿臂打ち), *jodan nagashi uke*, *tate uraken uchi* (縦裏拳打ち), holding breaks (first move in Tekki Nidan), throws (*kagi zuki* in Tekki Shodan and the second and third moves in Tekki Nidan), *gedan zuki* (下段突き), joint attacks, and arm-twisting techniques, to name a few.

2. Forward-facing *Bunkai*

Fundamentally, your imaginary opponent is in front of you and not necessarily to your side. You must not confuse the direction of the *bunkai* just because the steps taken in the *kata* are only to the sides. This *kata* is not teaching you to fight only in *kiba dachi*, which exposes your front (groin and midsection) to your opponent and is, of course, tactically unwise.

Look at the photo of Funakoshi on page 84 where he is executing *morote ude uke* (諸手腕受け) to his right side in a beautiful *kiba dachi*. Just try this. Place your hand over the bottom half of his body and see what his upper body looks like. What do you see? Doesn't he appear to be throwing this technique from a right *zenkutsu dachi*? In *bunkai*, you execute this technique from *zenkutsu dachi*, but in Tekki *kata*, you practice it from *kiba dachi* (for the purposes I have described here).

This *kata* was not designed as a method for fighting against a wall or in a narrow corridor as suggested in one of the Shotokan books that I've read, though I respect the opinion and work of that book's author. Rather, it was designed to teach a fighting method using restricted hip rotation by limiting the stance to *kiba dachi*. This is a perfect training method for short-distance fighting, where you are within grappling distance, and there is not much room to move. When you observe this *kata* as performed by Shorin Ryu (小林流) practitioners, you will witness a much more pronounced hip vibration with each technique.

Here are two photos that show Funakoshi and his student performing an interesting *bunkai* for the second and third movements in Tekki Shodan (*haishu uchi* and *enpi uchi*).

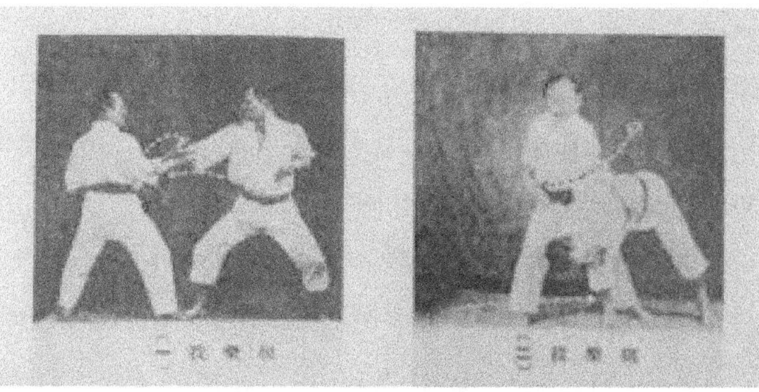

Here, Funakoshi uses *haishu uchi* (背手打ち) as *haishu osae* (背手抑え) or *otoshi uke* (落し受け). Then, he grabs the opponent's right wrist next and pulls him down as he takes one step forward and rotates his hips to bring the opponent's upper body down. During this process, he executes a left *enpi uchi* to the opponent's right elbow or rib cage, or he places his left hand on the opponent's elbow for leverage. A more aggressive interpretation (not shown in these photos) could be a *jodan enpi uchi* to the opponent's head instead of his elbow or rib cage.

By the way, this hip rotation and takedown cause him to face the opposite direction (his six o'clock) in this *bunkai*. If you are mentally trapped and believe that Tekki techniques must face only one direction, then you cannot even imagine this *bunkai*. In fact, this rotational move is incorporated into Tekki Mugen (鉄騎無限, 'Iron Horse Riding, Infinite').

Conclusion

I have shared only three key points of Tekki, but what did you think of them? Did these key points make sense to you? Have you now realized that these points are essential and fundamental elements for developing your karate, especially if you are an intermediate practitioner? I sincerely hope you have.

I recommend that all intermediate practitioners from fourth *kyu* to first *kyu* (and possibly even through *shodan*) put this *kata* into their regular training menu. I ask fourth-*kyu* practitioners particularly to not stop practicing this *kata* after pass-

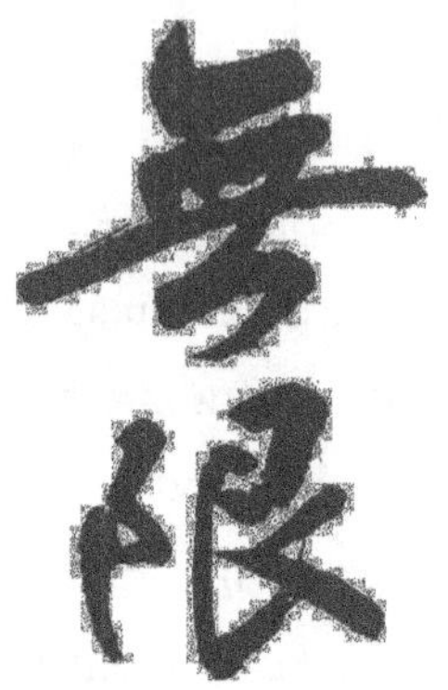

ing on to third *kyu*. I am aware that there are many new *kata* a brown belt needs to learn, but Tekki is a short *kata*, so it will not take too much time to include it in your routine. Spend five or ten minutes on this *kata* in each training session, and you can run it at least ten times.

If you learn the steps of Tekki Mugen, you can run this *kata* continuously for the full five minutes (or whatever time you wish to spend on it) without stopping at all. In addition, I must add that you can run Tekki Mugen along an *enbusen* (演武線) shaped like a circle, square, figure eight, or whatever other shape you wish. This simply makes it more fun to practice this *kata*.

As I delve further into the art of karate and find new meanings, I become more impressed with the ingenuity and wisdom of those ancient Okinawan masters who left us this treasure called *kata*.

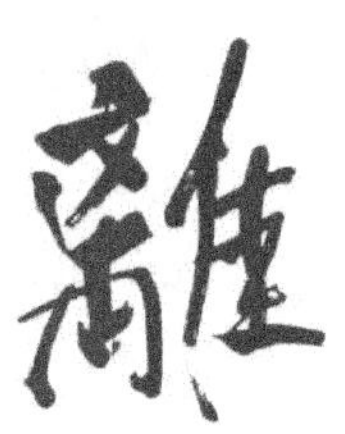

Chapter Ten
第十章

What Are Muchimi, Gamaku, and Chinkuchi?
ムチミ・ガマク・チンクチとは何ぞや

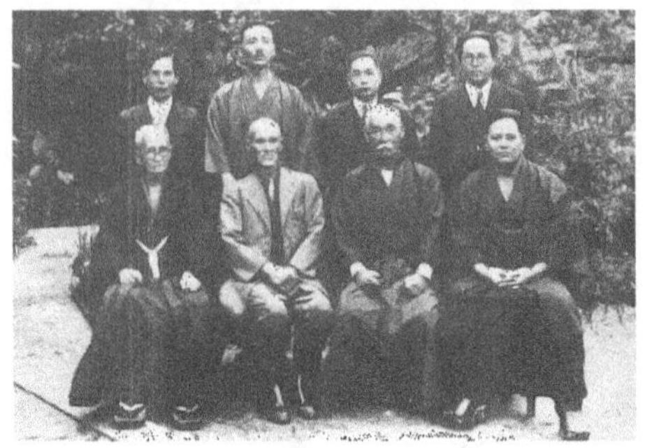

Have you heard of *muchimi* (or *mochimi*), *gamaku*, or *chinkuchi*? If you practice or have practiced an Okinawan style of karate, such as Goju Ryu, you may be familiar with these terms. In Okinawan karate, they are very popular and are considered to be critical if one wishes to achieve excellence in karate. As far as I know, these terms have not been used in Shotokan training. As a result, most Shotokan practitioners have never heard of them, though I believe Shotokan karate has ideas that are similar to one or two of the concepts stated here. I am not saying that Shotokan practitioners are totally missing something, but I hope you will agree that it is beneficial to investigate and see if we can find something we can learn from these concepts and methods.

I must confess that I have never been personally taught these words by any of the sensei I have had in the past. Just like most of you, I had never heard these terms in my regular dojo training or special seminars, either. I learned them mostly from the karate books that I have read during my research activities. What I did was compare what I read with the techniques I knew from Shotokan. What I have discovered is not only interesting but also insightful. So, after reading this chapter, I hope you will find the information beneficial to your training.

Before I go any further, I must emphasize that there are different variations in these techniques, depending on the different Okinawan styles. I also do not claim to have mastered these techniques or covered all of their meanings within this chapter. If I am incorrect or inaccurate in any way, I would be very happy to receive corrections. Let us start with the easiest one to understand, which also happens to be the easiest one to explain, *muchimi*.

What is *Muchimi* (ムチミ)?

There are two kinds of *muchimi*, and they are expressed with two different

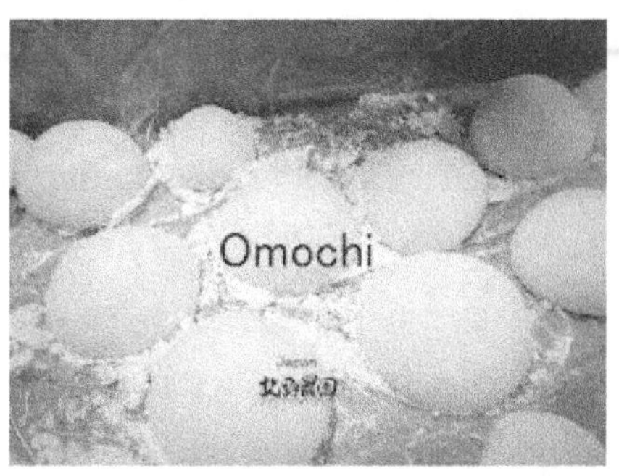

kanji, though the pronunciation is very similar.

The first kind is read as *mochimi* (餅身, 'rice-cake body'), which describes how a practitioner trains so that his body attains the character of *mochi* (or *omochi*), a popular food in Japan. To make *mochi*, rice is pounded into paste and molded into the desired shape. In Japan, it is traditionally made in a ceremony called *mochitsuki* (餅つき). Though it is eaten year round, *mochi* is a traditional food for the New Year period in Japan.

If you have eaten one of these *mochi*, you know the texture of this food. It has a lot of elasticity in your mouth, almost like rubber or chewing gum, as you try to chew it. You can naturally guess what the body needs to be like after learning the character of *mochi*. Thus, the elasticity of the body is expressed by the word *mochi* because of its similarity in character.

This technique is developed by using both the flexor and extensor muscles. The purpose of this chapter is not technical instruction, so I will not explain the mechanical details here. In short, the essence of body management comes from maximum contraction using the flexor muscles, which generates full extension of the extensor muscles. This may be too simplistic, but you tense your muscles to their maximum point and then let go to achieve maximum extension. The best analogy may be the mechanics of a spring. When compressed tightly, the spring will expand very quickly or, more accurately, will jump out explosively when the compression is suddenly released.

To make this more effective, the extensor muscles are trained to relax so that they can achieve their maximum extension. By mastering this, a practitioner can develop explosive power in his punches, even before the elbow is fully extended. This effect is most useful in short-distance fighting styles; thus, practitioners of Naha Te (那覇手) styles (e.g., Goju Ryu, Uechi Ryu [上地流], etc.), which use short-distance fighting methods, would naturally want to develop this technique.

One noteworthy point is that this technique, though very powerful, is not a sharp, whiplike punch. It is more like the sharp push of a *bo* (棒, 'staff'), and its speed is not as great as that of the whiplike technique used by practitioners of Shuri Te styles (mainly Shorin Ryu). I will explain the mechanics of the whiplike technique later in this chapter, but a punch that uses *mochimi* is more like a thrust than a snap. This is better suited to attacking a solid target, such as the chest or midsection of the opponent, rather than attacking a moving target, such as the head, which can easily bounce and move around, resulting in the reduction of the impact. Therefore, this technique is called *mochimi* (that is, '*mochi* body'), signifying the nature of the body mechanics involved.

By the way, if you watch the Naha Te *kata* Sanchin (サンチン), you will see only *chudan* punches. This demonstrates that the *mochimi* technique of Naha Te is most effective in the *chudan* area. Of course, to make a punch more powerful, other techniques must be applied at the same time. Among these are *tsukami* (掴み, 'grabbing') and *hikiyose* (引き寄せ, 'pulling in') as well as the use of *chinkuchi* (discussed in the third part of this chapter). Here is a video of Sanchin performed by the world-famous Morio Higaonna, tenth *dan*, Goju Ryu: www.youtube.com/watch?v=kybxNOlnl20. And, here is another interesting video clip showing Goju Ryu *muchimi* training: www.youtube.com/watch?v=1uOH54pLYmw.

OK, the other kind of *muchimi* is written as 鞭身, which means 'whipping body'. This was developed and taught by the masters of Shuri Te styles (mainly Shorin Ryu). Some Shuri Te practitioners may also call this one *mochimi*, but the core character of the technique is different. The same pronunciation has been used by some of them mainly because the name of the *mochimi* technique used by Naha Te practitioners became very popular, so Shuri Te practitioners chose to use the same pronunciation. Based on my study of the differences in the mechanics of each of these, though, I really think they are clearly two different techniques. Though they

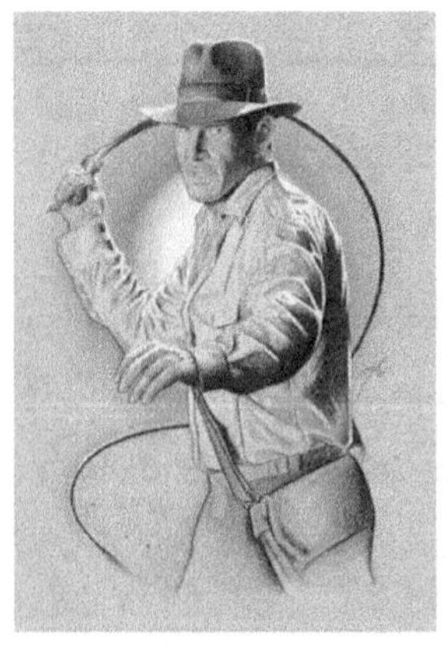

do share some common body mechanics, such as tension and relaxation, my personal opinion is that they are different enough that they should have two different names.

Let me briefly describe the application of *muchimi*. Simply put, it is a technique that utilizes a whipping action. What you need to do is relax the arms or the legs and then swing from the center of the body, namely, the backbone or the pelvis. Using this action, the limb will travel like a whip rather than like a stick.

Practitioners of Naha Te are known to focus on short-distance fighting; thus, their techniques include many short stances, such as *neko ashi dachi* (猫足立ち) and *sanchin dachi* (サンチン立ち), and short-distance techniques, such as elbow strikes, knee kicks, *mae ashi mae geri* (前足前蹴り, 'front-foot front kick'), and even headbutts. It is possible to execute a whiplike technique from a short stance without much body shifting, but they tend to use their body more like a stick than a whip.

Shuri Te, on the other hand, is a long-distance fighting method, so its practitioners prefer long stances and long-distance techniques, as the reader probably knows. So, the concept of long-distance fighting meshes well with the idea of using a whiplike motion. However, our arm is rather short and does not have many joints to make it into an effective weapon.

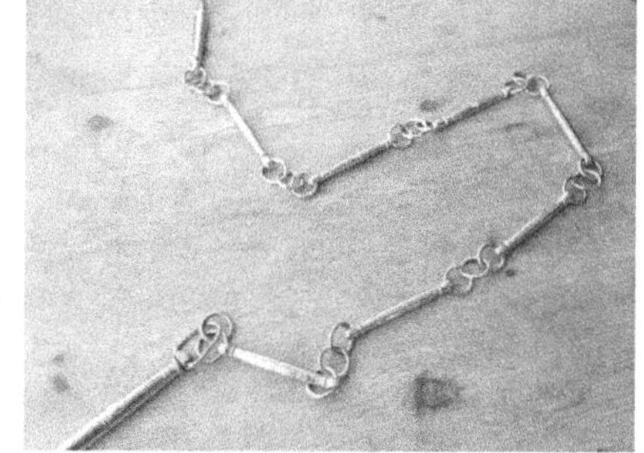

Take a look at the *kyusetsuben* (九節鞭, 'nine-section whip') in the photo to the right. This is one that I personally own. It has nine joints and a rather heavy anchor piece at the end to make it a lethal weapon. I use a *nanasetsuben* (七節鞭, 'seven-section whip') because the nine-section one is too long for me. Compared to these whips, our arm has only three joints (at the shoulder, elbow, and wrist). In addition, our anchor piece is our fist, which is obviously not as effective as the one on the whips.

So, what do you need to do? You need to use *muchimi* along with a pulling and a controlled tension movement called *chinkuchi*, which will be explained further in the third part of this chapter. Consider the following example to illustrate the concept. It is difficult to make a towel into a whip when it is completely dry, no matter how fast you swing it. But what happens when you get it wet? Yes, it becomes much easier to use like a whip, especially if the wet portion is just the whipping end or the whipping half of the towel, the part you are not holding.

The dry towel is the tension in your arm, and the key is that the water is fluid and extremely elastic. The water gives additional weight to the towel, but the more important effect is the energy and the body it gives to the towel. What I am trying to say here is that the tension you apply to *muchimi* must be minimal. Excessive tension will slow down the snapping motion, which will end up producing a poor whipping action or no whipping action at all.

The most common whipping techniques that Shotokan practitioners are familiar with are *uraken uchi*, a striking technique, and *mawashi geri* (回し蹴り), a kicking technique. However, if you understand and master the mechanics of *muchimi*, you can deliver other techniques much faster, as well, including the straight punch, *mae geri*, *yoko geri,* and all other techniques.

The ultimate technique is the one- or zero-inch punch. This utilizes a fundamental physiological method called *hakkei* (発勁), which literally means 'release of power', to generate power with minimal body motion. And, mastering *muchimi*, I believe, can aid in the development of the *hakkei* technique. Here are some interesting video clips for your reference:

Tekki Shodan by Michiko Onaga: www.youtube.com/watch?v=mCpkV-zSP-0
Tekki Shodan by K. Shinzato: www.youtube.com/watch?v=_DEVYxsihlE
Tekki Shodan by Tetsuhiko Asai: www.youtube.com/watch?v=WJqOeOGdm28
Body training by Master Asai: www.youtube.com/watch?v=L3jZcsfytl8

What is *Gamaku* (ガマク)?

At a karate dojo on Okinawa, you may hear a sensei yelling to the students,

"*Gamaku o irero*!" (ガマクを入れろ, 'put some *gamaku* in') or "*Gamaku o kakero*!" (ガマクをかけろ, 'apply *gamaku*'). I suspect the term *gamaku* must be very foreign to Shotokan practitioners unless they have had a chance to train in one of the Okinawan styles, such as Goju Ryu or Uechi Ryu. So, you may be asking, "What the heck is *gamaku*?" We will investigate this together to see if it is something new to Shotokan training or if it is something we already have.

First, let me explain the meaning of this word *gamaku*. It is an Okinawan term that describes the soft area at the sides of the waistline and at the top of the pelvis. This term is typically used for an Okinawan woman who happens to have a very small waistline. Of course, it is used for both men and women when it comes to karate training. This word is also used in Okinawan dancing, which has been closely related to Okinawa Te (沖縄手) for many generations. I have written about this in the past and also posted a video of Master Seikichi Uehara (上原清吉, 1904–2004) of Motobu Ryu (本部流) performing the dance Bu no Mai (武の舞). Here is the URL in case you missed it: www.youtube.com/watch?v=EdyD-NFJF1Q.

So, you may be asking, "What has the waistline got to do with karate?" It is obviously related to karate techniques, but the literal meaning could mislead us. There are two different methods of *gamaku*, and this fact, as with *muchimi*, may be causing some confusion even among Okinawan karate practitioners. Let me explain both and see if anything I describe is familiar or related to Shotokan training.

First, we need to define the area of the body that we use to execute a *gamaku* technique. Knowing this makes the difference between the two methods clearer.

The *gamaku* area for the first method covers not only the waistline but also the entire lower abdominal area, including the *seika tanden*, which is the core of the lower abdominal area. The photo to the right shows Higaonna Sensei executing *gyaku zuki* with a *gamaku* application. In this photo, a red circle indicates the *gamaku* area. I will discuss the actual mechanics of the *gamaku* application

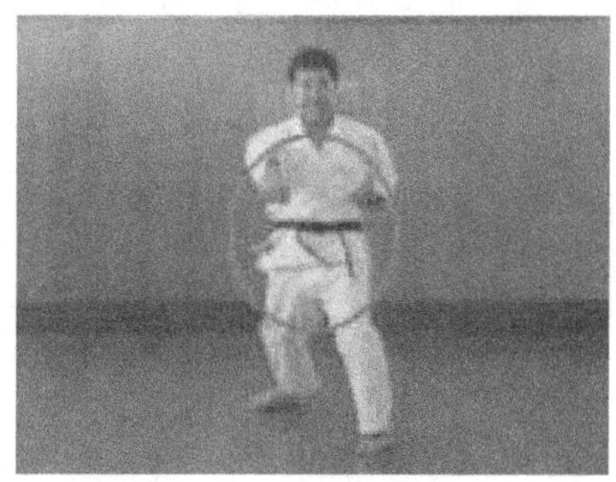

later.

The *gamaku* area for the second method is smaller (as shown in the photo to the right). This photo shows a *kagi zuki* technique that is supposedly being thrown with a *gamaku* application at the right hip region. The red circle pinpoints the particular area where *gamaku* must be applied. This is the very area that the original nonkarate term *gamaku* describes. The ancient masters probably borrowed this term to label the technique as the general area was similar to where it was to be applied. We will discover later, in the explanation of the second method, that this application is not limited to this small area.

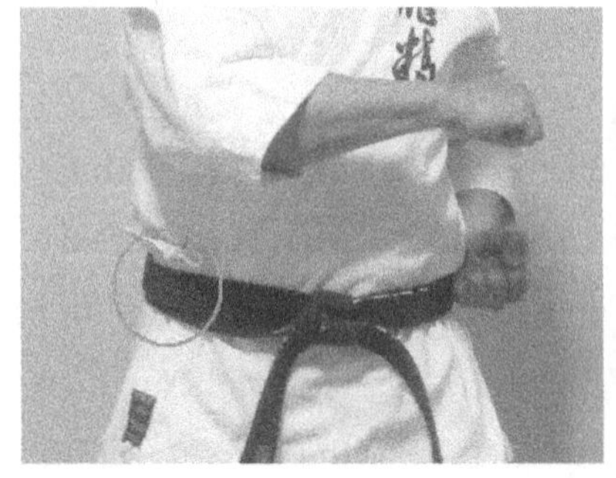

Now you know where the areas of the body that are used for these techniques are. Next, let me explain the methods and their mechanics, starting with the area of the body covering the entire abdominal region. Regardless of whether the first or second method is used, the objective of the *gamaku* technique is, in general, the same: to improve or increase power generation as well as body shifting and balance.

Then, how do you control and apply *gamaku*? Mastering *gamaku* control is not easy, but it is not too difficult to understand its mechanics. What you need to do is imagine that your abdominal area is a balloon or that you are holding a ball filled with water inside your abdominal cavity. An illustration of the mechanics is shown to the left. This ball or balloon may be small when you initially try to create these mechanics, so, naturally, the effect may also be small and partial. As you train more and thus become more efficient and gain more control, the balloon will be able to expand from the shoulder area all the way down to the upper knee area. Once again, look at the red circle shown

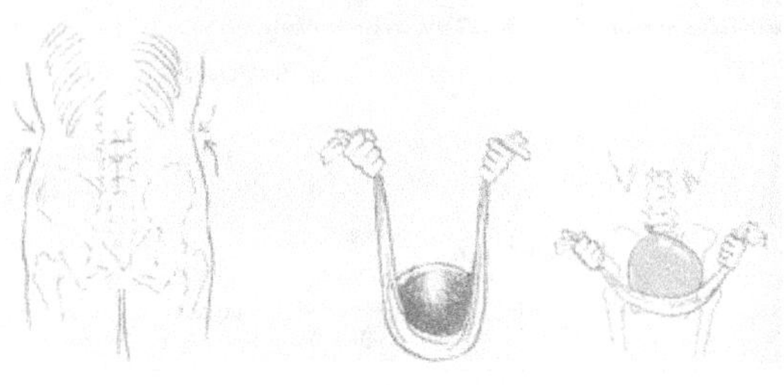

in the photo of Higaonna Sensei executing *gyaku zuki* for reference.

So, the mechanics are simple. If you wish to shift your center of gravity, you shift the "water" from side to side, top to bottom, front to back, etc. This applies not only to keeping your balance but also to creating a more lethal technique by increasing speed and power. These mechanics may be foreign to some, but they are definitely not ridiculous or unrealistic. We must remember that over fifty percent of our body is indeed made of water. We have a lot of internal organs in the abdominal area in particular, so the water content is naturally much higher there than in the rest of our body.

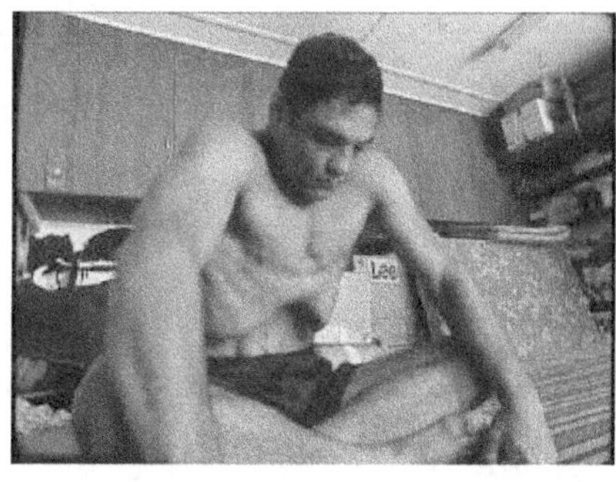

Using trained internal muscles, one can maneuver or shift a group of internal organs (the water) to carry out these mechanics. In the past, I have shared a video clip of Rickson Gracie (1958–) doing his yoga exercises, and one of them is used to train the internal muscles of the abdominal area. Here is that clip again so that you can observe how he trains the entire group of abdominal muscles: www.youtube.com/watch?v=CB_KRHXU1BA.

This exercise is excellent for your health—it is called *breath of fire* in yoga—but Rickson was not doing it for health purposes. I am certain he did this to train for his MMA fighting. Based on the way he trained his abdominal muscles, you can easily understand how he would be able to apply *gamaku* to whichever part of his abdominal area he chose. This is the very reason he was almost unbeatable on the ground once he was able to get on top of his opponent.

If you have never noticed the way he used to fight, I suggest you watch several of his fighting videos. You will notice that his strategy was not to knock the opponent down with punches from a standing position but rather to bring the opponent down to the mat, get on top of him, and beat him until he surrendered. By controlling his center of gravity, he was able to get on top of his opponent and remain there without being dislodged. The opponent simply could not get him off as he could maintain a perfect center of gravity no matter how hard the opponent tried to knock him off-balance.

OK, that is MMA. Okinawan *karateka* do not do as much ground fighting as students of Brazilian jujutsu, so why do they say it is critical to develop *gamaku*? When it comes to keeping balance or changing the center of gravity, you may tell me that you can use your arms and legs to accomplish the same task. This is true; you can do it that way. Our body is made up of many joints and small parts, so it is easy to shift our hip joints to keep balance. For instance, if you want to shift your balance to your left side without lifting your right leg, all you have to do is shift your hips to the left or simply lean your upper body to the left side.

This is easy, so what's wrong with it? You will know the answer only if you are practicing *bujutsu* karate. In *bujutsu*, which is life-or-death fighting, you must minimize your body movements to prevent detection by your opponent, or your slightest movement becomes a telegraph. Keeping balance by shifting *gamaku* enables you to move stealthily. This is why developing *gamaku* is indeed critical and important in *bujutsu* karate.

In modern-day sport karate, competitors constantly jump up and down, and in this environment, this subtlety is not needed. But, just imagine you were fighting a duel with another person, and each of you had a knife in your hand. Would the two of you choose the tactic of jumping around? Most likely not if you wish to survive. You would rather be moving very slowly and just a little bit, if at all. I respect the ancient masters, who considered this aspect to this degree, and their ability to create the exercises needed to build this technique.

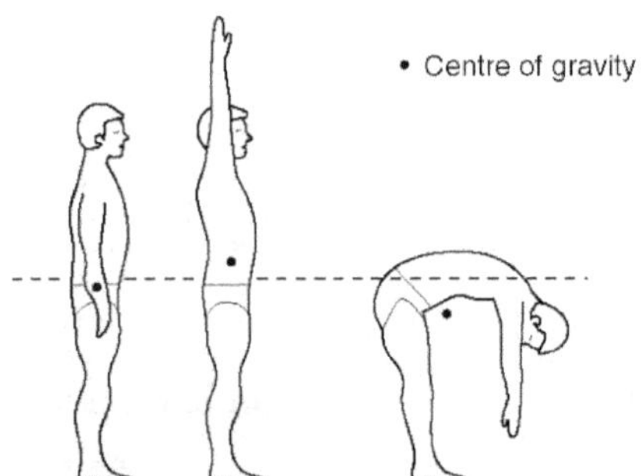

To understand how *gamaku* is applied, you need to understand the concept of our body's center of gravity. Now, this concept is not rare or unique to human beings. In fact, there is a center of gravity in almost everything we can put our hands on. Many readers already know that the center of gravity of our body when we are standing is located in our midsection, near the *seika tanden*. The exact location changes constantly as we move.

In addition to the concept of the center of gravity, there is another concept that is important in the martial arts: the center line of our body, which is called *chushinsen* (中心線, 'center line') or *chushinjiku* (中心軸, 'center axis') in Japanese. As we stand on our two legs, it extends from the top of the head to the tailbone as shown in the illustration to the left. It is aided by at least two more lines (drawn over the figure on the right in the same illustration), each of which is called *sokujiku* (側軸, 'side axis'). I will not go further into this subject here. I suggest you refer to Chapter 9: "Unstable Balance" of my book *Shotokan Mysteries*, in which I speak in depth about the body's center line and center of gravity.

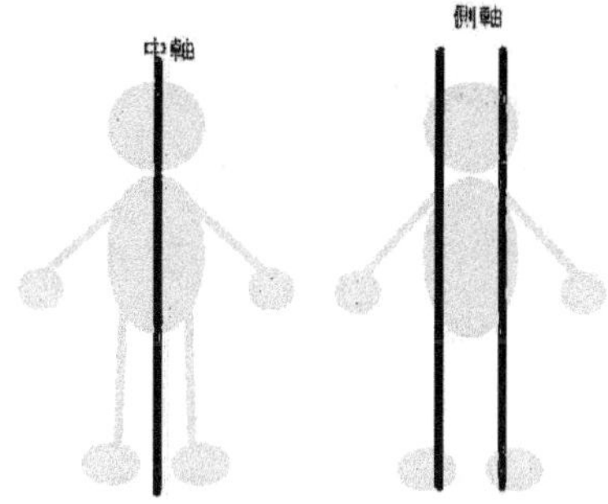

Let us do a small experiment. Stand up straight in *shizentai* in front of a large mirror. Pick a particular point in the reflection (something right behind your head if possible) and fix your eyes on it so that you can see if your body moves either left or right. Now lift up one of your knees—it does not matter which one—just as you would to prepare for *mae geri*. Did you notice that your body shifted toward the supporting (or standing) leg? This is a very natural thing and is needed for you to keep your balance.

Now try to do the same knee lift without shifting or leaning. Were you able to? If you did it slowly, you were probably not able to stay in the same position, but if you lifted your knee and put it back down very quickly, you might have been able to stay in the same position for a very short time. I suspect you tensed up your waist and abdominal area at the very moment you engaged in the quick motion of lifting your knee and then returning to *shizentai*.

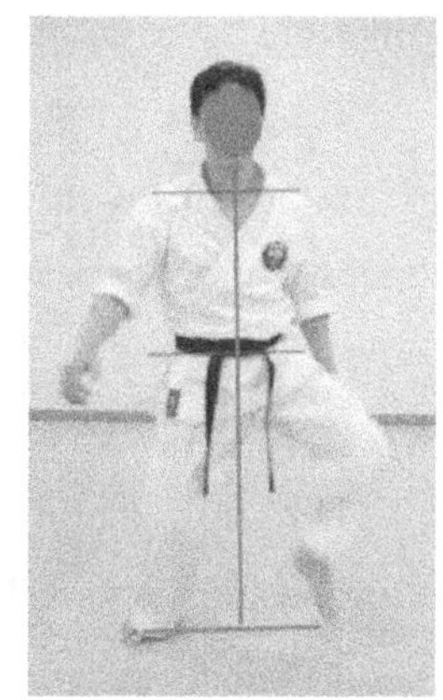

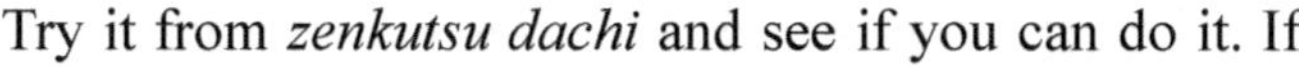

Try it from *zenkutsu dachi* and see if you can do it. If

you were able to do the knee lift, then try throwing *mae geri* without shifting or leaning. Were you able to? If you have not developed *gamaku* control, you will be unable to do this.

You probably have to lean, even if it is just a bit, to the supporting side to compensate for the loss of balance. But, a lateral leaning is so visible that your opponent will easily be able to detect your movement. What most practitioners do is lean to the supporting side or make some kind of feint (whether a step or a hand movement) to camouflage the kick since they cannot hide it. This is exactly why competitors in sport karate must jump up and down, but this is another subject, so I will not explain that any further in this chapter. To be able to kick without shifting, you need to apply a *gamaku* technique, an invisible shifting of the internal organs to compensate for the loss of weight on one side in order to maintain balance.

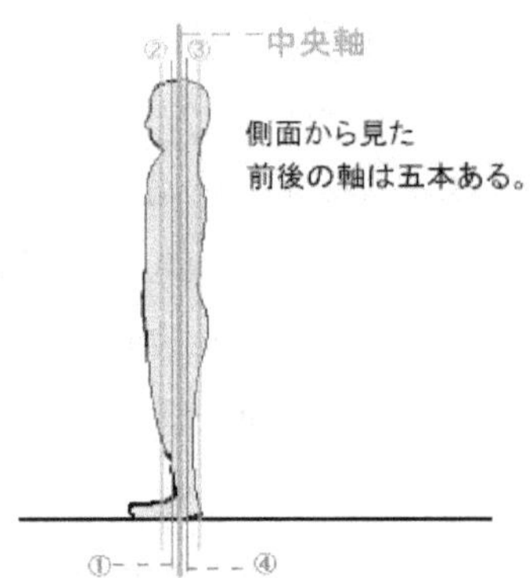

I need to add that there is also a center line as you look at the body from the side. Most readers already know that we have to shift our center of gravity forward if we wish to walk. This concept may be easier to understand as we walk daily. However, you may not consciously realize that we are indeed going through the fine movements of becoming off-balance and then recovering our balance every time we take a step. In fact, we cannot move or take a step in any direction if we do not first shift our center of gravity and become off-balance.

If you are a brown belt or above, you have practiced Bassai Dai many times, so you know the initial *kamae* where you are standing in *heisoku dachi* with your hands in the yin-and-yang position. You may have learned that the very meaning of *bassai* (抜塞) is 'to break into a fortress and capture it'. Thus, your teacher probably told you to have a very fast and powerful first step.

Do you remember that? Do you also remember whether he taught you anything besides just telling you to go faster? Probably not. I see many practitioners bend their knees in this initial stance. I know why. This position allows you to launch off the stance and jump forward much faster. However, I am sorry to inform you that you are not supposed to bend your knees in this stance. I see this error in Tekki Shodan, too. Did you know that you are not supposed to bend your knees here, either?

Believe it or not, these two *kata* are exactly the ones to run in order to learn how to develop *gamaku*. Bassai (Dai and Sho) teaches you how to catapult yourself to the front, and Tekki teaches you how to step quickly to the side by using *gamaku*. This particular technique is one of the important ones you are supposed to learn from those two *kata*. Yes, this is the method every sensei should teach for the first step in both Bassai and Tekki. As I mentioned earlier, I wrote about this particular subject in Chapter 9: "Unstable Balance" of my book *Shotokan Mysteries*. Please read that chapter for a detailed explanation on how to control and manage your body so that you have a fluid and explosive movement.

I need to go further with Tekki. It is amazing that this *kata* has so many important training points that are normally not explained in Shotokan dojo training. In the previous chapter, I introduced the concept of the invisible leg and how to develop it by using Tekki's *nami gaeshi*. Yes, some of the *bunkai* applications for this technique are a foot block, a kick to the opponent's knee, etc. But, unfortunately, it has been ignored and almost forgotten that the most important objective of the *nami gaeshi* technique is to develop strong *gamaku*.

I could share many photos of Shotokan practitioners demonstrating a beautiful invisible-leg technique, but I will just share one here (photo right). I believe this technique is being performed by Minoru Miyata (宮田実, 1916–1976) of the JKA. Of the two positions shown in the photo, the one on the right demonstrates the invisible leg. He has used his *gamaku* to keep his balance so that he can lift his right leg without leaning to his left.

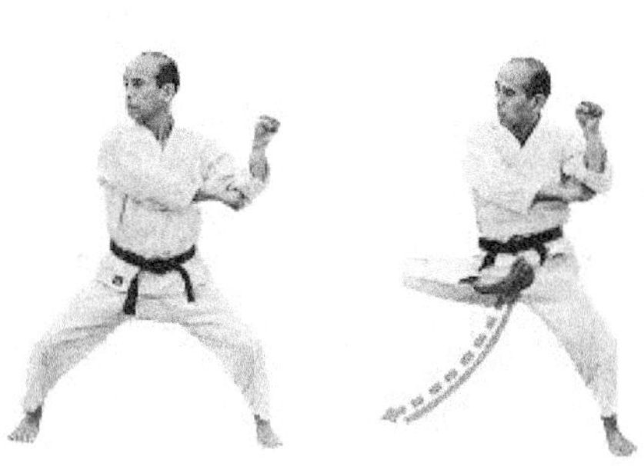

Almost any *yudansha* can do this for a split second with great effort, but it is difficult to keep the upper body relaxed while sustaining one's balance for half a second or longer in order to execute a proper *nami gaeshi* in Tekki. What you need to do is not only tense up the waist area on the right side but also—and this is even more challenging—shift the internal organs to the left side in order to keep your balance while the right leg is in the air. The more *gamaku* control you have developed, the longer you can stay in the air.

The benefit of this *bunkai* is an undetected kick as the opponent will not see the telegraph of your upper body leaning or moving while you throw the kick. Below are two training video clips by a Goju Ryu instructor explaining the application of *gamaku* with *mae geri*. Sorry, these are in Japanese only, but you should be able to pick out the main points he is trying to make.

Goju Ryu Gamaku Training 1: www.youtube.com/watch?v=oU-3jS9H38M
Goju Ryu Gamaku Training 2: www.youtube.com/watch?v=wVMJFA-AVps

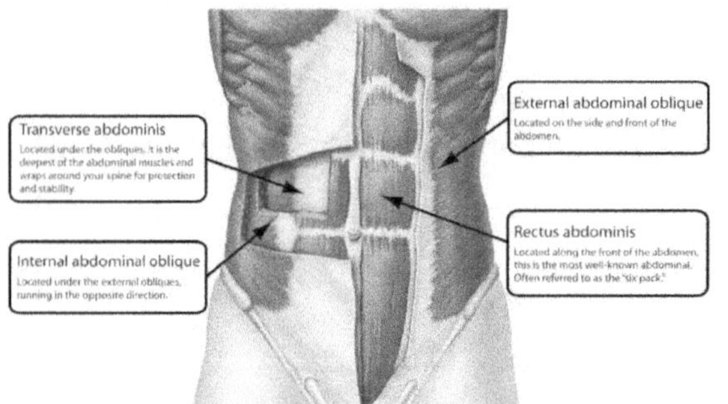

OK, let us go into the second *gamaku* method. This method emphasizes the side muscles called the *abdominal oblique muscles*, which connect the hips and the upper body. In fact, there are several layers of these muscles in the abdominal region. One is the internal abdominal oblique, and the innermost one is the transverse abdominis (illustration above).

Even if we are aware that these internal muscles exist, we cannot feel them, which is why the Okinawan masters had to refer to the soft area at the edge of the waist, which is mostly skin and fat, as *gamaku*. For this reason, if the application of *gamaku* is explained in a textbook showing this area as the part to be applied, it can cause some confusion. You need to receive an in-depth explanation from an expert to truly understand where it is applied. The hidden fact is that you use the internal muscles to stabilize the connection between the hip region and the upper body in order to achieve better balance and maximum power in the technique being executed.

I have explained that the quick forward shifting of Bassai can be used to train in the first *gamaku* method. For the second method, it is said that Seisan/Seishan (十三) is used. By the way, Seisan *kata* is the forefather of Hangetsu (半月), a familiar *kata* for Shotokan practitioners. In Seisan, the practitioner uses *sanchin dachi*; in Hangetsu, on the other hand, we use *hangetsu dachi* (半月立ち).

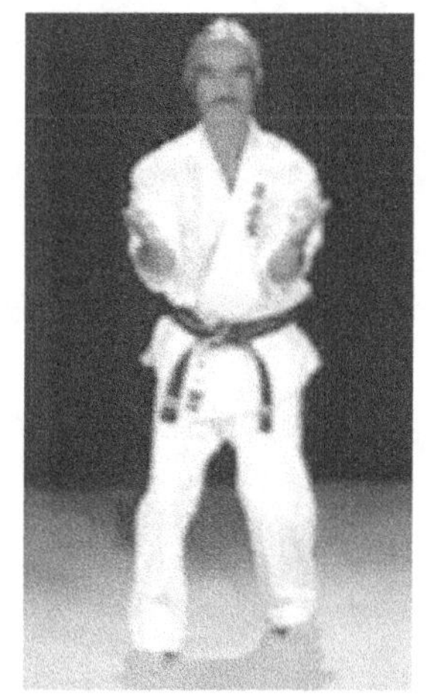

Sanchin dachi is a much shorter stance (as shown by the Uechi Ryu practitioner in the photo to the right), and you must learn how to generate power and stability by tensing up the inner muscles that are located at the sides of the waist. You tense the left and right muscles alternately as you step and execute the upper-body blocking and punching techniques. It is important to note that you must keep the muscles of the lower buttocks tight and pull the bottom of the pelvis forward all throughout the process so that the *seika tanden* area will also be pushed forward. As you take a step forward, the inner thigh muscles should be tense to create a stable stance when it is locked in. This maneuver is, in fact, a part of *chinkuchi*, which will be discussed later in this chapter.

The important point I must add here is that our body is holistic and works together. In other words, all the parts are not just physically joined together; they also coordinate with each other. In fact, you cannot move one muscle without affecting all the others, no matter how small the movement may be. So, when you apply the *gamaku* technique, it must coordinate with other mechanisms, such as *muchimi* and *chinkuchi*. By "coordinate," I mean that it must both increase and decrease tension in different parts of the body.

This may sound confusing, but think of the body as an orchestra with many different musical instruments. If all the instruments played loudly, they would not create music. Each instrument must coordinate and play its part (loudly, softly, slowly, quickly, etc.) to make beautiful music. The brain is the conductor, and it is up to the brain to conduct the different instruments, the muscles.

Anyway, the mechanics of inner-muscle tension are difficult to explain in words, but if you have been practicing Hangetsu with the deep breathing method, then the above explanation will easily make sense to you. I have written about Hangetsu previously, explaining the true purpose of this *kata* and the mystery of its stance. In that explanation, I did not, of course, refer to *gamaku*, but I did explain the necessity of tightening the muscles of the buttocks and connecting this to the use of the upper thigh muscles in order to attain the correct stance and generate power with the technique. For details on the execution and unique explanation of Hangetsu *kata*, please refer to Chapter 11: "Hangetsu" of my book *Shotokan Myths*.

I believe Tekki *kata* is also used to learn to apply *gamaku* to the right or left side of the waist. Examples of techniques from Tekki that would be best suited for this training are *kagi zuki* and *mawashi enpi uchi* (回し猿臂打ち), even though you can practice *gamaku* in every technique. In addition, as you progress in this method, you learn to use the reverse breathing method (expanding at the *seika tanden*, applying tension to this area as you exhale, and then releasing this tension as you inhale) to bring the internal organs up and down for better balance and for more sinking power, which aids with upper-body techniques.

In the second *gamaku* method, the emphasis, at least initially, is placed on the side of the waist instead of the entire abdominal area. I assume this stage of developing *gamaku* at the side of the abdominal area is only a start as it is more difficult to develop total control of all abdominal muscles. Eventually, the second method will advance to total control of the internal muscles of the abdominal region, which is the same objective as the first method.

In general, though the area that each method specifies is slightly different, the basic concept and the application of *gamaku* are very similar. A more important point for Shotokan practitioners is that, despite the fact that the term *gamaku* is foreign, the applications I have described above can be practiced by simply running some Shotokan *kata*. In addition, I believe we regularly practice the tightening of the buttocks and the pushing forward of the pelvis in our *kihon*.

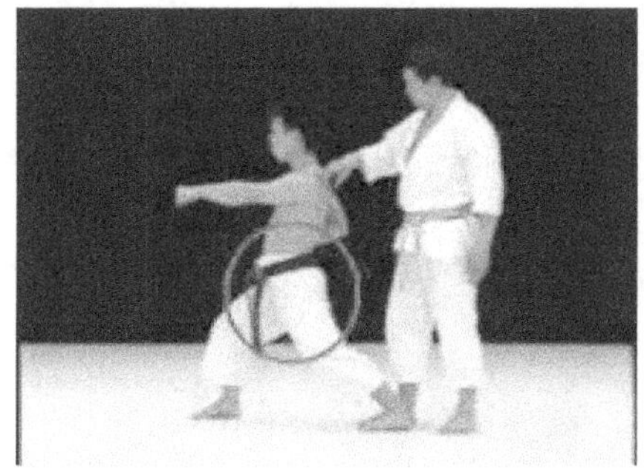

In the photo to the left, you can see that Masao Kagawa (香川政夫, 1955–) of the JKS is teaching a student a *gyaku zuki* technique. In fact, this photo comes from his instructional video, of which some readers may even have a copy. Here, Kagawa Sensei stresses the need for the punching shoulder to stay down and also the importance of the hip region that is connected to the supporting leg (the left leg if it is a left *gyaku zuki*). He does not use the term *gamaku*, but the concept he tries to covey is very similar to the second *gamaku* method described above.

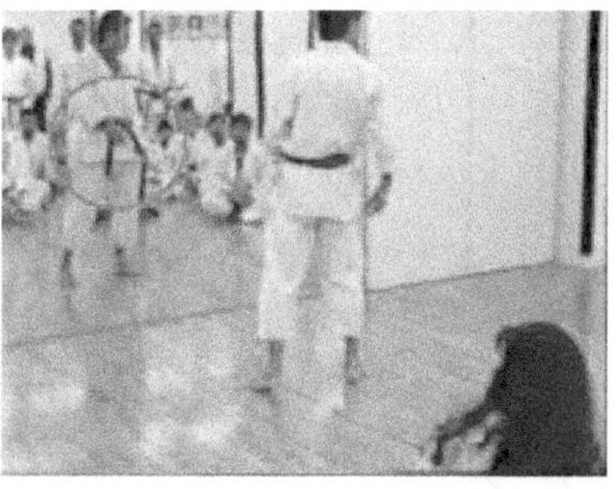

Other Shotokan experts and senior instructors, such as Tetsuhiko Asai, Hirokazu Kanazawa (金澤弘和, 1931–), and Mikio Yahara (矢原美紀夫, 1947– [photo right]), teach the importance of the *seika tanden* and the inner muscles, though they do not use the term *gamaku*. This means that the Okinawan karate concepts of balance and power generation have been handed down to modern-day Shotokan karate.

Unfortunately, it seems that some of the important objectives and methods of *kata* instruction have not been widely taught. I have noticed that the popularity of *bunkai* study is increasing, which is a welcome trend. I hope more Shotokan practitioners will include internal-muscle exercise and training as they practice the *kata* mentioned above.

I am confident that you will be able to improve your general karate technique as you develop your *gamaku* ability. Now that you have learned what *gamaku* means and that the training method is readily available to you, there is no excuse for you not to include it in your training.

What is *Chinkuchi* (チンクチ)?

Up to this point, I have attempted to provide explanations for and information on two Okinawan karate terms: *muchimi* and *gamaku*. My explanations covered the meanings of these foreign words and the basic mechanics of the techniques. We have discovered that these techniques can be found within the teachings of Shotokan, even though the same terms may not be used. Now we will look at the last term, *chinkuchi*, and investigate together whether this is a mysterious technique and also whether it is totally foreign to Shotokan instruction.

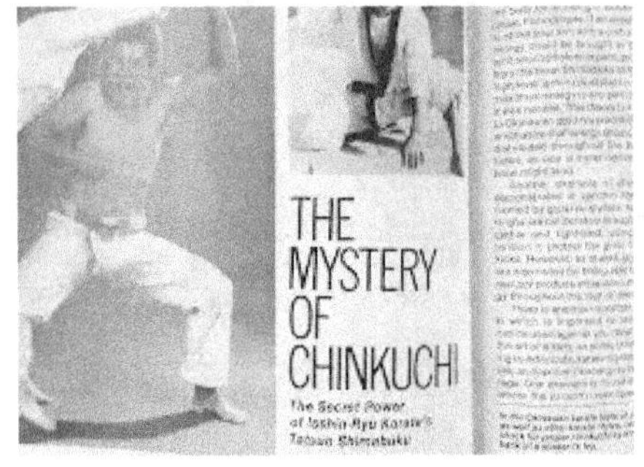

Excerpt from the December 1987 issue of *Black Belt* magazine

I have already mentioned that *chinkuchi* is also an Okinawan word. In fact, this word sounds strange even to non-Okinawan Japanese speakers. It is written in kanji as 一寸力 or 寸力, and this may give us a hint as to its meaning. The character 寸 designates a length of about one inch or simply a short distance. The combination of 一 and 寸 can be read as *issun* (いっすん), which literally means 'one *sun*' (about one inch), but it can also be read as *chotto* (ちょっと), which means 'a short distance' or 'a short time'. The character 力 means 'power' or 'energy'. Thus, a rendering of the entire construction could be 'one-inch energy' or 'small-movement power'. Now, isn't this getting interesting?

Now that you have learned what this term means, we need to look into how the technique is executed. According to Goju Ryu and Shorin Ryu, *chinkuchi* is described as a *gotaijutsu* (剛体術, 'hard-body technique'), which means that it is a technique that uses tension of the muscles of the body. One achieves this by tensing some muscles and the tendons around particular joints, namely, the elbows, shoulders, and hips.

This technique is considered to be extremely important among the Okinawan styles. It is emphasized in almost all Okinawan styles but is stressed more among those of the Naha Te group, which includes Goju Ryu and Uechi Ryu. When practitioners of a Naha Te style train in Sanchin, they frequently emphasize the application of *chinkuchi* to almost all the techniques in this *kata*. Allow me quote world-famous Goju Ryu master Morio Higaonna (photo below) as he describes this technique:

> [*Chinkuchi*] is used to describe the tension or stability of the joints in the body for a firm stance, a powerful punch, or a strong block. For example, when punching or blocking, the joints of the body are momentarily locked for an instant and concentration is focused on the point of contact; the stance is made firm by locking the joints of the lower body—the ankles, the knees and the hips—and by gripping the floor with the feet. Thus, a rapid free-flowing movement is suddenly checked for an instant, on striking or blocking, as power is transferred or absorbed. Then the tension is released immediately in order to prepare for the next movement.

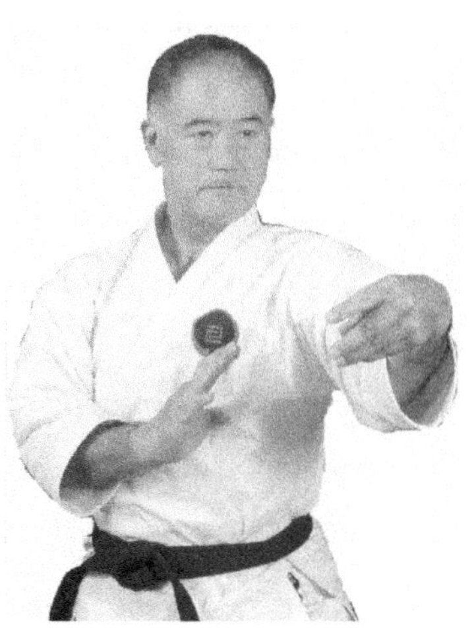

By now, many readers might have said in their mind, *Hey, this sounds like our* kime. *Is* chinkuchi *the same as* kime, *or are they different?* It's a very interesting question indeed, so let's investigate further and see if we can find the answer.

An important fact we must remember is that *chinkuchi* is often used in conjunction with *muchimi* and *gamaku* techniques. When *chinkuchi* is used with *muchimi*, it functions as an accelerator, though the action itself uses tension to stop movement. Yes, it can be confusing, so let's think of a whip as this will help you understand.

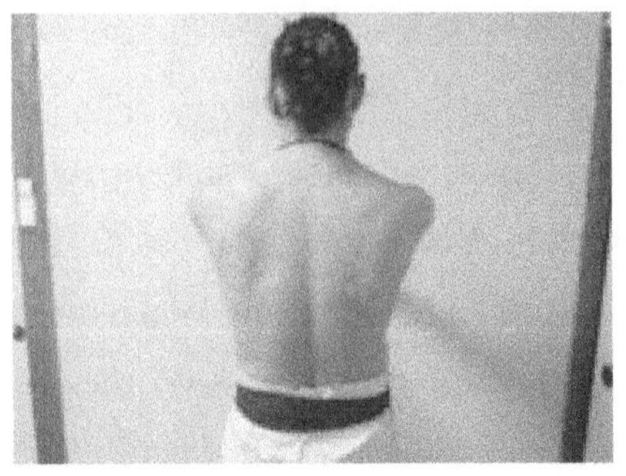

Imagine that you are holding a loose whip in your hand (understanding that this loose whip is an analogy for *muchimi*). You know that you need to swing your hand very quickly from the back to the front in order to crack the whip. And, what is important is that next you need to stop the motion very quickly by snapping your wrist. This action is *chinkuchi* except that you use your shoulder blade to do this to your shoulder joint.

When *chinkuchi* is used with *gamaku,* it functions in the lower abdominal area to provide a firm and stable stance as well as core tension in the hip and waist region.

I mentioned earlier that *gotaijutsu* is for tensing the muscles, particularly around the elbow, shoulder, and hip joints, in order to solidify the body. *Chinkuchi* seems to have two major purposes. One is that it tenses the body to receive the impact from the opponent's punch or kick. The other is that it contributes greater power to the techniques that one is delivering.

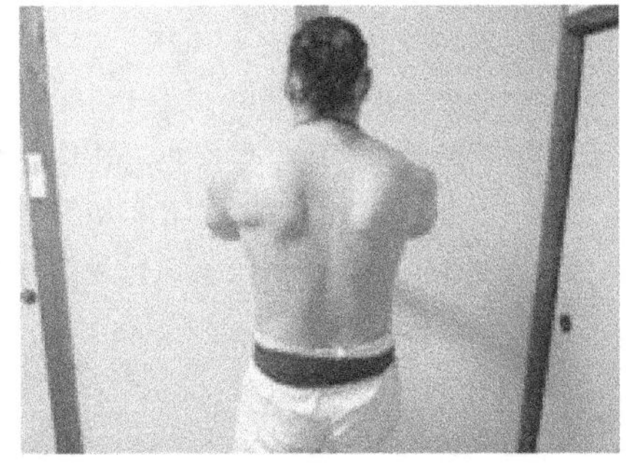

The first purpose is probably easier for us to understand as it is something we do naturally. Our body often experiences a natural tension when we get hit. Think of a situation such as bumping into a stranger in a busy subway station or on a city street, and I am sure that you will understand what I am referring to. The challenge most likely lies in understanding the second purpose, which will require further explanation. Supposedly, if you could achieve both purposes, this would be a perfect solution to both defensive and offensive strategies.

We need to investigate further just how *chinkuchi* can be achieved. I have already mentioned that to attain the power of *chinkuchi*, the entire body of the practitioner must be tense and must become one solid object (*gotaijutsu*). Doing this allows the weight of the whole body to be transferred to the point of contact, such as the punching fist, resulting in more destructive power. This almost sounds like an explanation of *kime* in Shotokan; therefore, I suspect Shotokan practitioners will not have any confusion or doubts about the explanation up to this point.

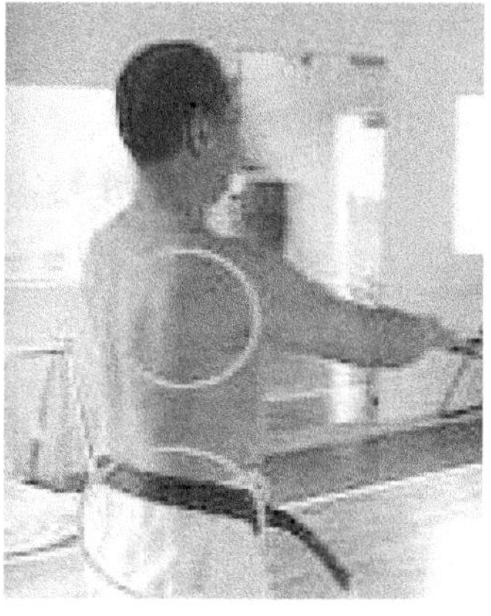

Let us now go more deeply into the application of *chinkuchi*. The application at the shoulders is frequently emphasized; however, the application at the hip area, namely, the iliopsoas, is also required. We can relate to this concept as Shotokan instruction emphasizes the importance of the *seika tanden* in generating *kime*. Once the practitioner becomes an expert in the application of *chinkuchi* in a comprehensive manner, he can generate a great amount of power with minimal movement. This is the reason this technique was named *chinkuchi*, 'small-movement power'. Understanding *chinkuchi* can provide an answer to the mysterious Shotokan technique of hip vibration.

Now we understand that there are two main joints where the practitioner must learn to acquire and develop *chinkuchi* techniques. One is around the shoulder and armpit region; the other is in the hip region. This concept should make sense to all of us as it is obvious that these two areas must be tight and locked in. Otherwise, the body will not be solid and thus will fail to provide a solid foundation for blocking and punching.

When we watch Goju Ryu and Uechi Ryu practitioners apply and train in *chinkuchi*, we can easily see that this is used for defensive purposes. Take a look at this video of Sanchin *kata*: www.youtube.com/watch?v=R5UIVObcmus. In the video, you can see that the sensei smashes his hands and feet all over the practitioner's body, but most of his hits are around the area of the shoulders, hips, and upper thighs. This exercise teaches the practitioner to bring the shoulders down and simultaneously tighten the inner muscles of the lower abdomen and upper thighs to create a solid stance and a good foundation.

I assume you will understand the objective here. By tensing all the muscles of the body, one becomes like a solid statue and consequently can absorb hard kicks and punches without feeling much pain. Uechi Ryu practitioners do this with open hands, so their movements may not look as stiff or rigid as those of Goju Ryu practitioners, who use closed fists (photos below).

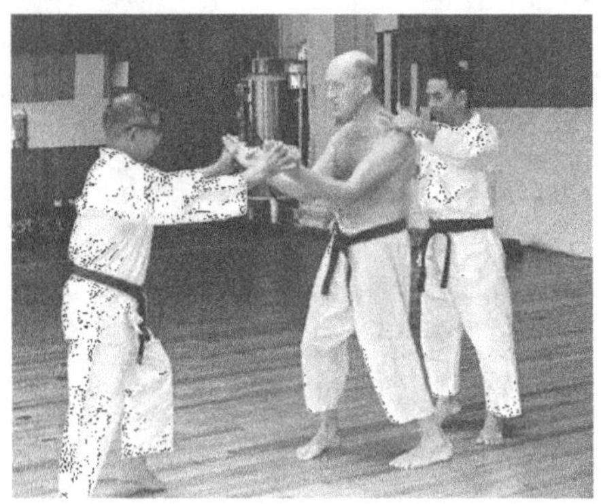

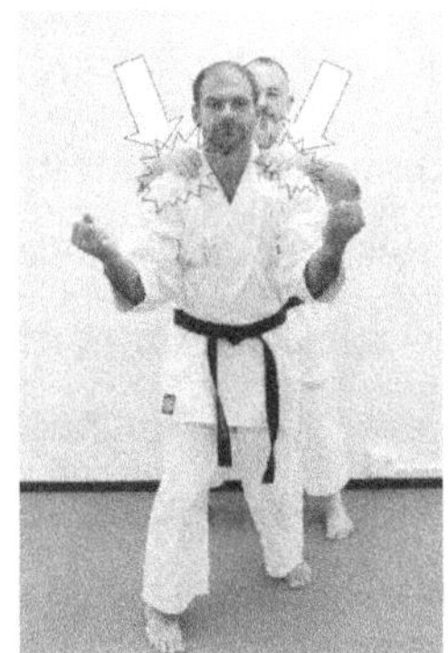

This concept of using *gotaijutsu* as a defensive tactic may be foreign to Shotokan practitioners. I must note that it was rejected by Master Funakoshi for the following reasons. His belief was that we should not receive any kicks or punches to the body as we are to consider the opponent's foot and fist to be a sword. He also rejected Sanchin *kata* and its training method, especially training half-naked.

As Okinawa is a subtropical region, it was (and still is) common to see many men walking around without a shirt. However, mainland Japan, particularly Tokyo, where Funakoshi immigrated to, is farther north, and being half naked in that area was and is considered to be impolite or uncultured.

Let me share a funny story. I will begin by saying that this story is not meant to degrade or ridicule Goju Ryu in any way but only to share an impression we had as beginners. This is a story from more than fifty years ago, when I was only fifteen years old. Anyway, when I started karate, I joined two different dojo: one Shotokan and the other Goju Ryu. I did this so that I could practice karate every day without knowing the grave consequences it could bring, but that is not what I want to share with you here.

What is funny is that I clearly remember that we beginners at the Goju Ryu dojo used to joke about the name of our style. Since the emphasis in our training was mainly on tension (*gotaijutsu*) and power generation, not flexibility, our impression of Goju Ryu techniques was definitely one of hardness or toughness. So, we had no problem with the first character, *go* (剛, 'hard' or 'tough'). What we joked about was the second character, *ju* (柔, 'soft' or 'flexible').

We did not see any *ju* in our training at all, so we used to say that a different character for *ju* would fit better. We picked 十, which means 'ten' or 'total'; thus, this alternate Goju Ryu (剛十流) would mean 'Totally Hard Style' or 'One Hundred Percent Hard Style'. We also used the character 重, which means 'heavy', so this Goju Ryu (剛重流) would mean 'Hard and Heavy Style'. I am not sure if this is funny to the reader, but we thought it was funny at the time.

Let us continue with the explanation of the body mechanics of *chinkuchi*. When you punch, you are expected to tighten the trapezius and deltoid muscles. The important purpose of this action is to accelerate the initial speed of the punch. In other words, it is like the initial explosion of gunpowder used to shoot a bullet. Now, this may be a little puzzling, and you may be wondering how this action can possibly accelerate the initial speed of the punch; however, the idea is simple. By tensing only the trapezius and deltoid muscles while keeping the other muscles around the shoulder relaxed, you can achieve an excellent level of explosive power and speed. While it may be rather easy to describe this concept, I am sure you will agree that executing it is not so simple.

This technique is said to be extremely important in short-distance fighting situations as it enables a powerful punch. If you are a practitioner of sport karate, I am sure you have had the experience of being at a distance that is uncomfortable for punching because your opponent is very close. The distance at which you cannot fully extend your arm is that uncomfortable distance. You sort of have to pull your punch. Otherwise, your fist will go "through" the opponent's head or midsection.

It is true that we have *ura zuki* (裏突き, 'inverted punch') for short distances like this. But, we do not practice this technique often, so we tend to use *seiken zuki*

(正拳, 'standard-fist punch') instead, which means our fist rotates. Then, what happens? The shoulder rises up, and maybe the elbow also. The arm looks as though we are throwing *mawashi uchi* (回し打ち, 'roundhouse punch' or 'round punch'), but that is only how it looks. The power is not there because we have to stop the punch prematurely. Otherwise, we will punch "through" the opponent's head.

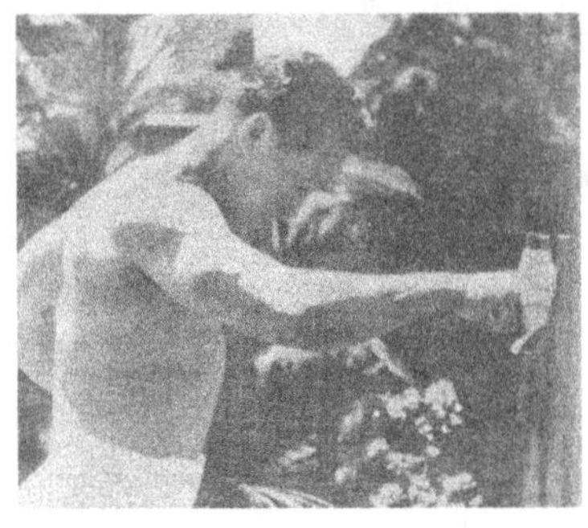

Now, here is an interesting photo (left). This is a young Mas Oyama punching a *makiwara*. I find this interesting because the form of his punching arm looks like what I explained above. Notice in particular that his elbow is not fully extended at the point of impact. Oyama practiced Goju Ryu, so I assume he is using the *chinkuchi* technique to generate power.

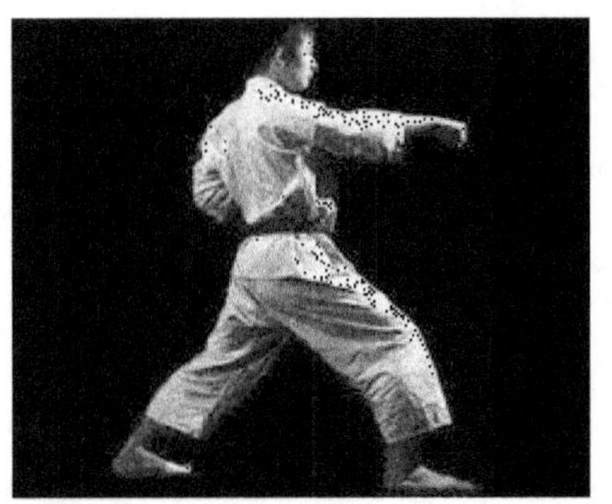

If you observe the way Goju Ryu or Uechi Ryu practitioners execute *choku zuki*, you will notice that their arm adopts a similar finishing position. In other words, despite the fact that it is a straight punch, their elbow is not fully extended (photo right). Maybe a Goju Ryu practitioner can confirm this or advise me if my assumption on the relationship between *chinkuchi* and the *choku zuki* arm is accurate.

Now let's look at exactly where the *chinkuchi* technique is executed. *Chinkuchi* is typically described as a technique involving the shoulder area, particularly the scapula, or shoulder blade. A frequent practice of Naha Te practitioners is to move the shoulder blades in and out to increase mobility and flexibility. High mobility of the shoulder blade is needed to enable the initial acceleration of the technique. It acts like the initial gunpowder charge for a bullet.

Many people still worship Bruce Lee, and more than forty years after his passing, there still exist some fanatics. I may receive some hate mail from these "believers" for my comments here, but true martial artists will agree with me. I give

Lee a lot of credit for being a great actor and for making Asian martial arts popular. However, having reviewed his performance outside of what is seen in the movies (as filmed action can be easily altered), I do not agree that he was a kung fu master.

Lee demonstrated his techniques at tournaments on a few occasions, the most notable of which was the one in Long Beach, California, in 1967. It is true that he greatly impressed the audience with a demonstration of his one-inch punch. But, no matter how many times I review the video, I still see a technique that is more like a five-inch push than a one-inch punch. If you look at the photo to the right, you can see that his upper body was leaning forward, his hips trailed behind, and his left foot lost its connection to the ground. You can also see that the punch is coming from his right shoulder.

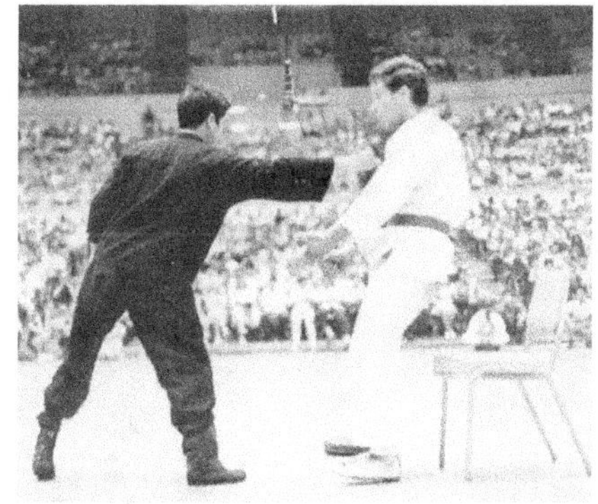

In a real one-inch punch, you use the power of the hips so that you do not need to lean forward as he did. He also turned his body sideways so that he could push. If it were a true one-inch punching technique, it would be more easily executed from a forward-facing position.

He made the demonstration spectacular by strategically positioning a chair right behind his partner (same photo above), so the poor guy had to fall dramatically backward. Without this chair, he would have just taken a few steps backward, which would not have been too impressive. In addition, the audience had never seen any technique at all, whether it was a one-inch punch or five-inch push, so they were easily impressed.

Though it may not be perfect, I have demonstrated a punch that is closer to a one-inch punch, which you can see in one of the Karate Coaching video classes and compare the two techniques.

Anyway, another thing I give Lee credit for is his excellent physical conditioning. He was known to have a big ego, and, as a professional actor, he obviously toned his body to show it off on the big screen. Consequently, his excellent physi-

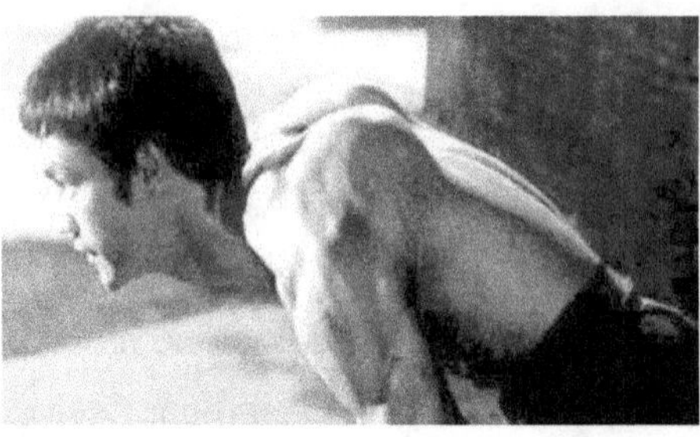

cal condition must have helped his martial arts performance. He not only developed his muscles but also worked on the mobility of his shoulder blades (photo right).

One other important part of the body that is needed to complete the *chinkuchi* technique is the *seika tanden* area. In fact, the necessary region extends beyond the *seika tanden* to include the iliopsoas muscle group (photo below left) and the quadratus lumborum muscle (photo below right). We have already discussed the importance of these muscle groups in the sections on *muchimi* and *gamaku*.

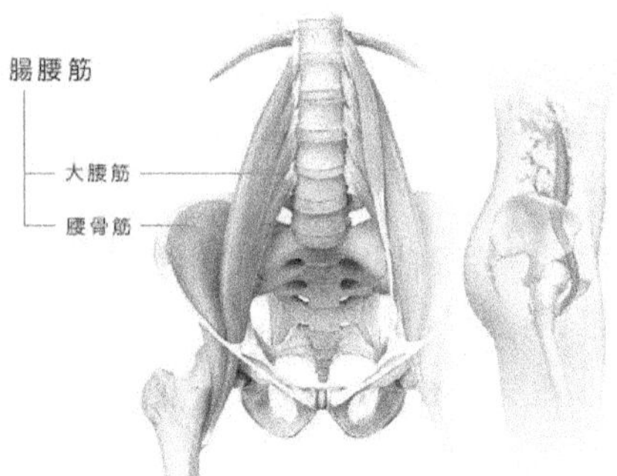

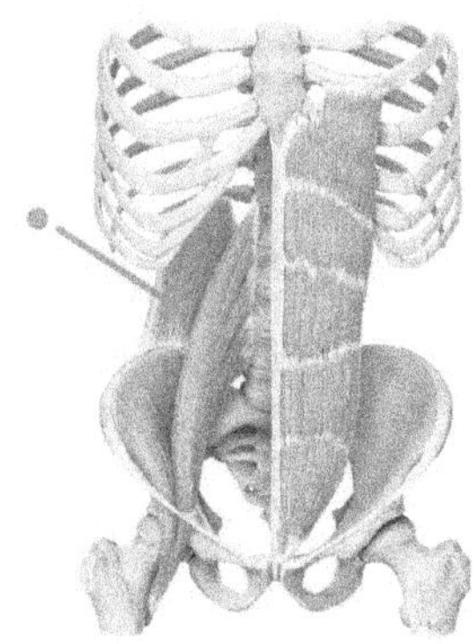

Here is what is important about the *chinkuchi* technique. The starting point for a punching technique does not reside in the shoulder area, though the technique in the shoulder is important. The true starting point is a proper *chinkuchi* technique in the legs, which serves to both stabilize the stance and send power to the upper body. This movement is very subtle and oftentimes invisible, which is quite different from the very visible motion of the typical Shotokan hip rotation found in *gyaku zuki*.

Yes, the hip rotation in *gyaku zuki* also generates power for the reverse punch, so there is nothing wrong with it. But, I feel that there is an overemphasis on its importance in Shotokan training. The biggest handicap in this approach is the time it takes to complete a full hip rotation. In *bujutsu* fighting, speed in power generation is important. Thus, when Shotokan practitioners advance, they are exposed to another technique called *hip vibration*, which is very similar to the concept of *chinkuchi*. Unfortunately, your average Shotokan dojo training does not include very much explanation or training in this area.

The important thing is that, surprisingly, the ability to perform *chinkuchi* is not a high-level technique. Almost everyone can tense his body, but the challenge comes only when one wishes to be skillful enough to control the tension so that he can tense and relax certain muscles and also tense only a specific area or areas of the body at will. You can say that you have mastered this skill if you are able to combine *chinkuchi* in peaceful harmony with *muchimi* and *gamaku*.

Conclusion

The Okinawan masters created these techniques to accelerate and/or modify the body's "natural" movements in order to maximize their efficiency and performance. We also learned this in the previous sections on *muchimi* and *gamaku*. But, these two are not stand-alone techniques. They must be applied in conjunction with the main technique, called *chinkuchi*, in order to increase the effectiveness of a given technique. In other words, you need to have good *chinkuchi* to have effective *muchimi* or *gamaku*. Even if you develop good *gamaku*, you cannot have an invisible leg if you do not apply correct *chinkuchi*. The same goes for the relationship between *muchimi* and *chinkuchi*.

Now that you have learned about *chinkuchi*, what do you think? Was this something new to you? Though this term, along with the other two terms, might be new to practitioners of Shotokan, the concepts themselves are probably not so foreign. I believe that similar concepts and techniques have been handed down to the Shotokan instructors (at least those within the Asai Ryu group).

My understanding of *chinkuchi* came from my understanding of the Shotokan techniques and teachings I received from my sensei. I would like to receive feedback from practitioners of the Okinawan styles as I wish to find out whether or not my understanding of *chinkuchi* is correct. I am always open to constructive criticism and the opportunity to learn from other styles.

Below are some video clips that show *chinkuchi* movements and training. The first three feature Katsuhiko Shinzato (新里勝彦, 1939–) of Shorin Ryu.

Pin'an Shodan: www.youtube.com/watch?v=lhQL5zce7Gg
Seiken zuki: www.youtube.com/watch?v=mXiB0l7MseM
Karate expert: www.youtube.com/watch?v=9tp2Vpm6-hQ
Goju Ryu *chinkuchi* training: www.youtube.com/watch?v=F1-Eqquri0o
Traditional training tools: www.youtube.com/watch?v=rgF6XzMAfKQ

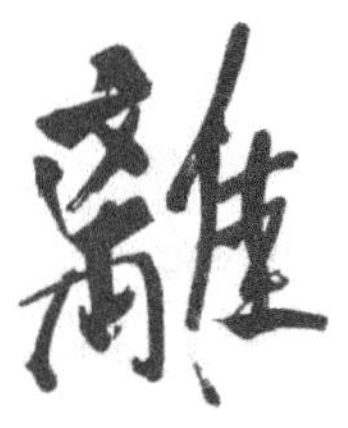

Chapter Eleven
第十一章

The Relationship between Choku Zuki and the Elbow Position
直突きと肘の位置の関係とは

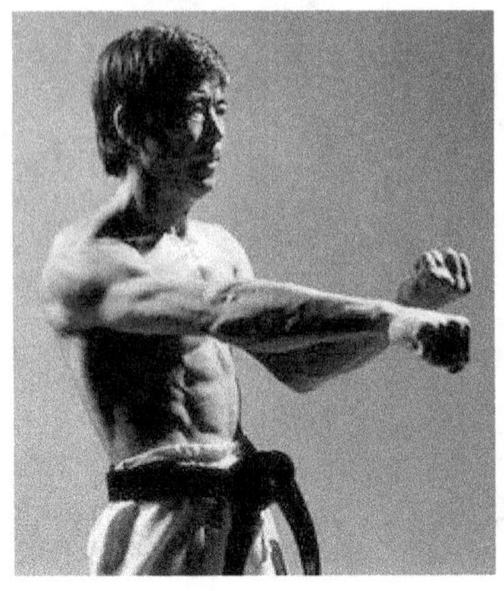

When you execute *choku zuki*, do you pay attention to your elbow? I expect most Shotokan practitioners do not. Your sensei may tell you to have a strong stance, keep your shoulder down, and possibly check your fist. If your sensei tells you to bring your shoulder down and tense your armpit, then he is giving you an excellent suggestion. It is even better if he explains to you the relationship between the tension of the shoulder, the armpit, and the upper back (the area around the shoulder blade). I am sure many senior Shotokan instructors can, and in fact do, teach these points. However, I am afraid not very many can explain further how to use the muscle groups in the forearm.

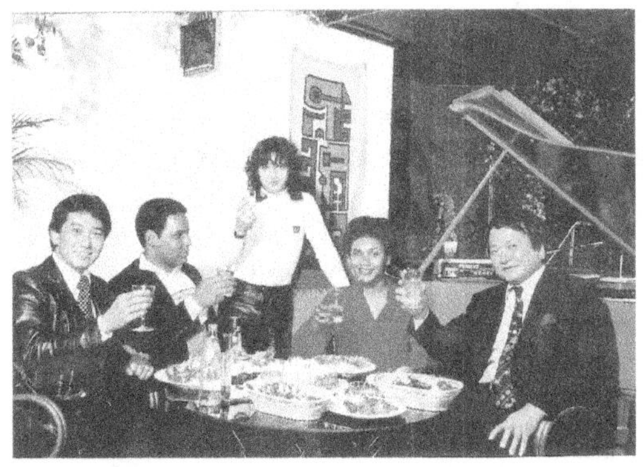

I remember one day in the early eighties when Jun Sugano (菅野淳, 1928–2002) and a few of the assistant instructors were in his bar. The photo to the right shows Sugano Sensei (far right) and the author in his younger days (far left). Sugano Sensei was my first sensei in Kobe, Japan, and he had his own small shop, where only a dozen or fewer people could fit. This bar is where Sugano Sensei would talk about karate techniques.

The customs in Japan are quite different from what the reader might be used to. Japanese sensei do not typically talk about the history and philosophy of karate or other in-depth concepts regarding karate techniques in the dojo. Yes, if you are doing your techniques incorrectly, they will correct you. They will not correct you with kind words but rather by either hitting your arm, leg, or hip with a *shinai* (竹刀, 'bamboo sword') or tapping one of these areas with their fist or foot. The Japanese sensei who live outside of Japan and those who visit foreign countries do not do this these days. They have learned that the culture is different outside of Japan.

Anyway, Sugano Sensei's bar was one of the few places where he relaxed and shared his thoughts and knowledge. It was an honor to be invited by him after a regular training session. We loved to tag along, and most of the instructors wanted to drink, but I had a different objective. I wanted to ask him some questions about karate techniques. Believe it or not, we could not ask any questions in the dojo. In fact, we were not supposed to talk at all. The only word we could say was *osu* (オス), regardless of the instructor's question or command.

So, that evening, Sugano Sensei rolled up his sleeves and said, "Look!" He showed us his extended arm in a *choku zuki* position. He was built like a bear, and his arms were like thick logs. He was probably about 5 feet 9 inches (175 centimeters) tall and weighed over 220 pounds (100 kilograms). He then asked, "What do you think?"

We were not sure what he was asking. His big fist was impressive and almost scary to look at, so we said something like "Your *choku zuki* looks strong!"

"Fools! What do you see in my arm?"

I was not sure what he was getting at, but I noticed that his arm was bent slightly downward, so I said, "Ah, your arm is bent."

"No, it is not bent. When you really hit someone in front of you, you need to tighten your arm this way."

This was more than thirty years ago, so I don't quite remember all of the explanation he gave. I only remember that he used the word *shime* (締め), not *kime* (極め). *Shime* means 'tighten', 'contract', or 'squeeze'. It's similar to *kime* but a little different, and it is difficult to explain the fine nuances between these two words.

I remember that he showed us the position of his elbow and stressed the importance of having it in the right place. It looked funny and was pointing straight downward. I tried to imitate his elbow position but was not able to do it at that time. He laughed and said, "This is how you punch in a street fight." I thought my punching was good enough for a street fight, so I was perplexed and frankly felt a little upset.

He saw the expression on my face and followed up by saying that if I were to punch a *makiwara* many times with my arm in that position, it would harm my shoulder and especially my elbow. I did not understand what he meant or why he had said it at that time, but I do now. So, I wish to share this with you in case you are not paying much attention to your elbow when you execute *choku zuki*.

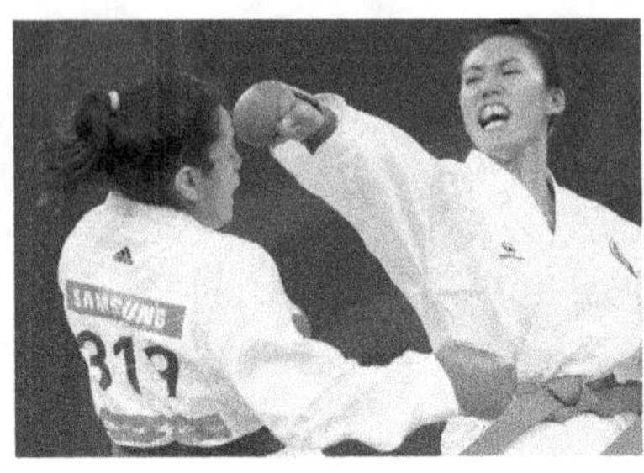

If I told you that there are two basic kinds of kicks, *keage* (蹴上げ) and *kekomi* (蹴込み), I am sure you would concur with my statement. How about if I told you that there are also two striking methods? You might quickly think of the two types of *uraken*, one with a snapback and one with a thrust (*uraken uchikomi* [裏拳打ち込み]), and I would be glad to hear that you understood these mechanics. So, how about with *choku zuki*? Most would probably say, "No, there is only one way," and they would be partially correct because there is no snapback with *choku zuki*. However, there is another method called *tsuki hanashi* (突き放し) just as there is actually one more kicking method, *keri hanashi* (蹴り放し) or *kebanashi* (蹴放し), which is where you let your fist or foot go without a snapback or tension (*kime*).

In the case of *mae geri*, for example, it is more effective to "ride" your kick in and kick through if you are in a real fight. However, in a tournament, you cannot do this as you would injure your opponent and most likely not score a point. You need to have a quick snapback to earn a point. The same mechanics can be applied to *choku zuki* (both the *oi zuki* and the *gyaku zuki* version). So, most of the time, a fast *choku zuki* in a tournament is *tsuki hanashi*, which doesn't use *shime*.

Why *tsuki hanashi*? First, the distance is greater in a tournament situation as the competitors are typically more than three feet (one meter) apart. Second, punches are faster when there is less tension. In a *sundome* (寸止め, 'one-inch stop') noncontact tournament, you cannot punch through, so what do you do? You quickly pull your fist back to your hip.

I am sure you have seen this action. Just like the snapback with *mae geri* or *mawashi geri*, the use of a pullback with a punch is required to score a point in many cases. If you punch through and knock the opponent out, though this would be a win in a street fight, it will be regarded as a *hansoku* (反則, 'foul').

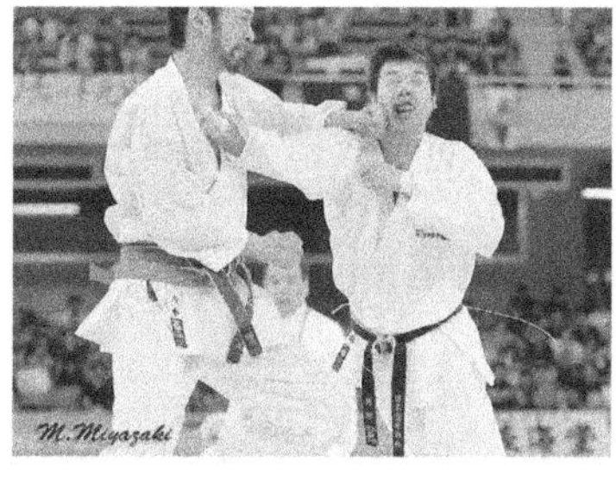

In the photo to the left, the competitor on the left has a good punch that has connected with the opponent's *jodan*. If he had extended his arm, he could have knocked the opponent down. But, I suspect that he probably will not score a point as this would be considered too close since his arm is not fully extended. We can see that the competitor on the right, on the other hand, has missed the target. However, since he has extended his arm, if the judges fail to catch that he missed the target, this competitor may get a *waza ari* (技有り).

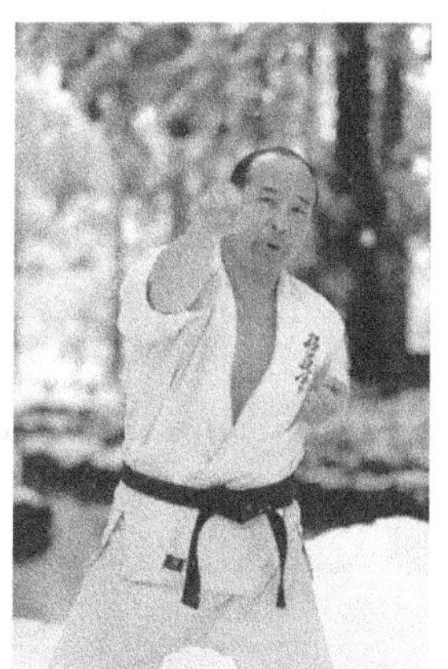

Let's look at another punching method called *tsuki* with *shime*. Look at the photo to the right of Mas Oyama punching during *kangeiko* (寒稽古, 'winter training'). You can see that his elbow is pointing downward here. He is applying *chinkuchi* in his arm and upper back. This tightens his armpit muscles (latissimus dorsi and teres major) as well as the muscle in his upper arm (triceps brachii). You may not see this type of arm positioning in Shotokan karate training anymore. However, if you punch a *makiwara*, you will understand that bringing the elbow down is better. You will absorb the impact much better, mainly at the elbow but also at the shoulder.

Look at the photos below.

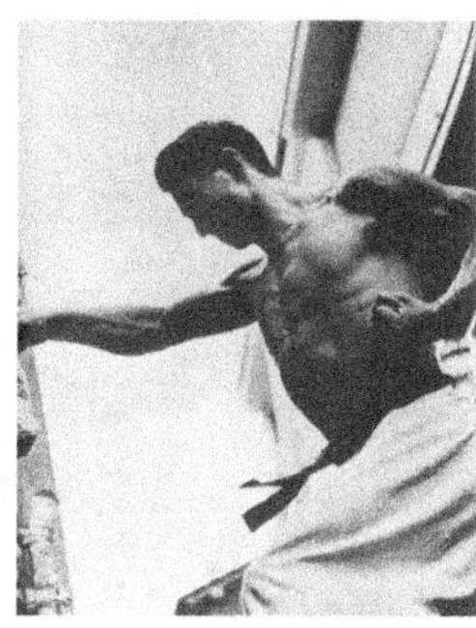

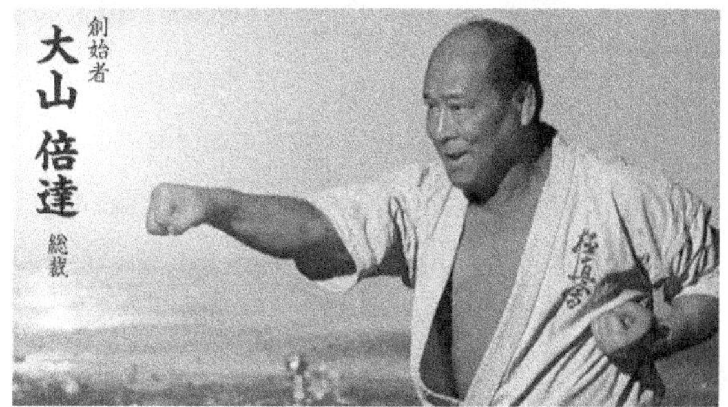

The one on the left is Hidetaka Nishiyama (西山英峻, 1928–2008), and the one on the right is, again, Mas Oyama. Notice the arm and elbow position of these two sensei. When you punch a *makiwara*, you cannot punch with *tsuki hanashi* as you would damage your shoulder, your elbow, and possibly your wrist. You must have good *shime* ('contraction') to absorb the impact.

If throwing *seiken zuki* with the elbow pointing downward is difficult to do, then I suggest you punch the *makiwara* with *ura zuki*. You may never have done this before, so it may feel uncomfortable. In order to hit the *makiwara* square to your fist, you have to either bend your wrist backward a little (no more than ten or fifteen degrees to avoid a wrist injury) or get closer to the *makiwara* and punch at a lower level. You may still feel uneasy punching this way as it is new to you, but I am sure you will find that your elbow is pointing downward.

You will not experience any elbow problems when punching like this. However, you may say, "The distance is too short. I want to hit the *makiwara* from a greater distance." In this case, punch with *tateken* (縦拳, 'vertical fist'). With this fist position, you can punch almost as far as with *seiken zuki*, and you will find that you can keep your elbow pointed downward, too. I recommend that almost all who want to train with the *makiwara* always use *tateken* to prevent elbow injuries. This is a very safe way to punch, even when fully extending the arm. Maybe the Chinese martial arts experts in ancient times knew from experience that *tateken* was the safest position because some kung fu styles, such as tai chi, use only *tateken* in their training (illustration left).

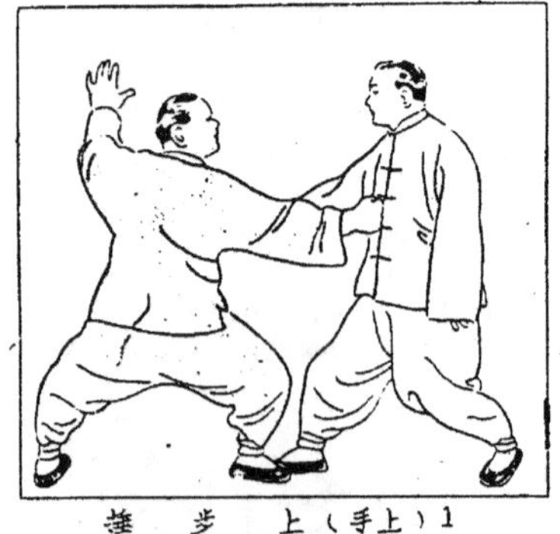

捶 步 上（手上）1

You may say, "But, these two punching techniques, *ura zuki* and *tateken zuki*, only extend the arm. They do not have the rotation of the forearm that is supposed to increase punching power." This corkscrew motion is a punching method that has been used even by famous boxers such as Muhammad Ali (1942–2016). It is true that the final turning of the forearm generates extra power, so the Okinawan masters—and probably the masters of the kung fu styles, as well—improvised a special way of keeping the elbow down while enabling the forearm to rotate at the end of *seiken zuki* or *choku zuki*. Here is how you train your arm to execute *seiken zuki* without rotating the elbow:

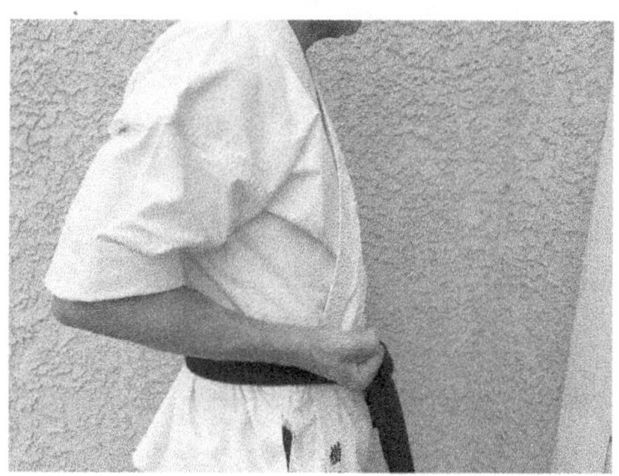

1

Start from the hip.

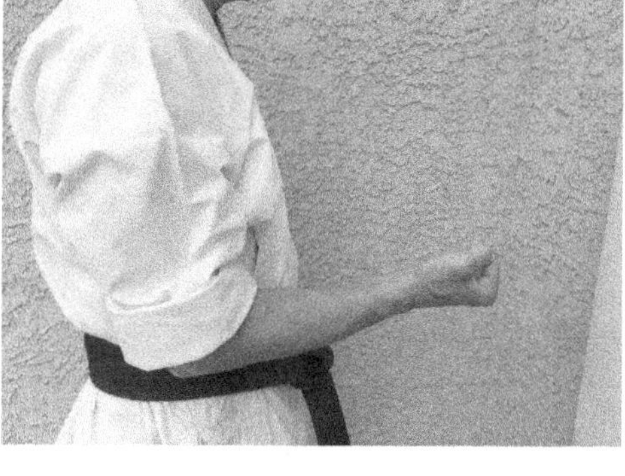

2

Start to extend the arm. Be sure to keep the elbow pointing downward.

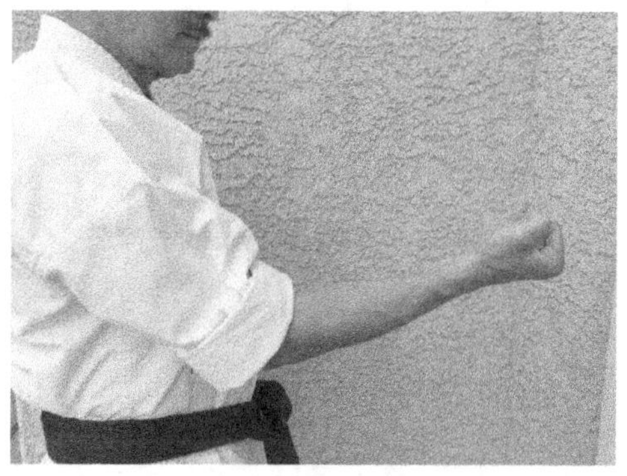

3A

Extend the arm further, keeping the elbow down as if you were executing *ura zuki*.

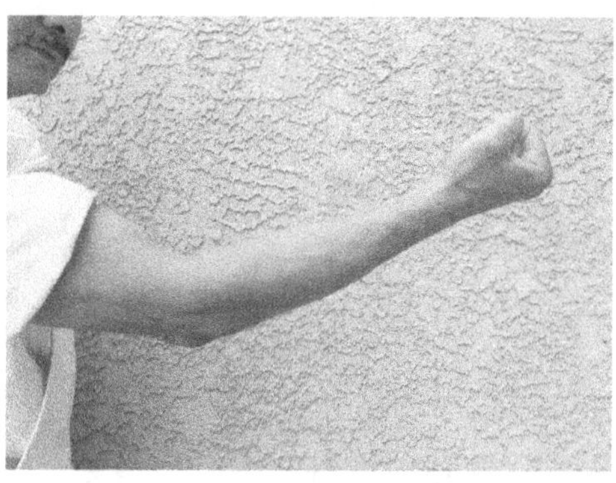

3B

The sleeve has been rolled up in this photo to show the elbow position more clearly.

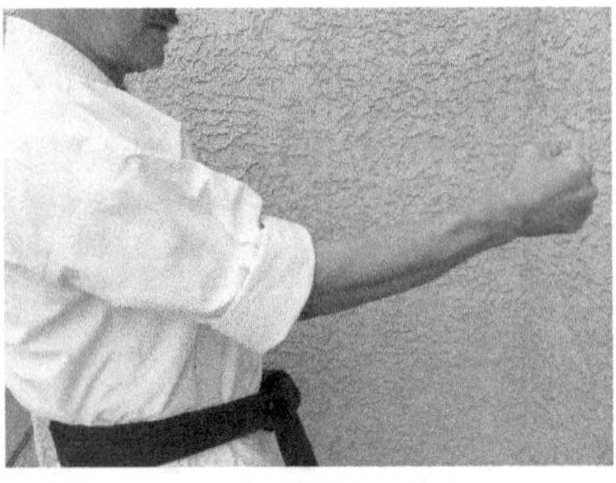

4A

As you extend the arm, begin rotating the forearm, but keep the elbow pointing downward as if you were executing *tateken*. Imitating the *tateken* movement allows you to more easily keep the elbow down.

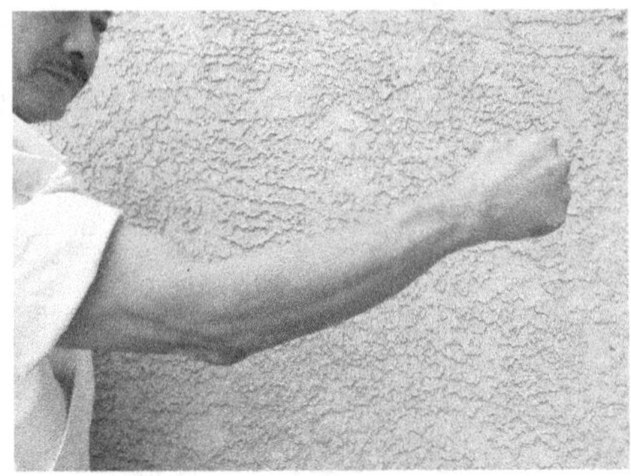

4B

The sleeve has been rolled up in this photo to show the elbow position more clearly. The process should not have been too difficult up to this point. The next step is the real challenge.

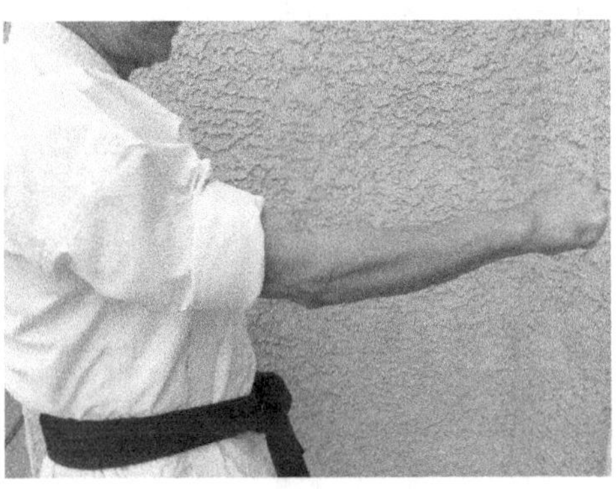

5

The arm is now ninety percent extended. Rotate only the fist and forearm. Do not rotate the elbow.

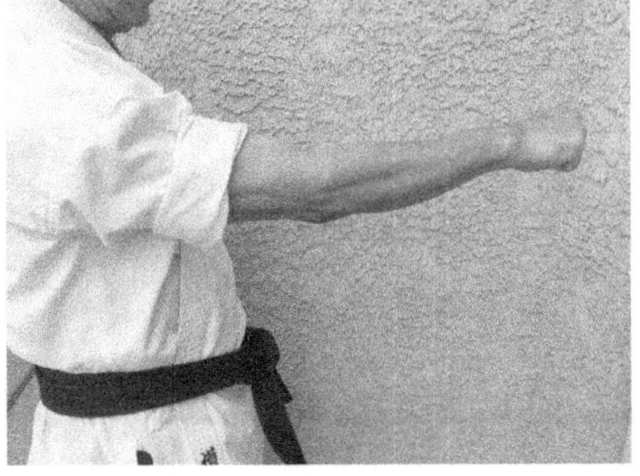

6

Choku zuki is now fully extended. The arm looks as though it is bent at the elbow. This is because *chinkuchi* has been applied at the armpit and the upper back, which causes the arm to appear to have been pulled back while the elbow has been kept down.

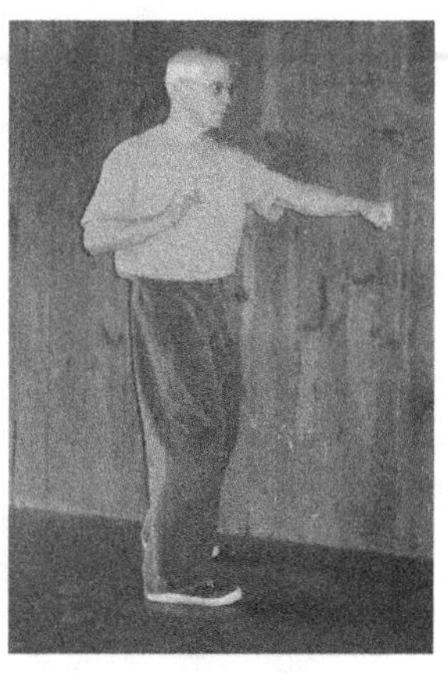

To the right is a photo of a Western practitioner of Goju Ryu punching with *chinkuchi*. You can see the slight bend at the elbow as he tightens his armpit and keeps his shoulder down and his elbow pointing downward.

Even if you do not believe that this punching method has been practiced by Shotokan *karateka* in the past, it is worth trying in your *makiwara* training. I am sure you will feel what will hopefully be a positive difference when you punch this way.

What I am presenting here is two types of *choku zuki*: *tsuki hanashi* and *tsuki* with *shime*. These are used in different situations and for different purposes. On the surface, neither method seems to be better or worse than the other. Because of the popularity of tournament *kumite* and also the lack of *makiwara* training, the long-distance punching method, *tsuki hanashi*, is used by most practitioners these days. Consequently, few instructors train in or teach the short-distance punching method, *tsuki* with *shime*.

OK, so a sport karate practitioner may say, "I am only interested in tournament *kumite*. If the long-distance (extended) punching method is a better fit for tournament *kumite*, then why should I care about the other punching method?" If you do not have any problems with your elbow, then you may not care about the other method. But, the extended punching method involves pointing the elbow outward and thrusting the forearm in without any braking action, which may result in tennis elbow for some practitioners.

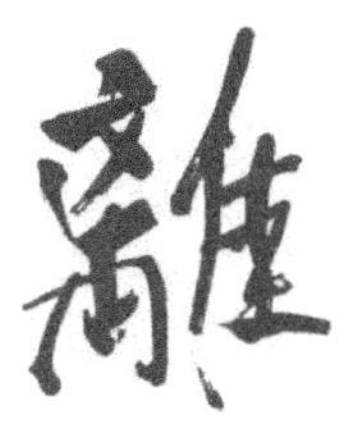

Chapter Twelve
第十二章

There Is More Than One Tanden
丹田は一か所に非ず

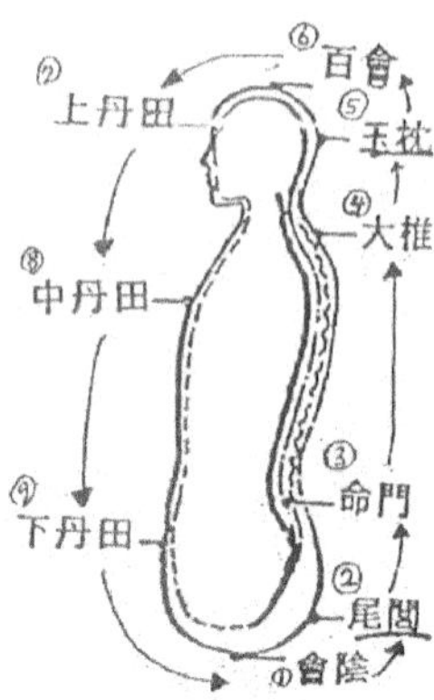

Tanden (丹田) is a popular Japanese word in the areas of Zen (禅), the martial arts, and the Far Eastern medical traditions. This is a very unique and involved subject, so I could write an entire book on it, but in this chapter, I will attempt to introduce the concept and explain it briefly. Since it is an important concept, I may write a longer essay to explain it sometime in the future.

Since this is a very popular term in Japan, I expected to find it in the dictionary, but I was wrong. In order to find a general definition, I had to use *Wikipedia*, even though I prefer not to use this tool. Surprisingly (at least to me), the word was not listed on *Wikipedia*, either. I was redirected to an article under the Chinese name of this concept, *dantian* (or *dāntián*). If you are interested in a general explanation of *tanden/dantian*, here is the URL for that article: www.wikipedia.org/wiki/Dantian.

Let's first try to understand the literal meaning of *tanden*. *Tan* (丹) has several meanings. It can refer to a red clay that is a compound of sulfur and mercury, an element that was made from lead with sulfur and saltpeter added, or a particular medicine that is supposed to be an elixir of life. *Den* (田) means 'field' or 'paddy'. So, the combination of these two characters, *tanden* (丹田), is used as a technical term for a specific area (physical/anatomical) or energy field (physiological/energetic) where one cultivates or produces ki (気 or 氣) and its energy.

In Chinese medicine, they regarded the *tanden* (particularly the lower one) as the body's furnace. The life essence, ki, was considered to be fire. By consciously breathing air and rotating the ki in your body, the ki "burns" and is strengthened.

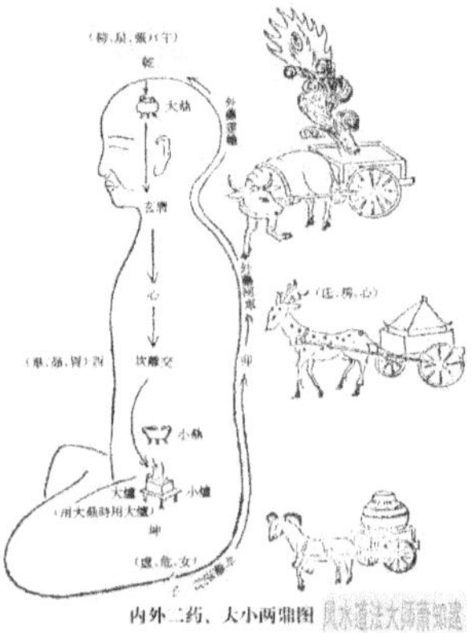

The word *tanden* is quite old. We find it recorded in some ancient books from the third and fourth centuries, but it may be even older than that as we have no way of knowing its precise origin and history.

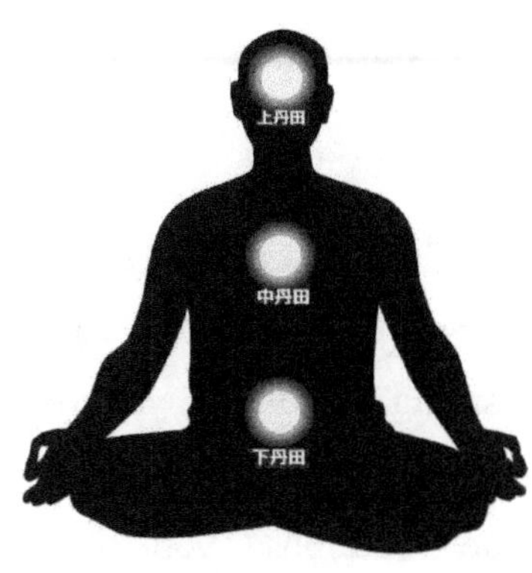

Many Shotokan practitioners, especially the senior ones, may know about the *tanden* and refer to it as the area just below or directly behind the navel in the lower abdominal area. However, few know that there are three—some believe there are even five—*tanden*. The one we are familiar with in the martial arts is the lower *tanden*. The other two are the upper *tanden* and the middle *tanden*. OK, let me give you a brief explanation of each of the three.

The Upper *Tanden* (*Jotanden* [上丹田])

This is supposed to be located between the eyebrows, deep inside the forehead. Some people call it the *third eye*. This cauldron is supposed to store *shin* (神), which literally means 'god', but the understood meaning is closer to 'inner spirit'. You may want to consider this *tanden* to be the brain *tanden*. By developing a strong *jotanden*, you can coordinate the right and left hemispheres of the brain, which results in a creative mind and possibly allows you to achieve a greater perceptive ability (third eye).

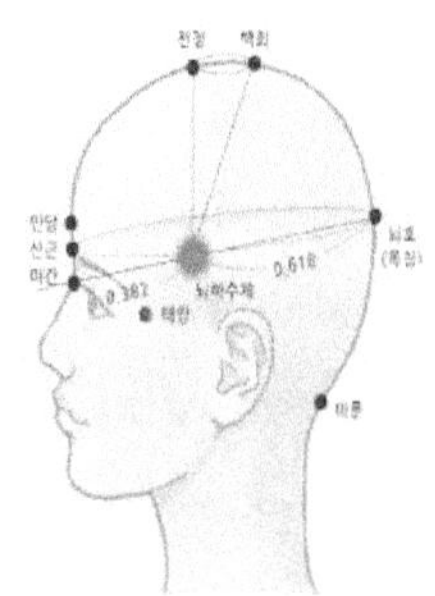

Upper *Dantian* (blue dot)

One example of someone who developed such a *jotanden* may be Edgar Cayce (1877–1945), an American who claimed to be a psychic with the ability to channel answers to questions on various topics while in a self-induced trance. Another example may be Michel de Nostredame, frequently referred to as *Nostradamus* (1503–1566), who was one of the world's most famous authors on the subject of prophecies. His most famous book is *Les Propheties* (1555). And, one final example may be Saint Teresa of Ávila, also called *Saint Teresa of Jesus* (1515–1582), a Spanish mystic, writer, and reformer in the Carmelite Order.

The Middle *Tanden* (*Chutanden* [中丹田])

This is located in the middle of the chest. It is also called the *crimson palace* and is associated with storing ki (気), which is life energy. The *chutanden* could be considered the heart *tanden*. When you develop a strong *chutanden*, you also develop strong love and aspiration. Some excellent examples of people I consider to have possibly developed a strong *chutanden* would be Steve Jobs (1955–2011), Bruce Lee, and Mother Teresa (1910–1997).

The Lower *Tanden* (*Getanden* [下丹田])

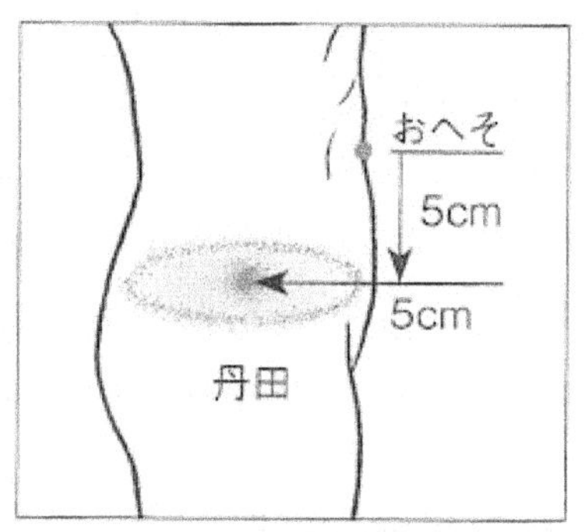

This is located about three finger widths below and two finger widths behind the navel. It is also called the *seika tanden* (臍下丹田, 'lower abdominal *tanden*'), *kikai tanden* (気海丹田, 'sea of ki *tanden*'), *kinro* (金炉, 'gold furnace'), or *shinro* (神炉, 'god furnace'). It is supposed to store *sei* (精), which means 'energy' or 'vigor'. Examples of those who may have developed a tremendous *getanden* would be Yukiyoshi Sagawa (佐川幸義, 1902–1998), a famous *jujutsuka* (柔術家); Tesshu Yamaoka (山岡鉄舟, 1836–1888), a famous samurai who helped the Meiji Restoration; Harumichi Hida (肥田春充, 1883–1956), founder of Hida Shiki Kyokenjutsu (肥田式強健術, 'Hida Health Strengthening Method'); and Rickson Gracie.

The three elements mentioned above, *shin*, ki, and *sei*, are essentially the same thing or could be considered different stages of ki. They are also called the *three treasures of life* as they give us vitality. There are no physical organs in the three areas mentioned, so the three *tanden* must be considered to be the consciousness or the mind in these areas.

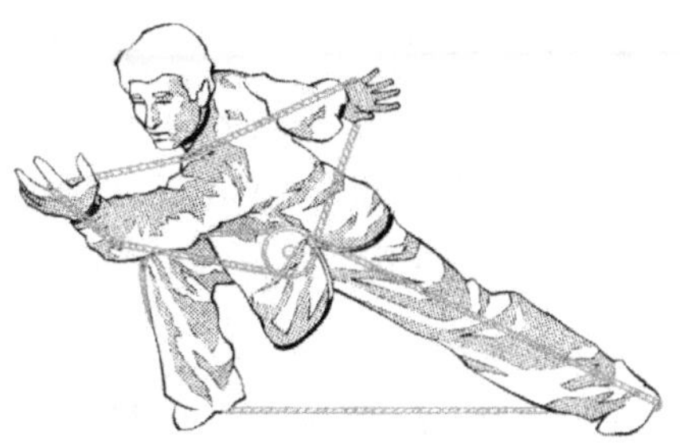

Of the three *tanden*, the *getanden* is considered to be the most important one, especially in the martial arts and Zen. The *getanden* is thus also called the *seitanden* (正丹田), which means 'true *tanden*', 'correct *tanden*', or 'main *tanden*'. When we use the term *tanden* in a martial arts context, we are referring to the *getanden*.

The *getanden* exists deep inside the lower inner abdominal region. Having consciousness in this area can produce at least three benefits.

1. It stimulates autonomic nerves, which enables a peaceful mind. It has also been proven that stimulation of the autonomic nerves leads to increased immunity.
2. It stimulates the inner organs, which normally do not get any exercise. Deep diaphragmatic breathing causes the inner organs to be pushed down and pulled back up. This massaging stimulus produces healthy inner organs and thus good health in general.
3. It stimulates the inner muscles that tie the spine to the lower limbs, which is necessary and critical in the development of martial arts skills.

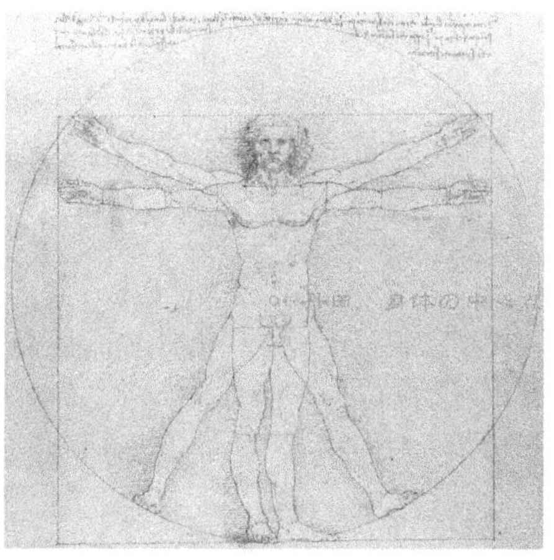

So, now you have a better understanding of the *tanden*. I am sure you wish to improve not only your karate but also your general health. It is better to coordinate your deep breathing with meditation to get the best results. If you are not into having a meditation routine, then introduce slow and deep breathing into your daily activities. As you breathe slowly, just focus on the lower belly area, where you can develop your *seika tanden*. There is not much to lose by trying this ancient method of health improvement. What do you think?

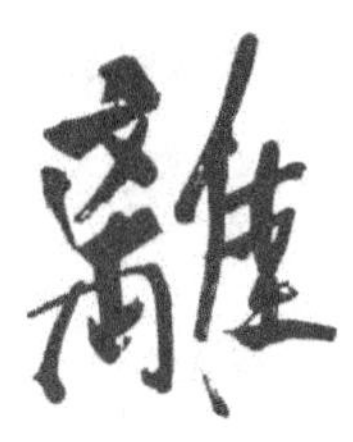

Chapter Thirteen
第十三章

The Mystery of the Arch
土踏まずの不思議

As *karateka*, we are aware that most of us have a gap under the middle part of our foot when we are in a standing position. This middle section is raised slightly off the ground, and we know that this part is called the *arch of the foot* or simply the *arch.*

This construction of having an arch in our foot feels so natural that we think nothing of it unless we happen to have flat feet (fallen arches), which means that there is no arch or that the arch is very low (illustration right). However, this does not necessarily mean there is a problem. They say that a significant number of people with flat feet experience no pain and have no problems.

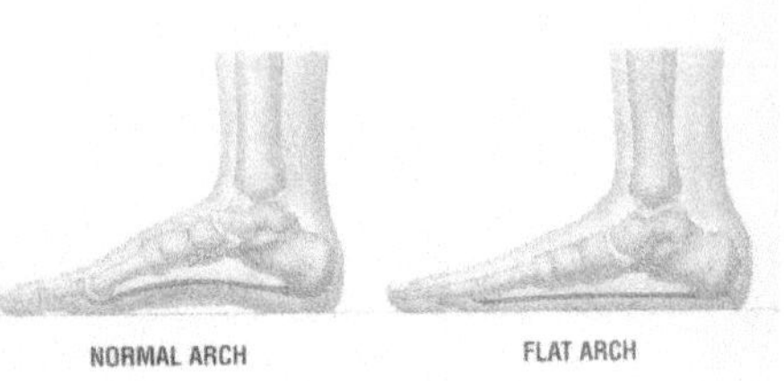

On the other hand, some do experience pain in their feet, especially when the connecting muscles and ligaments are strained. The leg joints may also be affected, resulting in pain. If the ankle turns inward because of flat feet, the areas most likely affected will be the feet, ankles, and knees. But, we will not go any further into the problem of flat feet here as we are focusing on the mystery of the arch in this chapter.

I call this a mystery because we human beings are the only animals who have an arch in our foot. Did you know this? If you did, then why do you think we have this peculiar construction? The more I learn about the body and its construction, the more I am convinced that someone or something great (called *God* by some) has designed our body and made it into a fine masterpiece. I truly believe this. It is true that most four-legged animals, such as dogs, horses, etc., can run faster than we can. But, look at all the skillful things we can do with our two-legged body, such as cycling, skiing, skating, surfing, dancing, and karate, to name a few. Few dogs and horses can imitate any of these feats.

OK, let us get back to the subject of the arch. So, the question is why we have this arch. Believe it or not, it all comes down to the fact that we are the only mammal that walks on two legs. You may say, “So what?” I know most people are not very interested in this subject as they are not aware that this fact can be critical. Actually, just knowing this fact itself may affect the way you move your legs, specifically your feet.

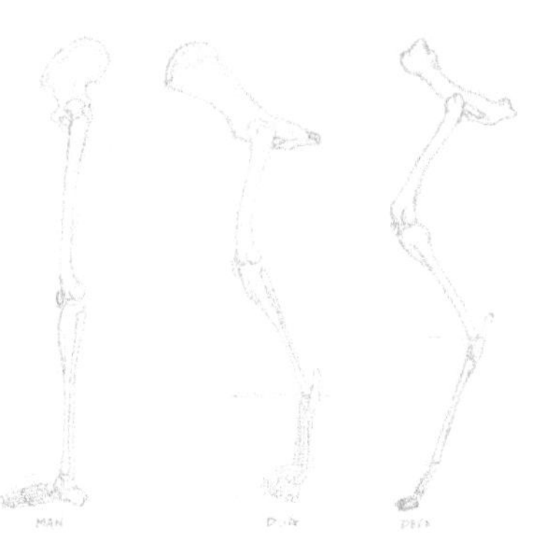

I will explain how this can affect your physical movements, but first let us observe the leg constructions of a man, a dog, and a deer (illustration right) to see if there are any differences. Isn't this interesting? Yes, indeed it is. The first one, of course, is from a human. We know how we stand and what our bone structure looks like. The second one is the rear leg of a dog. The third one is that of a deer.

So, now you can see the differences in bone construction. What differences do you see? Yes, our leg is straight, whereas that of the dog and the deer are bent or crooked. Is this important? Yes, it is, but I will explain why it is important later. What else do you see that is different? Do you see the horizontal lines crossing the bone structures of the dog and the deer in the illustration above? Those lines, believe it or not, show where their heels are.

Look at the photos below so that you can clearly identify where the heel of the rear leg is located.

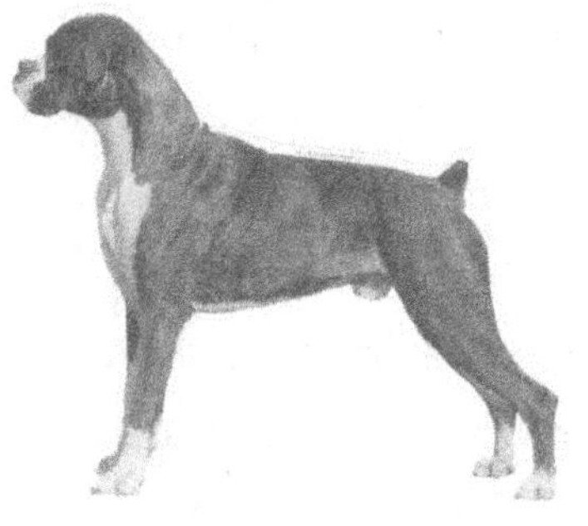

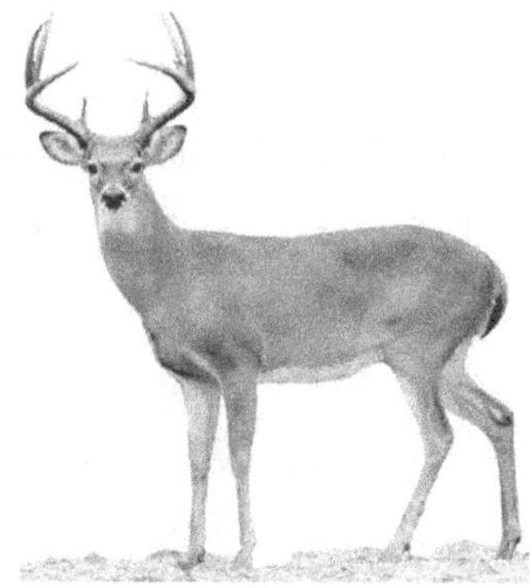

What do you think? Their heels are located very high and do not touch the

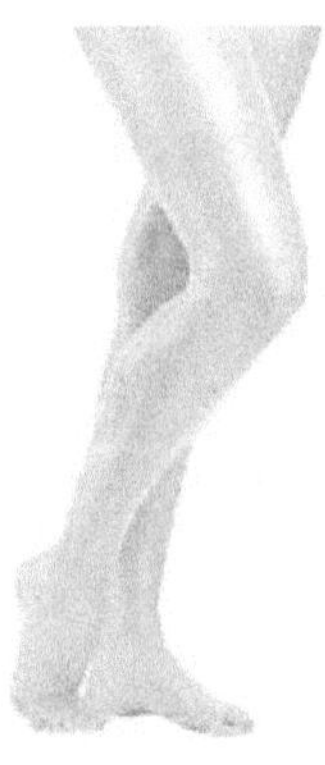

ground as ours do. If we walked on the balls of our feet (as the dog or the deer does), then our leg position would be like the right leg shown in the photo to the left.

Our feet would get tired very quickly, though, so we could not walk in this fashion for a long period of time. However, it looks as though ladies like this style of walking more than men, so they invented special shoes, high heels (photo below right). These shoes certainly make you taller and make your legs look longer; however, we also hear about the possible harm that comes from wearing this type of shoe for a long time. Again, we will not go into this subject here as we are focusing on our feet in a normal standing posture.

So, back to the photos of the dog and deer on the previous page. The dog stands on its paws, which are the equivalent of a combination of our toes and the ball of our foot. In the case of the deer, there is a hoof, which is the tip of the toe of an ungulate mammal (horse, rhinoceros, cow, etc.), strengthened by a thick, horny keratin covering. In other words, these animals walk on their toenails as ballerinas attempt to do. But, look at the toes and toenails of the ballerina in the photo to the left. Obviously, we are not fit for this way of walking.

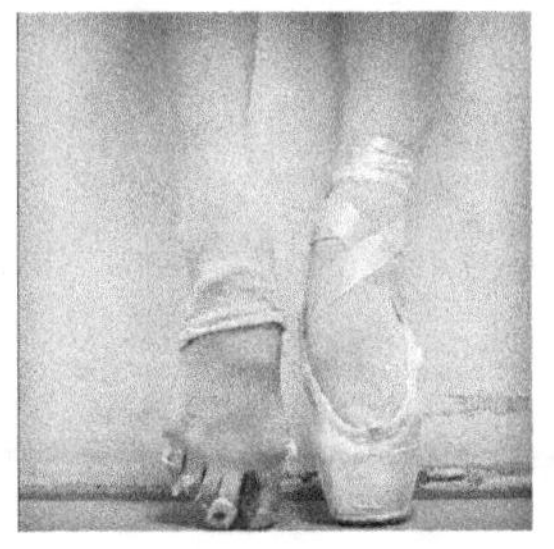

Also, notice that their front legs are rather straight, similar to our legs. Though the heel of the front leg does not touch the ground, it is much lower. This is important, and we need to find out why.

Let us look at the biomechanics of our sample animals, the dog and the deer. If we compare the front leg to the hind leg, it becomes obvious that the hind leg has bigger muscles, which means it is used mainly for acceleration when running. Of course, the front leg is also used to pull—the best example being the cheetah, the world's fastest land animal—but the main power comes from the hind leg's push against the ground. So, the front leg is used more or less for balance and thus does not need to be bent at the knee.

Does a dog put the heels of its hind legs down on the ground? Yes, it does but only to sit down or to balance itself as it lifts its front legs up (photos below).

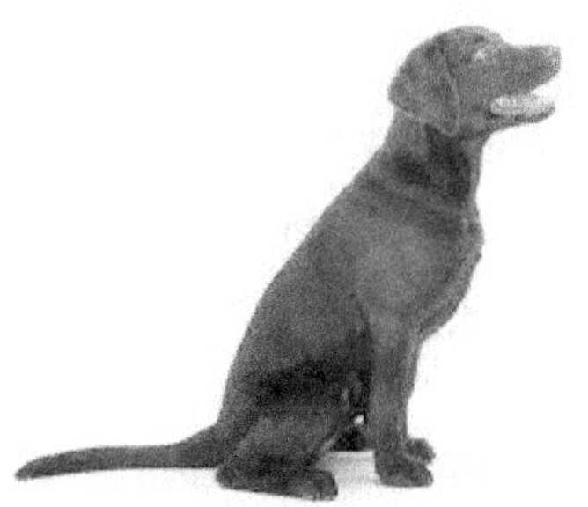

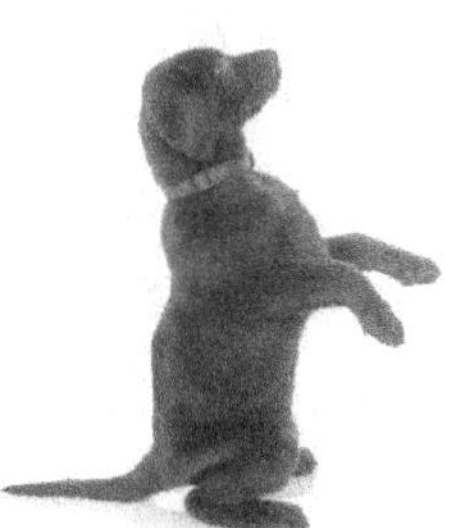

These positions are definitely not for action or quick movements. When a dog wants to jump forward, it brings its rear up and lowers the front of its body. A cat also usually assumes this position before pouncing on a mouse or a squirrel. It bends its front legs as it needs to raise its rear higher in order to bring its momentum forward when it starts to run. The photo to the left shows a big cat assuming this position, ready to pounce on its target.

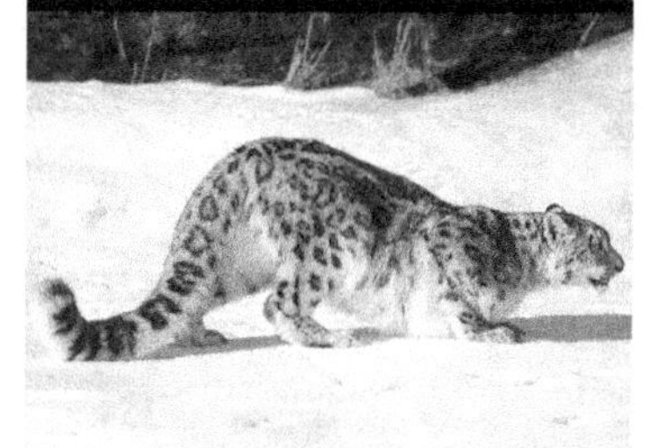

OK, now you may say, "I understand the biomechanics of cats and dogs, but what does that have to do with us, especially with our karate?" Thank you for asking as I was waiting for just this question. This is exactly where I am going.

To the right is an interesting photo that I would like you to take a look at. What do you think? Yes, it is the starting position for a short-distance runner. So, when you want to maximize acceleration at the start, you have to get down into this position and look like the big cat above. Doesn't this tell you something? To move quickly, it is better to be down on

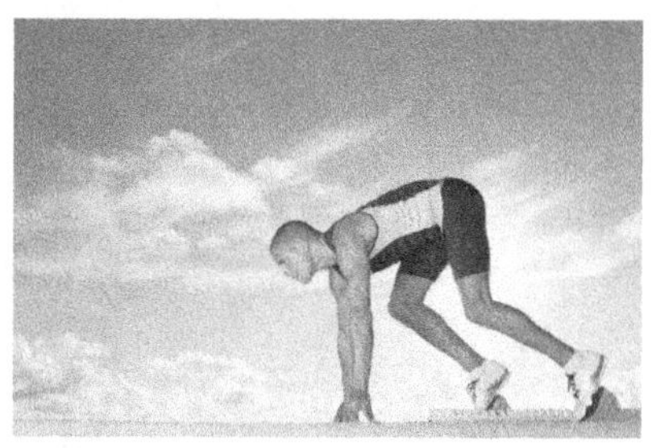

all fours (at least at first).

Now you may be saying, "OK, I understand that four-legged animals are in a ready-to-run position even when they are standing still. I also realize that it is better for humans to crouch down and put their hands on the ground in order to get a quick start in a sprint. But, what does this have to do with our feet, especially the arch that you are supposed to be explaining?"

Wonderful! Now I can get into the real subject, which I believe I am the first person to introduce into the karate world, though it may be well known in the medical and sports-science worlds. You may or may not agree with my theory, but let me explain how our feet function for us.

When we decided to lift our front legs up and start walking on two feet hundreds of thousands of years ago, we (or our Creator or Designer) made a remarkable adjustment to our feet. Yes, it was our arch! How? OK, let's take a closer look at our foot.

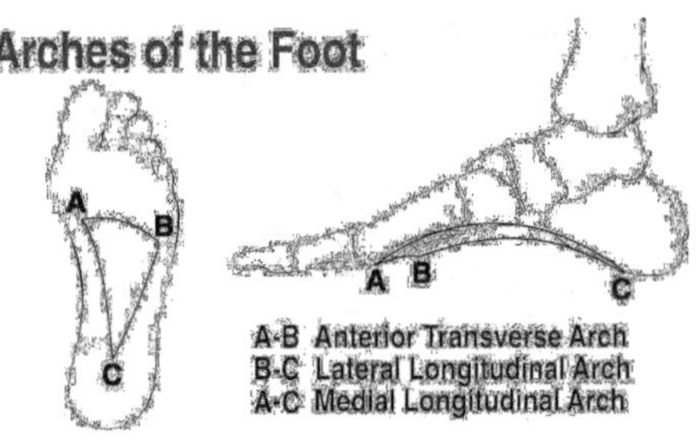

The illustration to the right shows that there are, in fact, three arches in our foot. (This is a very interesting key point that I will explain later.) Now, if you look at the bone structure, you can see that there are two parts to our foot that make firm contact with the ground: the ball and the heel. As you are a smart reader, you can probably guess what I am going to propose here. Yes, these two contact points function as the front foot and the hind foot. To be precise, we actually have three contact points instead of just two (Points A, B, and C in the illustration).

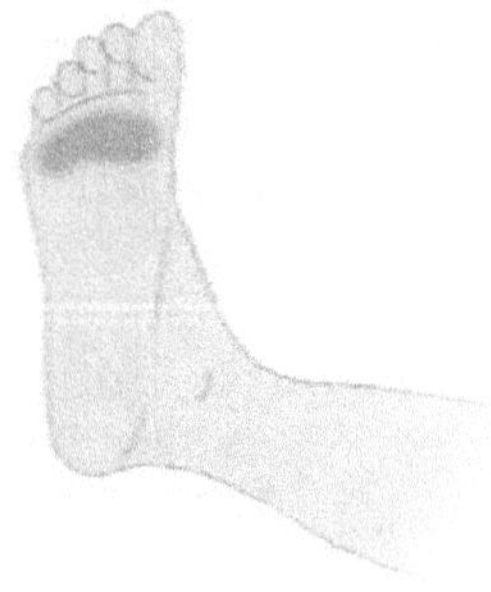

This is amazing in that, if trained—and that is the key word—we can have four front feet! We normally do not train our mind and our body to differentiate between the contact points on the ball of the foot. Most of us consider this to be one spot (illustration left). When you reach the expert level of dancing, ballet, football, basketball, or even track and field, you know the difference between these two points and use each one differently. Certainly, a martial arts expert should know this, too.

Though you must use both points (A and B) of the ball of the foot, I recommend that you use Point B rather than Point A when you are moving forward. I will not go into the details of this in this chapter, but I may write a more thorough piece on this very point with a detailed explanation as to why it is better in the future. Regardless, the Designer of our body allowed us to have four "feet," and we must remember that, because of this fact, we can perform some incredibly complicated body movements, such as dancing, figure skating, skiing, gymnastics, and martial arts, just by skillfully manipulating these three points on each of our feet.

Even if you do not pay attention to the two points on the ball of the foot, I hope you at least agree that the foot has two points of contact: the ball and the heel.

OK, what is next? I want you to compare the rear leg of a human to that of a dog again (Picture 1). When a dog stands on its hind legs, what does it have to do? It must sit down by bringing its heels down if it is to maintain balance (Picture 2). If it needs to move forward—moving backward is almost impossible—it certainly cannot walk like a person, so it has to hop with both legs together (Picture 3).

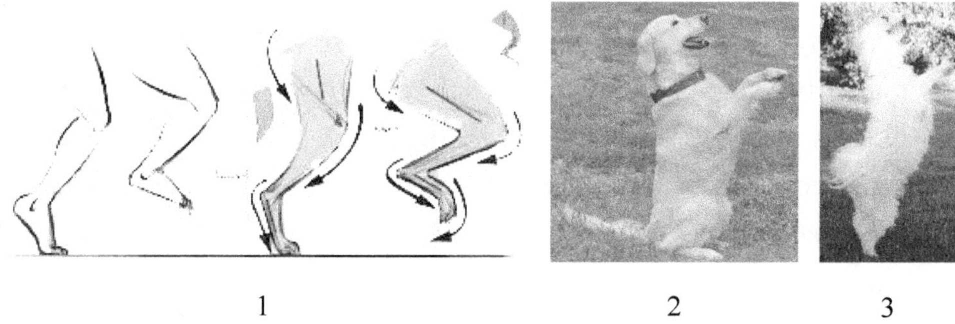

1 2 3

So, how does this tie in with our karate movements? How does a hopping dog relate to karate? I will attempt to explain here.

Recently, someone asked me a question. He said he had gotten into *kumite* competition in the eighties. He learned the free-sparring style and hopping footwork commonly seen at World Karate Federation (世界空手連盟 [WKF]) tournaments, where competitors are either standing on the balls of their feet or hopping around (Picture 4). However, as he watched the JKA *kumite* videos from the sixties, the seventies, and even the eighties, he noticed that those competitors would stand in a flat-footed position with their heels planted firmly on the ground (Picture 5). He asked me why this occurred.

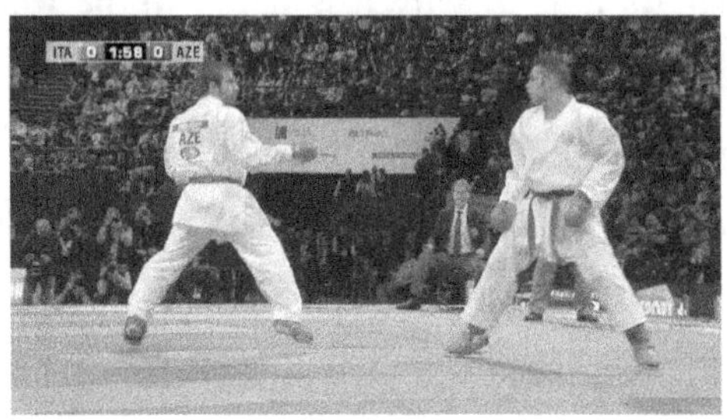

4

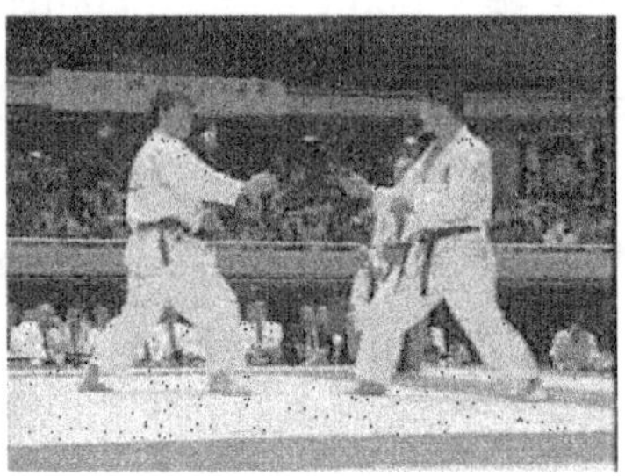

5

Here is my answer to his question. In 1981, our karate, specifically the *kata* and *kumite* of the JKA, experienced a change. I will only talk about *kumite* in this chapter. That year, the JKA joined the Japan Karatedo Federation (全日本空手道連盟 [JKF]) so that JKA competitors could compete for the first time in the Kokumin Taiiku Taikai (国民体育大会, 'National Sports Festival'), or Kokutai (国体) for short.

The thirty-sixth Kokutai was to be held in Shiga Prefecture (滋賀県) that very year. I know this because I represented my prefecture, Hyogo (兵庫県), as one of the competitors. Luckily, I had won first place in the JKA Hyogo Prefecture championship that year and had captured the opportunity to participate in the sports festival.

I was, of course, a traditional JKA competitor with my feet flat on the ground, so I was a little shocked to witness the hopping-style *kumite* that had already been adopted by Shito Ryu competitors and those of other styles, as well. We JKA competitors had to change our fighting style because we could not win with the flat-footed style. This was certainly not because the JKA competitors were slower or less powerful. We simply found that the *kumite* rules were different.

There were two major differences, though they were somewhat interconnected. Let me explain.

The first difference was distance. As you know, in JKA *kumite*, you basically have to make contact to get a *waza ari*. Bloody noses and lips were very common, and nobody got disqualified, even if a competitor knocked his opponent's tooth out.

At the Kokutai, on the other hand, we were strictly prohibited from touching or making contact with the opponent, especially to the *jodan*. Even if it was a light touch to the opponent's face, we would be automatically disqualified. The *chudan* was similar, though very light touching to that area was tolerated. Even if your fist was one inch away (with a fully extended arm), it was considered a *waza ari*.

The second difference was the posture and power (or lack thereof) behind the technique. At a JKA tournament, techniques had to be heavy, meaning that the punch or kick had to be supported by having the whole body behind it. If a punch was thrown with a fully extended arm, but the body was turned sideways, it would not be considered to be effective or worthy of a *waza ari*. So, the techniques I was familiar with were of the one-punch-one-kill variety.

The techniques that were allowed at the Kokutai, on the other hand, were very fast and light to me. Jumping in and throwing the arm out quickly seemed to be enough to score a point. From that perspective, it made sense that the competitors were hopping. So, remember that this hopping movement performed by karate competitors is based on the same biomechanics as the movements of a dog hopping with both feet together to move forward or just to move around.

If you happen to practice kendo (剣道), you may say, "In kendo, we lift our rear heel up, even though we do not hop." This is true. But, I have to say, with all due respect, that the techniques of kendo have become sportlike, even though its practitioners say that they maintain the *budo* spirit. I am not a practitioner of kendo or kenjutsu, but I can say this based on my understanding of the concept of *budo* and *bujutsu*. This is important, so I will explain it further.

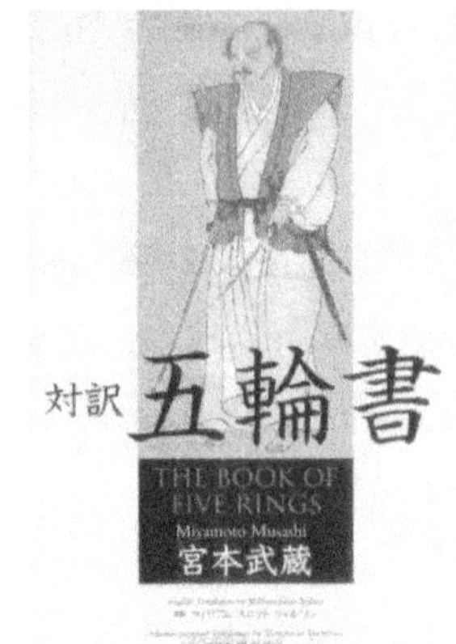

In *Gorin no Sho*, Miyamoto makes a statement that is puzzling to modern-day kendo practitioners. He writes that the heels must be firmly planted on the ground when fighting (with swords). In other words, he warns practitioners not to lift their heels up while assuming *kamae* and attacking.

This statement is puzzling because kendo practitioners now lift their rear heel (typically the left) off the ground (Picture 6). But, if you compare this to iaido (居合道, 'sword-drawing art') or the *koryu kenjutsu* (古流剣術, 'ancient sword arts') shown in Picture 7, you will notice two differences. One is the distance, and the other is the heel position.

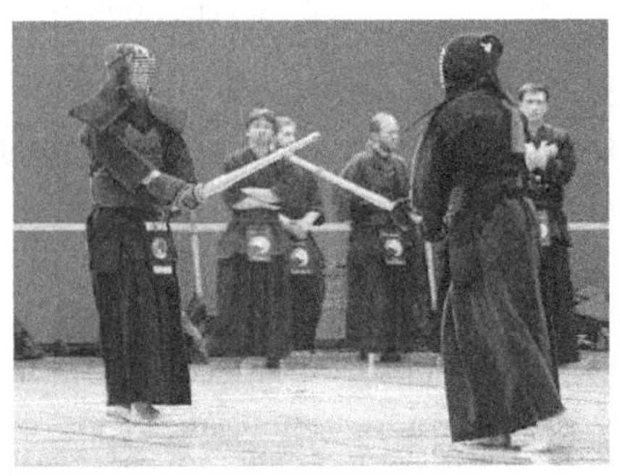

6

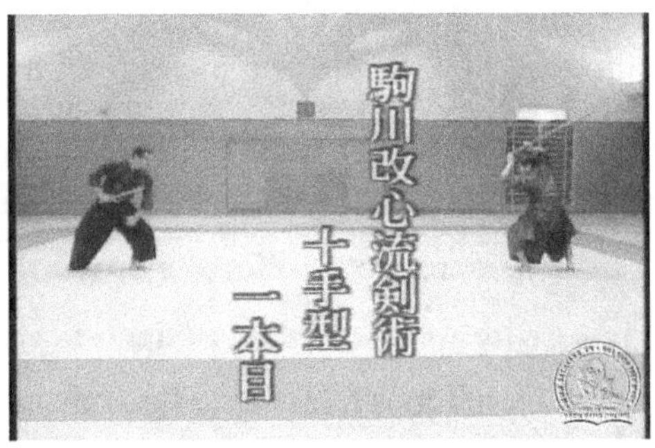

7

The *maai* (間合い, 'distance') used in *koryu kenjutsu*, which is practiced with either a wooden sword or a real sword, is typically much greater than that of kendo. In kendo, the distance is short, and one opponent can strike the other by taking one step forward. Why? It is simply because there is no fear of getting cut by the sword. You may feel some shock to the head if you get hit by a *shinai*, but the fear factor is tremendously less than when you are facing a person with a real sword.

Regarding the position of the heel, it is obviously raised in kendo in order to get a faster jump, which is the same reason WKF competitors stand on the balls of their feet. In *koryu kenjutsu*, however, the heels are down because the cuts are heavy, so the strikes need the full weight of the body behind them, which is the same concept as a karate punch or kick with *kime*.

Conclusion

We are bipedal, which means that we walk on two legs. This is very unique as we are the only mammal that does this, and it requires fine-tuned balance. Think of riding a bicycle. You can easily keep your balance when you are moving forward, but once you stop, it is tremendously difficult to keep the bike balanced without putting your feet on the ground. We have been walking since we were one year old, so we feel that it is almost natural to be able to stand up and walk. However, we must remember that it took us a whole year (or even longer for some) to acquire our bipedal walking ability. This topic can also be found in Chapter 9: “Unstable Balance” of my book *Shotokan Mysteries*.

To compensate for our lack of front legs, we now have an arch, which creates two contact points on the ball of the foot (Points 2 and 3 in the photo to the right). If we consider the heel (Point 1 in the same photo) to be a hind foot, then we now have two front feet on each leg for a total of four front feet! This is not a joke. By being able to manipulate and utilize these “feet,” we are capable of doing some very intricate body movements (dancing, figure skating, gymnastics, martial arts, etc.) that are impossible for other animals to do.

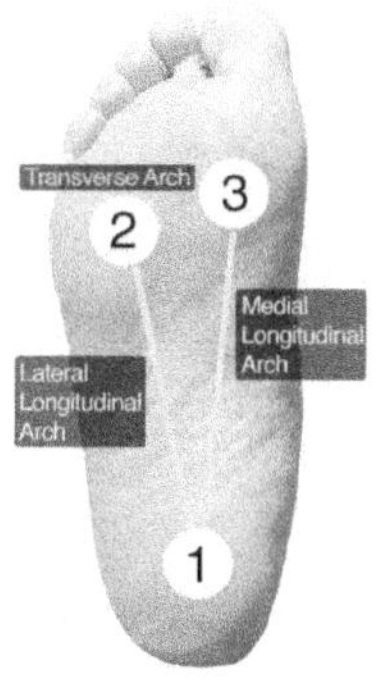

In sport karate, there are different objectives; thus, competitors hop on the balls of their feet. In *budo* karate, we must learn to keep our heels firmly on the ground as we do in our *kata*. At the same time, we must learn how to move forward, move backward, and turn, using the correct parts of our feet. I talk about the subject of turning in Chapter 4: “What Part of Your Foot Do You Use When You Turn?” of my book *Shotokan Transcendence*. If you are interested in this topic, please refer to that chapter.

The more we find out about our body and its incredible design, the more we can appreciate what we have and the tremendous potential of what we can do with it.

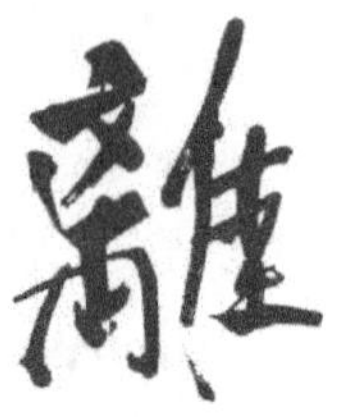

Chapter Fourteen
第十四章

The Difference between Wanting to Win and Not Wanting to Lose
勝ちたいと負けないの違い

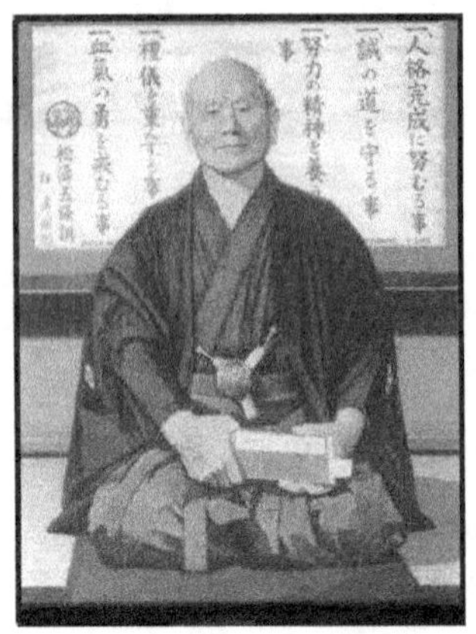

Most Shotokan practitioners, as well as many practitioners of other traditional karate styles, know that Gichin Funakoshi is the father of modern-day karate and that he brought Okinawa Te to mainland Japan in the early twentieth century. In the Epilogue of my third book, *Shotokan Transcendence*, I wrote about Funakoshi's *Niju Kun* (二十訓, '*Twenty Principles*'). These principles have been translated by many people, but I decided to provide my own translation as I had not found any that satisfied me. If you have not read that book, please get a copy from *Amazon*.

In *Shotokan Transcendence*, I cover the meaning of each of the twenty *kun* in depth. Here, however, I would like to single out one *kun* in particular to discuss further. The one I would like to talk about is the twelfth one, which states the following:

> 勝つ考えは持つな負けぬ考えは必要
> *Katsu kangae wa motsu na makenu kangae wa hitsuyo*
> Do not think of winning. Think, rather, of not losing.

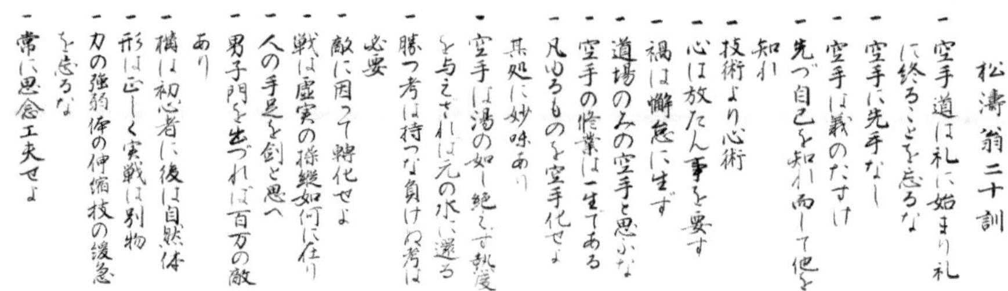

松濤翁二十訓

一 空手道は礼に始まり礼に終ることを忘るな
一 空手に先手なし
一 空手は義のたすけ
一 先づ自己を知れ而して他を知れ
一 技術より心術
一 心は放たん事を要す
一 禍は懈怠に生ず
一 道場のみの空手と思ふな
一 空手の修業は一生である
一 凡ゆるものを空手化せよ其処に妙味あり
一 空手は湯の如し絶えず熱度を与えざれば元の水に還る
一 勝つ考は持つな負けぬ考は必要
一 敵に因って轉化せよ
一 戦は虚実の操縦如何に在り
一 人の手足を劍と思へ
一 男子門を出づれば百万の敵あり
一 構は初心者に後は自然体
一 形は正しく実戦は別物
一 力の強弱体の伸縮技の緩急を忘るな
一 常に思念工夫せよ

I have decided to discuss this *kun* further because of an experience I had during my recent visit to Japan (January and February 2016). I wish to explain this important *kun* in depth through a story of an event that took place in Japan. It is a rather long story, but after reading it, you will better understand what this *kun* really means.

OK, are you ready for this long story? On a freezing day in February 2016, I visited the third-largest city in Japan to exchange a very important agreement document with a certain Japanese karate organization. The signing and the ceremony went well, and we had a small party afterward. We had a very nice seafood dinner, a glass of beer, and a *kanpai* (乾杯, 'toast') to celebrate the agreement, even though I do not drink beer. The party went well, and, as usual, we had discussions about karate, which I always enjoy very much.

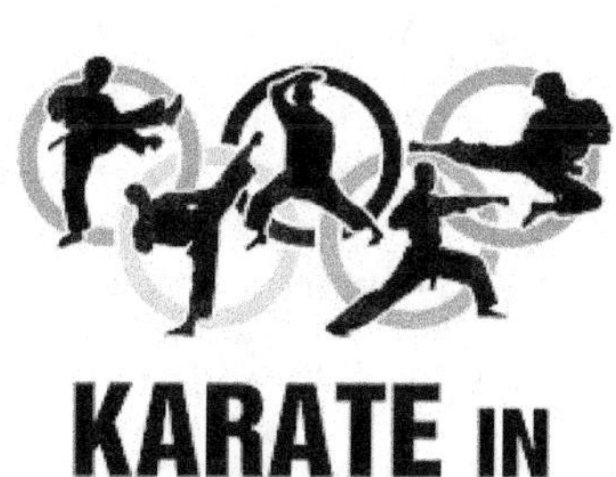

We started off our discussion with a few subjects that were related to karate techniques. After a period of time, one sensei from northern Japan who was there as a special guest asked me how I felt about the possibility of karate's being included in the Olympic Games. My answer was clear. I was totally against the inclusion of karate. He expressed that he was in favor of it and asked why I was against this possibility. I explained that the main reason for my opposition was the fear that the *budo* spirit would be ignored and forgotten once it was included in the Olympics.

This sensei respectfully disagreed and said that he taught his young students not only discipline and hard training but also courtesy and etiquette. He proudly stated that his students would be a good example of *budo* karate for the rest of the world. I congratulated him on his teaching methods and also told him that I respected him for running his dojo that way.

Now, I know that he teaches his students how to be courteous and demonstrate good etiquette. The students' parents, without being asked, take brooms and trash bags when they accompany their children to a tournament. With these tools, they are prepared to clean up the tournament site before they leave, though this gesture is totally voluntary and is not expected by the sensei or by the tournament management. For this reason, I sincerely hope his team will have an opportunity to demonstrate their behavior at the 2020 Tokyo Olympics.

Although I respect this sensei very much and understood what he was saying, I still had to disagree with him. I could foresee what karate would become from watching the current behavior of karate tournament competitors. He asked me why I was so strongly opposed to the idea of karate's being in the Olympic Games, and what follows is the explanation I gave him.

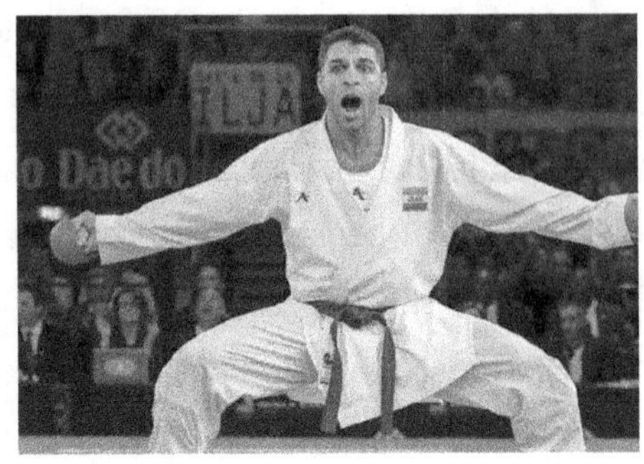

The trend of recent tournaments has been toward establishing winning as the ultimate goal. I fear that this trend will become even more significant now that karate has been included in the Olympics. I told him that this was the reason I had said karate would lose the *budo* spirit. He said, "I am sorry, but I do not understand."

So, I asked him, "Sensei O——,"—I refrain from revealing his real name here out of respect for his privacy—"do you know the twelfth *kun* from Funakoshi's *Niju Kun*?" He did not, so I told him the *kun* that is written at the beginning of this chapter: "*Katsu kangae wa motsu na makenu kangae wa hitsuyo*" ('Do not think of winning. Think, rather, of not losing.').

He said, "Frankly, this *kun* is very confusing to me. I do not see the difference between 'thinking of winning' and 'thinking of not losing.' Do you?"

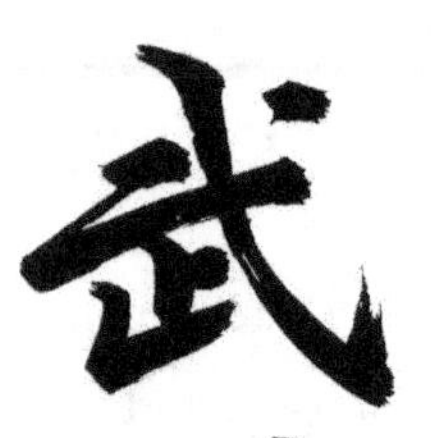

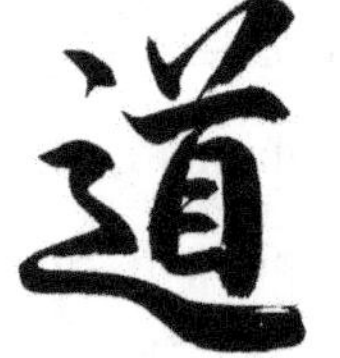

I suspect this is what most readers also think. I answered, "Yes, I do know," and explained to him that there was a big difference between these two attitudes or desires. Here is my explanation.

If winning is your ultimate goal in a match, you tend to do anything to accomplish that end. I am not saying that winning is bad or wrong in and of itself; I am referring to the process of winning. In other words, even if an action is dishonest or is unbecoming of *budo*, you choose to take it anyway in order to win.

As an example, imagine that one competitor is leading by one point and has only ten or fifteen seconds left in the match. What will this competitor do? He will most likely stay back and not take any chances so that he doesn't risk losing by letting the opponent score. This means that he will stop fighting. Even if he is not obviously running away, he will still maintain a safe distance from the opponent.

I asked this sensei if he would encourage such a competitor to stay back or to fight more aggressively if he were his coach. He answered, "If the rule allows the competitor to be dormant or nonaggressive, then he can use this rule to his advantage. So, I would coach the competitor to stay back and secure the win. There is nothing wrong with this."

His reply was exactly what I had expected. So, I continued, "Sensei O——, let's change the situation to that of a cashier in a store." He was OK with this, so I asked him a silly question: "Would you allow your students or your children to steal money from a store?"

"Of course not!" He quickly replied.

I had expected this reply, too, so I continued, "Imagine that there were a rule stating that store management will not press charges or conduct an investigation when the cash register is only short by one penny. If this were the case, would you allow your student or your child to steal a penny?"

"Definitely not!" He emphatically stated, "Taking even one penny is still stealing!"

I told him that I agreed and that this was exactly my point. I asked why he would let his student or child carry out an action unbecoming of *budo* in a tournament just because a rule allowed for it and what he thought the difference was between this action and that of stealing a penny.

He said, "Well, I understand your point from your analogy. Then, what about trying not to lose? Isn't that the same thing? If you do not want to lose, then won't you become less aggressive in that particular situation?"

This is the challenging point that many people misunderstand about this *kun*.

My answer was as follows: "No, I do not think that is what Master Funakoshi wanted to tell us. My understanding of his intended meaning is that we should not make winning the ultimate goal in a tournament. This means that karate practitioners must not place winning above the principles of *karatedo*. Therefore, a karate practitioner must not cheat or act dishonestly in order to win. In other words, the competitor in the earlier situation must continue to fight with the same fighting spirit during the final ten seconds. He will be careful not to let his opponent score against him, but he will certainly not run away from the opponent or waste time just to run out the clock."

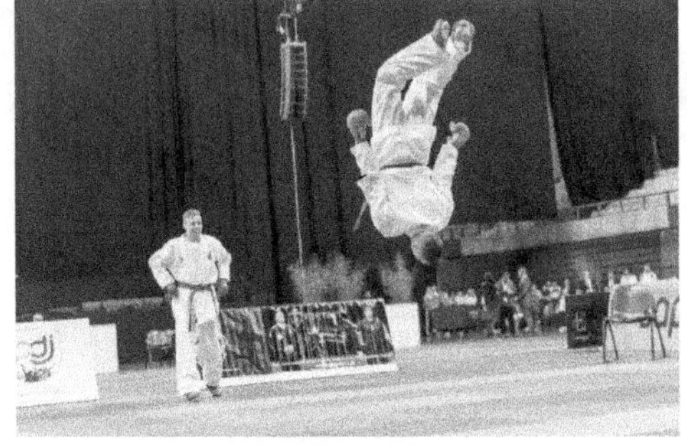

I told him that, in *budo*, we (particularly the Japanese samurai) seek the beauty of losing with honor rather than winning by dirty or dishonest means. I concluded that this kind of attitude or way of thinking would not be developed or cherished by Olympic competitors or their coaches. He agreed and uttered weakly, "You are right, Yokota Sensei, but that is a big challenge. I am a coach, but I am not sure if I can guide my students to seek a clean loss and forget about winning."

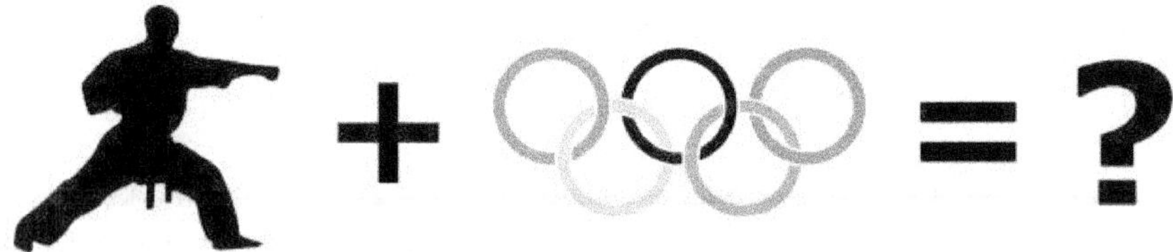

An honorable loss is much better than a dishonest win. But, now that karate has become an Olympic event, I doubt very much that this spirit will be honored or carried out by most competitors. Therefore, I will conclude by saying that I hope Sensei O—— will see the educational value of Funakoshi's *Niju Kun*, particularly that of the twelfth *kun*. This would allow him to add the true value of *budo* to his teachings when training his young students. He is still in favor of having karate in the Olympics, so I sincerely hope that his students will be a model for the world by demonstrating true *karatedo* spirit and actions when they compete.

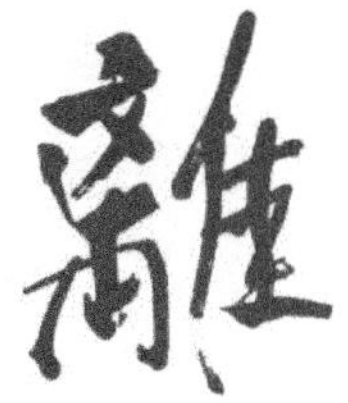

Chapter Fifteen
第十五章

What Is the Most Important Training Point in Budo Karate?
武道空手の稽古において一番重要な要項とは如何に？

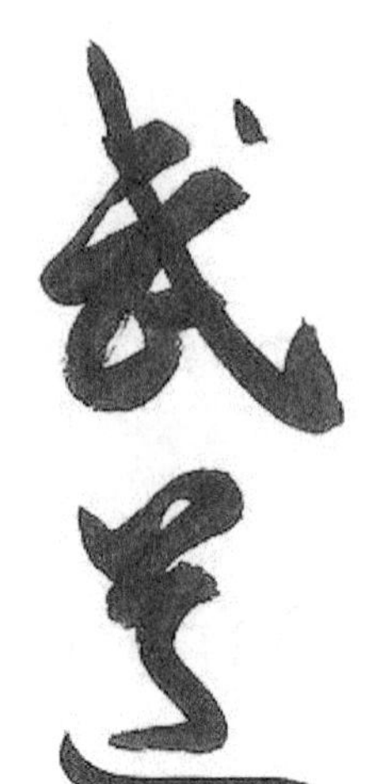

Before you try to answer the question in the title of this chapter, I ask that you pay attention to the fact that I placed the word *budo* in front of *karate*. In other words, my question is specifically geared toward *budo* karate (martial art karate), not sport karate.

OK, then we need to define *budo* and agree on a concept so that we can discuss this question. The reader most likely knows that *budo* is a term describing modern Japanese martial arts. Literally translated, *budo* means 'martial way' and may be thought of as 'the way of war'. *Budo* is a compound term that is made up of two characters. The first character, 武 (*bu*), means 'war', 'martial', or 'military', and the second one, 道 (*do*), means 'path' or 'way'. I am sure we all agree on this translation.

Thus, in *budo* karate, we train to defend our lives in critical situations. Therefore, I am sure you will agree that the purpose of our training in *budo* karate is not to learn how to score a point in a *kumite* competition or perform a *kata* in an attractive way in order to earn a high score in a *kata* competition. So, now that we have agreed on this, what do you think the most important element in karate training is?

Some people may pick speed, power, or distance as the most important; other people may say it's *bunkai*; and some old-timers may insist that it's *kihon* or *kata*. There are so many other important elements, such as breathing, concentration, etc., that it is quite difficult to pin down which one is the most important. So, what do you think?

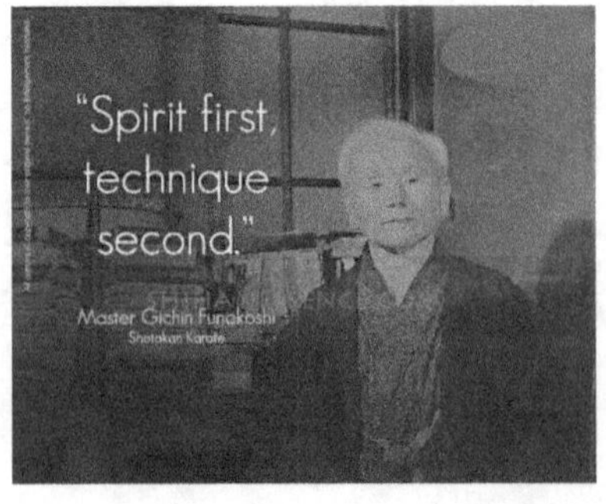

Yes, all of the points listed above are indeed important. I do not disagree with this. But, you may be surprised when I tell you that none of them is the most important element in *budo* karate. Then, what is the most important one? As far as *budo* karate is concerned, the most important element, by far, is mind-set. If you do not agree, check the fifth *kun* of Funakoshi's *Niju Kun*:

> 技術より心術
> *Gijutsu yori shinjutsu*
> Mentality over technique.

I am truly impressed that Master Funakoshi put this short *kun* in the fifth place out of twenty important precepts. It is very obvious that he considered it to be one of the most important teachings. As I mentioned in the previous chapter, I included a deeper translation of Funakoshi's *Niju Kun* a few years ago in the Epilogue of my book *Shotokan Transcendence*. I quote my explanation of the fifth *kun* from that book below:

> This translation needs further explanation to understand the deep meaning of this *kun*. Let me explain the meaning of each word, and that should help us understand this important *kun*. *Gijutsu* (技術) means 'technique', but *gi* (技) itself means 'technique', and *jutsu* (術) means 'art', 'way', 'method', or 'means'. So, it means 'technical method' or 'technical way'. So, it does not necessarily mean 'karate techniques'. When we say the word *gijutsusha* (技術者), that is, '*gijutsu* person', we mean 'engineer' or 'craftsman'. Regardless, by "*gijutsu*," he was referring to karate techniques.
>
> Then, what is *shinjutsu* (心術)? *Shin* (心) means 'heart', 'mind', or 'intelligence'. So, we may quickly translate *shinjutsu* as 'mind way' or 'intelligent way'; however, this translation is not exactly what Funakoshi really wanted to say.
>
> The Japanese word *shin* has many meanings, and it is a very important word in Japanese. *Shin* can mean 'center' or 'core' (*kan* [幹]) and even 'stomach' or 'guts' (*hara* [腹]). The samurai considered *shin* and *hara* to be the center of their samurai spirit or value. This is why they cut their belly open when they committed *seppuku* (切腹), or *harakiri* (腹切), to show that their center was pure.
>
> I do not think Funakoshi was thinking of *harakiri*, but he was thinking of the samurai spirit. He was thinking of the *gojo no toku* (五常の徳), which are the five cardinal Confucian virtues. These virtues are *jin* (仁, 'benevolence'), *gi* (義, 'justice'), *rei* (礼, 'courtesy'), *chi* (智, 'wisdom'), and *shin* (信, 'trust'). I will write about Bushido in the near future and will include further explanation of the *gojo no toku* at that time.

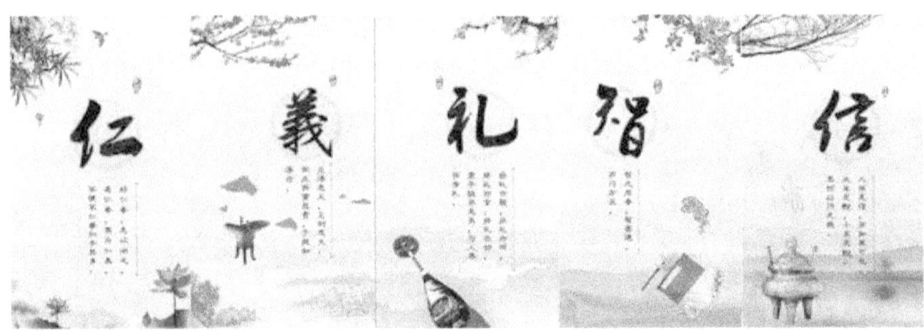

The samurai also believed in the importance of *hara* and *shinjutsu*. Some kenjutsu styles, such as Jigen Ryu (示現流), have dropped almost all techniques. You are taught to raise your sword over your head and just bring it down. That is it. Practitioners of Jigen Ryu also practice by repeatedly hitting bundles of sticks with a *bokken* (木剣, 'wooden sword'). In fact, karate historians suspect that this practice is the forefather of karate's *makiwara*.

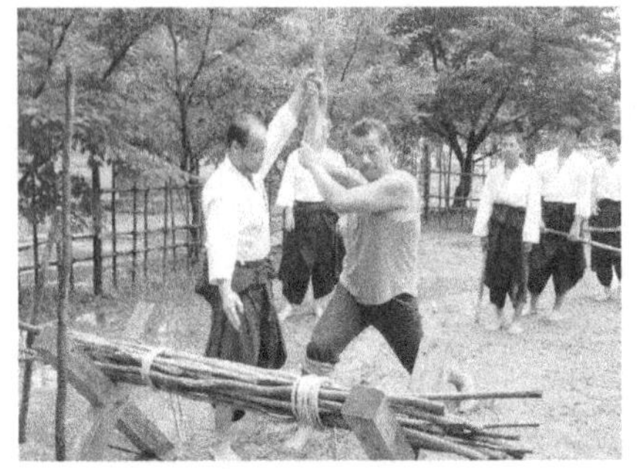

Jigen Ryu was invented in the Satsuma Domain (薩摩藩), which was in the southern part of Kyushu (九州), the island nearest to Okinawa. Following the occupation of Okinawa by the Shimazu Clan of Satsuma in 1609, some of the Okinawan karate practitioners visited Satsuma to learn their style of kenjutsu, Jigen Ryu. It is easy to guess that these Okinawan *karateka* learned this practice of hitting sticks with a *bokken*, took it back to Okinawa, and, from there, invented the *makiwara* for karate training purposes.

OK, that is enough of that side story. So, back to the main subject. The samurai believed in the importance of *hara* and *shinjutsu*. After reading the quote from *Shotokan Transcendence* above, did you think I had covered the full explanation of *shinjutsu*? I am sure you did not. You must have felt that something was somehow missing. Yes, I purposely left out one thing in my explanation, which is that *shinjutsu* must include *heijoshin* (平常心, 'presence of mind') to explain why Funakoshi put it above *gijutsu*.

OK, so what is *heijoshin*? *Hei* (平) means 'flat', and *jo* (常) means 'constant'. As you know, *shin* means 'heart', 'mind', or 'spirit', so the combination of all three characters literally means 'flat and constant heart'. In our daily life, it is difficult for us to keep a peaceful mind as we become surprised, upset, angry, sad, or even frightened. So, *heijoshin* refers to the ability to maintain a peaceful mind, and *shinjutsu* refers to the techniques and training methods used to form and build *heijoshin*.

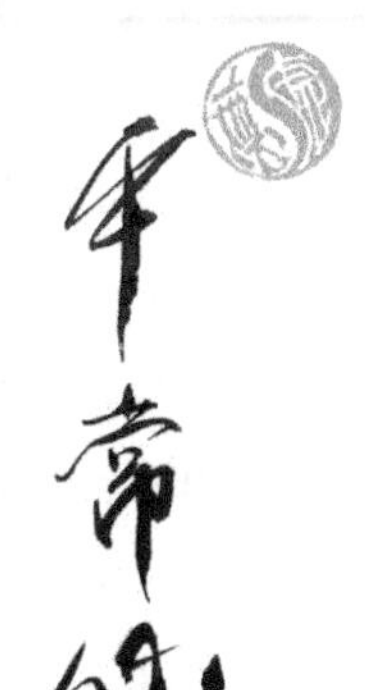

A sport karate enthusiast may come back and say, "Hey, we also need *heijoshin* to prepare ourselves for a tournament, especially for big events such as national and world championships. So, why do you specify *budo* karate?" It is true that tournament competitors need to have a calm and peaceful mind. I respect them for their enthusiasm and dedication to their karate training. If they are nervous, upset, or shaky, then they will not be able to perform to the best of their ability.

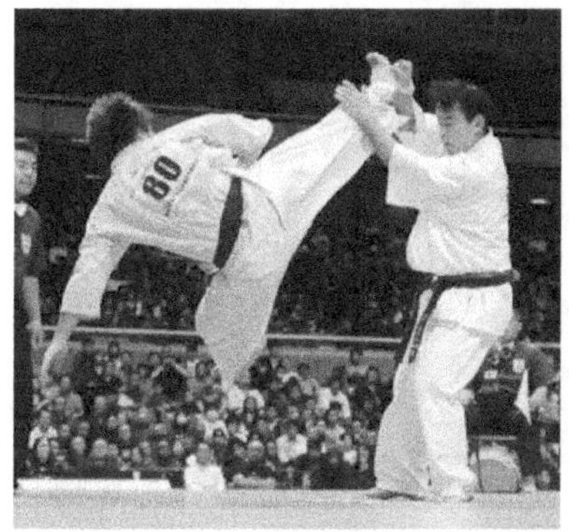

Having said that, I am afraid the degree of stress in tournament competition is vastly different from that of *budo* karate. In *budo*, we practice on the assumption that what we are fighting for is a matter of life or death. I am sure you will agree that facing an assailant with a gun or a knife is quite different from facing an opponent in *kumite*, even if it is a full-contact tournament.

When an assailant with a gun or a knife is facing you, a serious degree of control is naturally required. First, you must control your fear. Second, you need to be able to make quick and correct judgments. You must quickly determine if this is the time to fight or to surrender, depending on the intentions of the assailant. If he simply wants to take your money, or even your car, it is definitely wiser to let him have it rather than risking your life to avoid material loss. On the other hand, if this person intends to harm you or a family member, you may have to fight. If he is thinking of killing you, then you have no choice but to fight to save yourself or your family members.

This is, indeed, a life-or-death fight and is exactly when a cool head is most needed. Even if you have no fear, you will fail and possibly be killed if you are too excited and become reckless. At this critical time, you need to be able to execute the techniques as you have practiced them many times in your dojo. It is easy to say this, but being able to do all these things is considerably more difficult than you can imagine.

In this situation, your physical techniques may be important, but your ability to use your mental techniques (*heijoshin*) is needed first. In other words, if you can keep a cool head, your karate techniques can be average or, in extreme cases, not even necessary. Even if you have little karate or martial arts training, if you can punch or kick, you may be able to defend yourself in a critical situation by keeping a cool head and making the right decisions.

So, how can you develop and maintain *heijoshin*? Well, this was a core question for the samurai all throughout the feudal period (from the late twelfth century up to the first half of the nineteenth century). I am sure they were scared of fighting and dying in battle. *Heijoshin* certainly did not come naturally or easily even in the period of the samurai, and it is certainly more difficult now. If this mind-set did not come naturally to the samurai, then how did they learn it or train in it? This is an extremely important question that more martial artists should ask themselves, but I am afraid this particular area, which is of extreme importance, is often ignored in martial arts training, including that of karate.

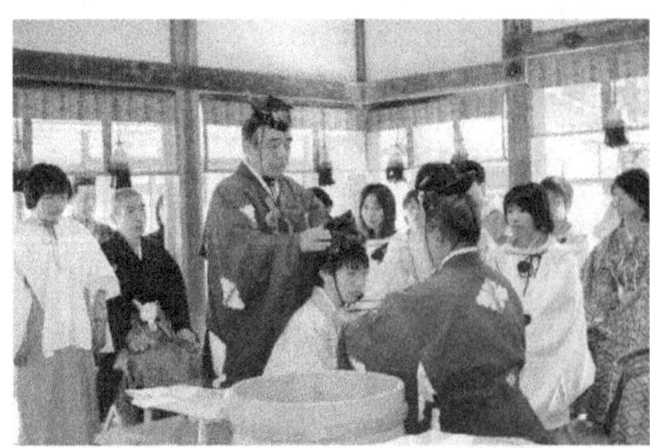

Samurai children started their training early. At the age of seven, boys would receive a knife from their father. At their *genpuku* (元服), the male coming-of-age ceremony typically held between the ages of twelve and sixteen, male children would receive a set of *ka-*

tana (刀, 'swords'), which consisted of both a long and a short sword, and would learn the detailed method and etiquette of *seppuku*. They were also forced to watch the *seppuku* of other samurai and the beheading of criminals in order to get used to the sight of blood and killing. The homes of high-ranking samurai would have a small room specifically saved for the *seppuku* ritual. Children were taught about this room and were told never to step inside other than for the specific purpose of committing *seppuku*.

Of course, samurai children as young as three to five years old would start training in the martial arts, including kenjutsu, sojutsu, kyujutsu (弓術, 'archery'), etc. During the *Sengoku* (戦国, 'Warring States') period of the fifteenth and sixteenth centuries, samurai children were required to join a fighting group and experience battle after their *genpuku*.

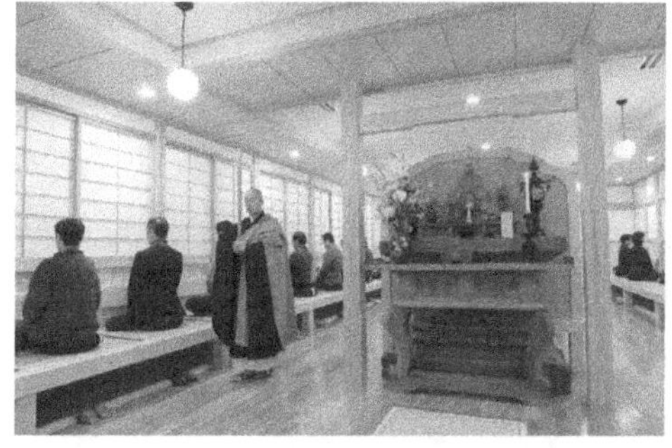

One practice the samurai relied on was *zazen* (座禅, 'seated Zen meditation'). I will not go deeply into this subject in this chapter, though it is an interesting one. Most readers know that this is a special meditation practice typically performed by a certain sect of Buddhist monks who open their temples for commoners to practice, as well. Regardless, it is probably very difficult for most Western readers to find such a temple in the U.S. or Europe. So, though this is a very useful method, I will not cover it here. Maybe I will focus on this subject sometime in the future as it is a fascinating practice.

The samurai would also polish their swords periodically. They would take care of their long swords, which they used to kill others, as well as their short swords, which they used to kill themselves. So, the samurai faced death and learned about it very often, mostly for the purpose of preparing their minds.

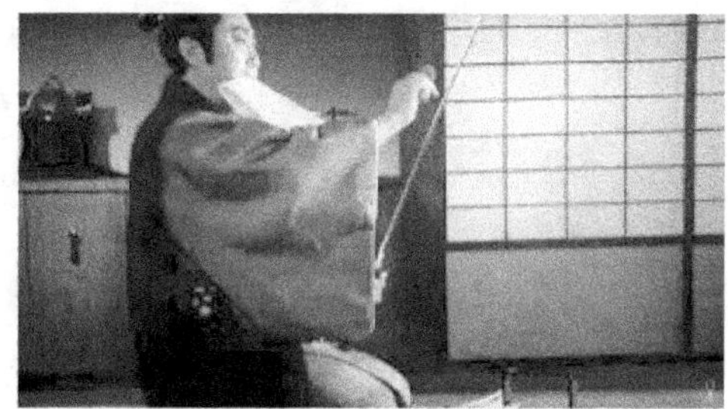

OK, but we are living in the twenty-first century, so we cannot have such experiences. Does this mean there is no method for us to develop *heijoshin* other than just wishing for it? No, do not be discouraged. In fact, there is a method, and it is easy enough that anyone can practice it. I am happy to share it with you here, but before I go into explaining the training method, I need to give you a brief historical background to set the stage.

After the Battle of Sekigahara (関ヶ原の合戦) in 1600, the Warring States period ended, and the Edo (江戸) period began. This was a peaceful period of some two hundred fifty years (covering the entire seventeenth and eighteenth centuries as well as the first half of the nineteenth century), during which there were no major battles. During the Warring States period of the fifteenth and sixteenth centuries, killing and battles had been very common. Therefore, it was natural that the samurai were accustomed to seeing death all around them. During the two and a half centuries of peace that followed, on the other hand, it became less and less common for the samurai to see people getting killed or to get involved in fights in which they might kill someone. Though there were some incidents of *seppuku* every once in a while, surprisingly, many samurai would never have to draw their sword even once (for the purpose of fighting) throughout their lifetime.

So, the period they lived in became similar to our modern-day environment. Ironically, it may be more dangerous in the twenty-first-century U.S.A. than it was in eighteenth-century Japan. But, despite their "peaceful" society, the samurai still had to carry their swords all day. If they were ordered to kill themselves or someone else, they had to follow the order without protest or objection. That was the samurai code, and almost everyone followed it to the letter without questioning it.

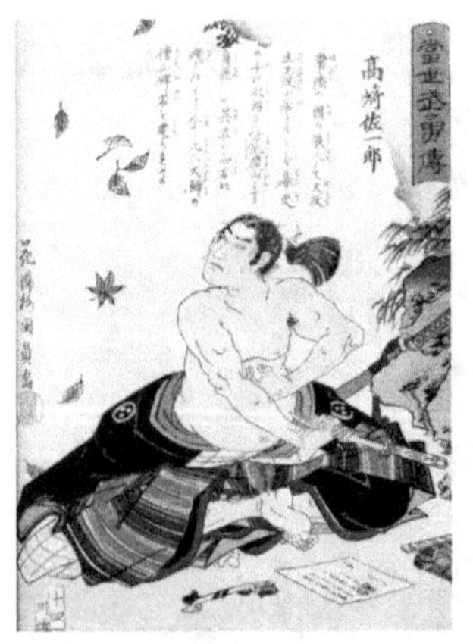

Though the situation of the samurai looks similar to that of our modern-day soldiers, it differs greatly in that the samurai had to follow orders without asking why, and a samurai's refusal to follow an order, or even his failure to carry it out, would mean his death. Even for the samurai, it was naturally a scary thing to face death, especially in the case of *seppuku*. Theoretically, any of the samurai could be ordered to commit *seppuku* if they failed in their daily duties. So, they had to do something to overcome this fear.

Of course, most of them practiced kenjutsu and other *bujutsu* to build up *budo* and the samurai spirit. They practiced Zen meditation and all the other special ceremonies and samurai customs, but most of these do not apply to modern-day people, including Japanese people. So, what can we do? This is the main point that I want to share with the reader and present as a model that we can practice.

So, what else did they do? Believe it or not, it was a simple thing that they did. Many of them recited daily that it could be their last day and promised to die with honor if death were necessary. They did this first thing in the morning when they prayed in front of the household shrine (*kamidana* [神棚]) or altar (*butsudan* [仏壇]) before eating breakfast. This practice is based on the same concept as reciting the *Dojo Kun* (道場訓) after every training session. I also understand that many Christian people recite the Lord's Prayer daily. I am sure other religions have similar practices of reciting something important.

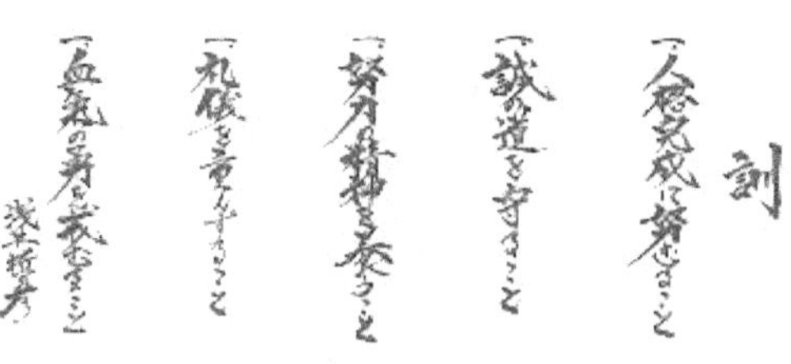

I do not know if reciting, "Today may be my last day," will help you to develop *heijoshin*, but this is what I picked up many years ago. We'll see if this helps me at my critical moment, which may or may not be dramatic, but one thing I am one hundred percent sure of is that my last day will come one day, even if I do not know when. No matter what situation I may be in at that moment, I want to be ready. I say this because I believe that, at that very moment, the way I finish my last day will determine whether or not I died as a samurai.

Now, some people may object to my statement, saying, "Your title said, 'The most important training point,' but what you do does not happen in the dojo." This is true. I recite this when I am in my bed (as I do not have a *kamidana* in my house), when I wake up, or when I look at myself in the mirror right before washing my face in the morning. This may be one of the biggest differences between sport karate and *budo* karate.

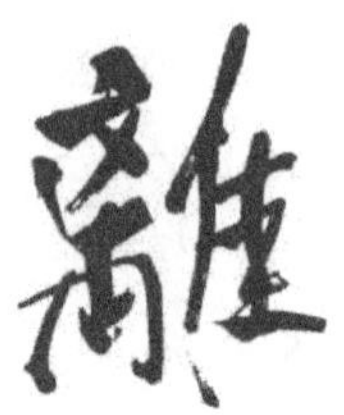

Chapter Sixteen
第十六章

What Is the Kenpo Hakku?
拳法八句とは？

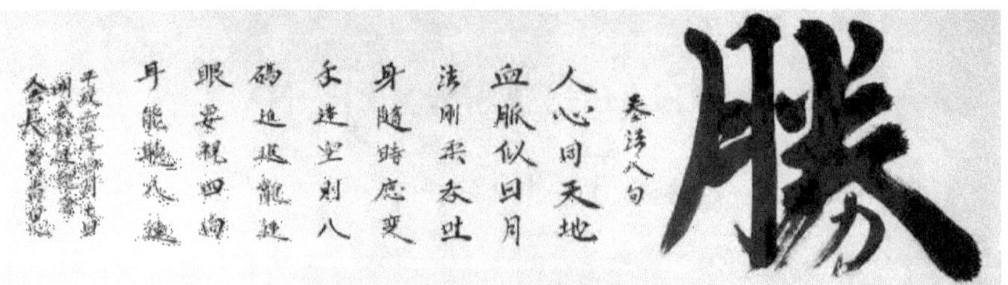

Shotokan practitioners know of Funakoshi's *Niju Kun*, and I have written previously on this set of teaching guidelines. The other styles also have similar precepts. In this chapter, I would like to investigate the *Kenpo Hakku* (拳法八句, '*Eight Verses of Kenpo*'), which has been handed down in Goju Ryu.

The *Kenpo Hakku* was a favorite poem of Chojun Miyagi (宮城長順, 1888–1953), the founder of Goju Ryu. In fact, Miyagi named his style *Goju Ryu* by taking a part of one of the verses of this poem. We know what *kenpo* means, but what is *hakku*? It means 'eight verses' and refers to the eight precepts or teachings of kenpo, that is, karate.

Even though the teachings of the *hakku* have been handed down only in Goju Ryu, I believe they are beneficial to all karate practitioners, and that is why I have decided to share them with the practitioners of Shotokan. But, before we go into the interpretation of the *hakku*, let me introduce Goju Ryu and its founder, Chojun Miyagi, for they may not be too familiar to many Shotokan practitioners.

Goju Ryu is one of the four major traditional karate styles (Shotokan, Goju Ryu, Shito Ryu, and Wado Ryu) in both Japan and Okinawa. One of Chojun Miyagi's top students, Jin'an Shinzato (新里仁安, 1901–1945), was involved in the naming of the style in 1929, but Miyagi later approved it in the thirties, and *Goju Ryu* became the official name of his style.

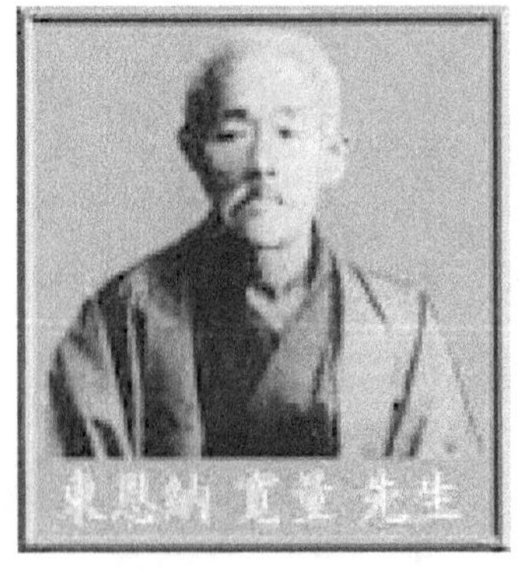

Goju Ryu is the representative style of Naha Te. Miyagi combined the teachings of his master Kanryo Higaonna (東恩納寛量, 1853–1915 [photo left]) with some of his own modifications. Kanryo

Higaonna was also known as *Higaonna West* as there was another master by the name of *Kan'yu Higaonna* (東恩納寛裕 1849–1922), who was known as *Higaonna East*. These two are often confused due to their having the same last name. We must remember that Miyagi learned from Kanryo Higaonna, that is, Higaonna West.

According to *Wikipedia*, Goju Ryu features a combination of hard and soft techniques (hence the name *goju*, which literally means 'hard and soft'). Both principles, hard and soft, come from the famous martial arts book *Bubishi* (武備志, '*Treatise on Armaments and Military Provisions*' [1621]), which was used by the Okinawan masters during the nineteenth and twentieth centuries.

The character 剛 (*go*), which means 'hard', refers to closed-handed techniques and linear movements. The character 柔 (*ju*), which means 'soft', on the other hand, refers to open-handed techniques and circular movements. Thus, Goju Ryu incorporates both linear and circular movements into its curriculum. It combines hard striking attacks, such as kicks and closed-handed punches, with softer circular techniques for attacking, blocking, and controlling the opponent with open hands, such as locks, grappling, takedowns, and throws.

Major emphasis is placed on a certain breathing method called *ibuki* (息吹き) in all of the *kata*. This is particularly true for Sanchin, which is one of two core *kata*, the other being Tensho (転掌), which means 'circling palms' and is used to teach the soft aspects of the system. The practice methods of Goju Ryu utilize various weights and tools called *hojo kigu* (補助器具, 'supplementary tools') for body strengthening and conditioning. The basic approach is short-distance fighting (*maai*, stickiness, power generation, etc.) and partner drills.

Goju Ryu's twelve *kata* are Gekisai Dai Ichi (撃砕第一), Gekisai Dai Ni (撃砕第二), Saifa (サイファ), Seienchin (セイエンチン), Seisan, Seipai (セイパイ), Shisochin (シソーチン), Sanseiru (サンセイルー), Kururunfa (クルルンファー), Sanchin, Tensho, and Suparinpei (スーパーリンペイ).

It should be noted that Chojun Miyagi began his study in Shuri Te at the age of eleven in the dojo of Ryuko Aragaki (新垣隆功, 1875–1961). But, in 1902, at the age of fourteen, he became a student of the Naha Te master Kanryo Higaonna and was devoted to the teachings of Higaonna throughout the rest of his life.

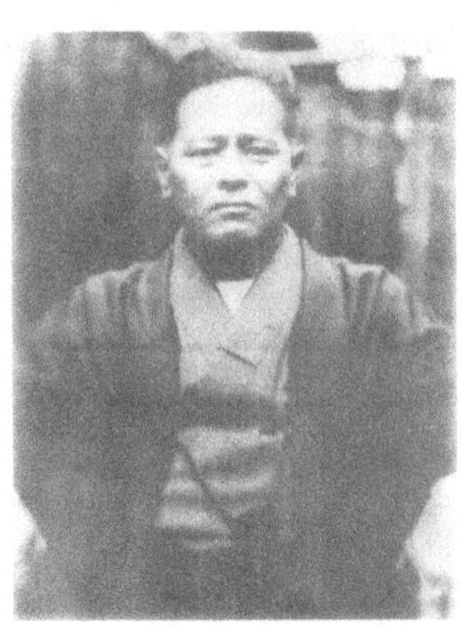

There is an interesting story about Miyagi in which he visited Funakoshi's teacher, Anko Itosu, one day and asked if he could learn some karate techniques from him. Itosu, the number-one Shuri Te master at that time, told him that there was nothing more he could teach him because Miyagi was the senior student of Higaonna and had already mastered Naha Te. I am not sure if Itosu really meant this or if it was just a diplomatic comment meant to show respect to Higaonna. Regardless, what is important to learn from this story is that Miyagi was open minded enough to seek instruction from a Shuri Te master.

One thing I must mention here is an important note on the *Bubishi*, the presumed source of the *Kenpo Hakku*. It is said that these eight verses (*hakku*) are found in the Chinese book *Bubishi*. But, one fact that we must know is that there are two different books that are referred to as *Bubishi*: a Chinese work called *Bubishi* (武備志 [read as *Wǔbèi Zhì* in Chinese]) and an Okinawan work called *Okinawa Den Bubishi* (沖縄伝武備志). This fact is not too well known, even among Goju Ryu practitioners, but it can cause some confusion. For instance, *Wikipedia* only lists the original Chinese *Bubishi* with no mention of the Okinawan work.

The original Chinese *Bubishi*, written in the seventeenth century during the Ming dynasty (明朝), is the most comprehensive military book in Chinese history.

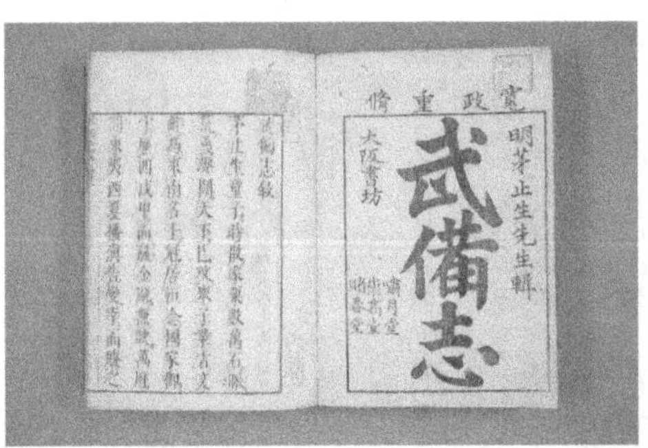

It was edited by a naval officer named Yuanyi Mao (茅元儀 [read as *Máo Yuányí* in Chinese], 1594–1640) and contains 240 volumes, 10405 pages, and more than 2,000,000 Chinese characters.

The work is divided into five sections. The first section contains military theories; the second describes more than six hundred specific examples of battle; the third introduces different ways of training troops; the fourth covers topics related to wartime logistics; and the fifth deals with weather and geographical features as well as traditional Chinese methods of divination, formation, and marine navigation. The third section is the most interesting to us because it includes martial arts training with different weapons.

The other *Bubishi*, whose official title is *Okinawa Den Bubishi*, is the one that was handed down by Miyagi. He had supposedly purchased a copy of the Chinese *Bubishi* in 1914, when he visited southern China's Fujian Province (福建省), which is the closest Chinese province to Okinawa. However, karate historians now believe that this work is a totally different book because its content is limited to White Crane kung fu, which is known as *hakutsuru ken* (白鶴拳 [read as báihèchuán in Chinese]).

The Okinawan book consists of approximately ten thousand characters and only seventy-two illustrations, while the original Chinese book has over two million characters and about seven hundred illustrations. *Hakutsuru ken* was developed and practiced mainly in the Fujian Province; therefore, it is very possible that the author of the Okinawan *Bubishi* may have "borrowed" the well-known name from the famous military book.

As this chapter is not about the *Bubishi*, I will not go any further into this subject. If you are interested in it, I recommend the book *Bubishi: The Classic Manual of Combat* (Tuttle, 2016 [photo right]) written by well-known martial arts historian Patrick McCarthy, which can be purchased from *Amazon* at this URL: www.amazon.com/Bubishi-Classic-Manual-Patrick-McCarthy/dp/4805313846/. In the future, I may venture into writing on the differences between the original Chinese book and the Okinawan book, but here we will focus our attention on the *Kenpo Hakku*.

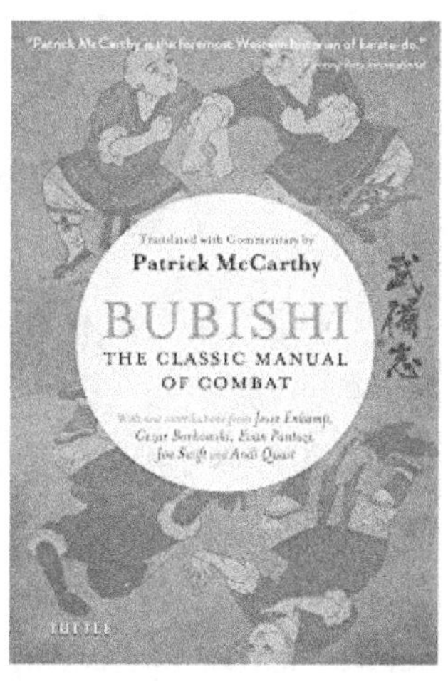

The *Kenpo Hakku*

The *Kenpo Hakku* is said to be a vital document for Goju Ryu as it holds the hidden meanings and secrets of the martial arts. As previously mentioned, Chojun Miyagi, one of world's most influential men in the history of karate, used one of the lines from this document to name his style, Goju Ryu.

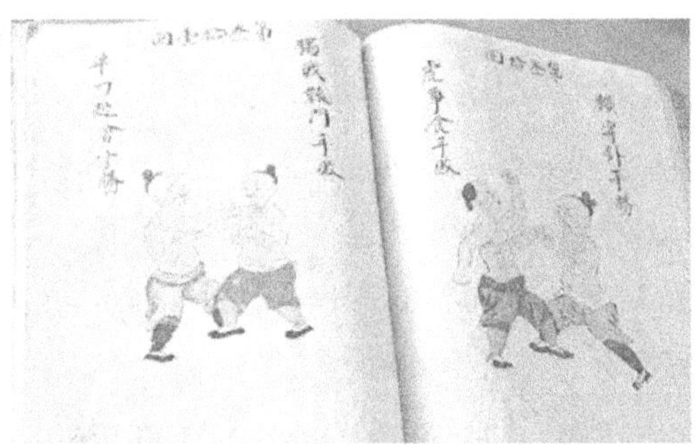

The *Kenpo Hakku* was written according to the sentence structure of Chinese poetry. Its interpretation can vary from one individual or practitioner to another. I reviewed several interpretations that are available online but was not totally happy with any of them. Thus, in this chapter, I have included my own interpretation of each verse based on the original Chinese text.

I am not a Goju Ryu practitioner and am new to these verses, so I am not sure if my interpretation is in line with what is typically taught at a Goju Ryu dojo. I welcome any input or corrections from senior Goju Ryu practitioners.

人心同天地
Jinshin wa tenchi ni onaji
The human spirit is the same as the sky and the earth.

Two interpretations I found were 'man is earthly as his spirit is heavenly' and 'the mind is one with heaven and earth', but these do not make sense. We need to think more deeply. My interpretation is that our mind is usually filled with worries and worldly things that hinder the martial arts mind.

My interpretation: we must be able to clear our mind so that we can unite with nature (heaven and earth) if we wish to excel and master kenpo (karate).

血脈以日月
Ketsumyaku wa nichigetsu ni nitari
The cycle of blood is similar to the cycle of day and night.

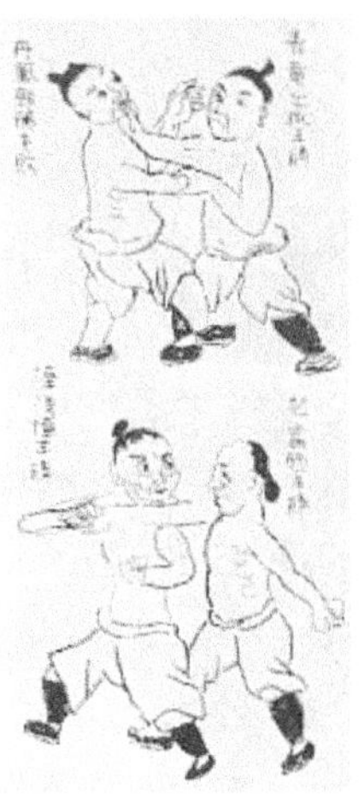

Other interpretations are 'the circulatory rhythm of the body is similar to the cycle of the sun and the moon' or 'the blood, arteries, and veins are similar to the sun and moon'. These do not make sense to me. When Asians talk about blood, we mean the bloodline of a family.

So, how is this related to the cycle of the sun and moon? I believe it signifies the unceasing universal design. The sun rises every morning, the moon comes up when the sun sets, and this happens every day and every night. So, this verse is saying that we must continue to pass on our karate heritage from one generation to another. Even though the relationship between teacher and student is not the same as the relationship between family members, I believe it is very common for us to consider the dojo to be our family.

My interpretation: we must continue our karate tradition and hand it down from generation to generation.

法剛柔呑吐
Ho wa goju o donto su
The law of strength and softness is inhaling and exhaling.

This verse must be the most important one for Goju Ryu practitioners to understand. It is said that Miyagi used this verse to name the style. The literal meaning of this verse is why, I suspect, Goju Ryu practitioners consider the style's unique breathing method, *ibuki*, to be an important exercise within its syllabus.

One interpretation I found was 'to inhale must be strong and to exhale gentle'. With all due respect, I disagree with this interpretation. It may be correct for beginners, but as you practice further and better understand the secret of breathing, you

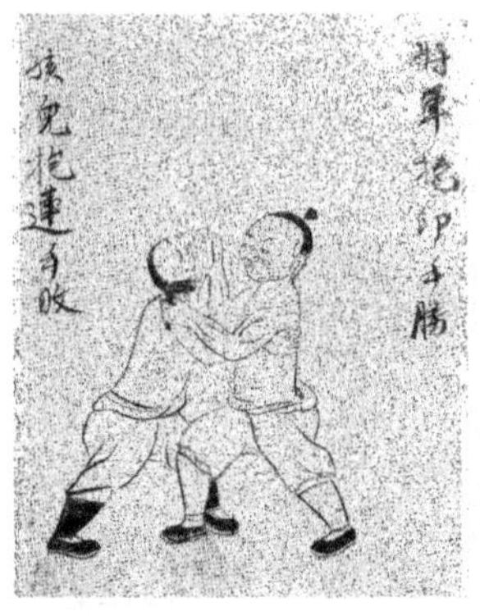

find that breathing methods are much more complex than this. In other words, you can generate power as you exhale as well as when you inhale. You also learn that your breathing can be a combination of half inhalation and half exhalation. Then, you learn that the proportion of inhalation to exhalation is not limited to fifty-fifty but rather can vary quite a bit. This law applies not only to breathing but also to the application of power as you execute techniques.

My interpretation: just as we can control our breathing methods, we must be able to control our body very naturally so that we can apply both strong and soft techniques at will.

> 身随時應変
> *Mi wa toki ni shitagai hen ni ozu*
> Actions vary according to time and conform to changing situations.

This one is not too complex, though the meaning is deep.

My interpretation: our mind must be able to work in harmony with our body so that our body can move regardless of time, situation, or circumstance.

> 手逢空則入
> *Te wa ku ni ai sunawachi hairu*
> When the hands meet emptiness, then they enter.

This verse is a challenging one. The literal translation is easy, but catching the true meaning is hard. This translation does not make any sense, of course. *Te* (手) means more than just 'hands' and should be translated as 'techniques'. *Ku* (空) means 'emptiness' and refers to the state of mind. *Hairu* (入) means 'enter' and is talking about the execution of the techniques.

My interpretation: our techniques must come out naturally without any conscious thought, once again teaching the importance of the harmonious unification of body and mind.

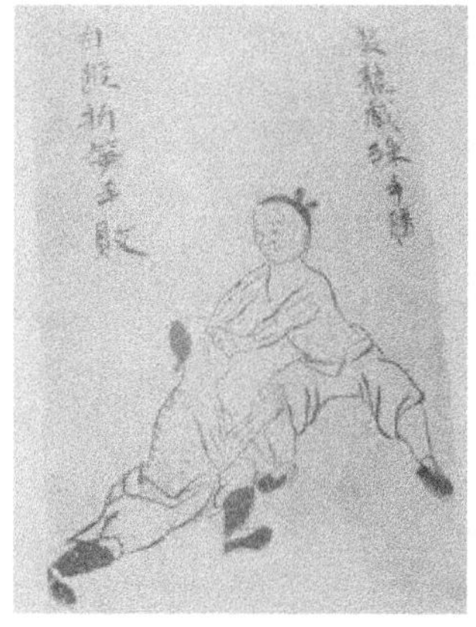

碼進退離逢
Shintai wa hakarite riho su
Advance and retreat; part and meet.

The literal meaning does not make much sense. I figure this verse is talking about footwork.

My interpretation: our body and mind must unify with heaven and earth so that our feet can move swiftly and precisely.

眼要視四向
Me wa shiho o miru o yo su
The eyes must look in all four directions.

This one seems to be simple based on the literal meaning. However, I suspect the ancient masters must have thought something deeper than the obvious.

My interpretation: we must be able to see with more than the eyes, developing eyes in our heart so that we can sense all things around us that are not visible.

耳能聴八達
Mimi wa yoku happo o kiku
The ears must listen in all eight directions.

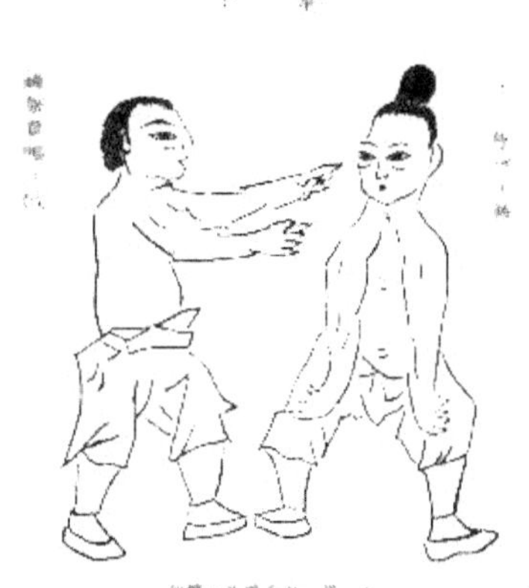

This one is similar to the previous one.

My interpretation: we must listen not only with our ears but also with our heart so that we do not miss anything that cannot be heard.

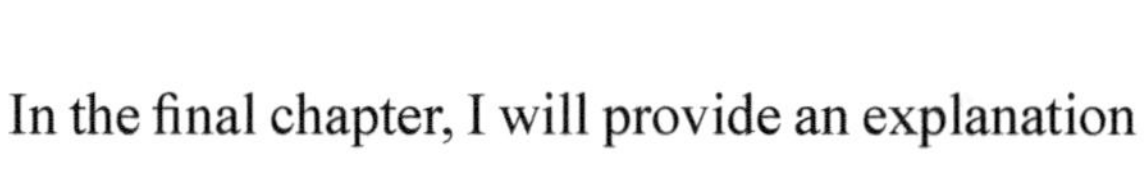

In the final chapter, I will provide an explanation

of Itosu's *Ten Precepts of Karate* to conclude this book.

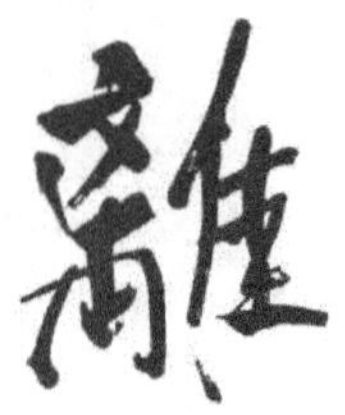

Chapter Seventeen
第十七章

Itosu's Ten Precepts of Karate
糸洲安恒先生遺稿(唐手心得十ヶ條)

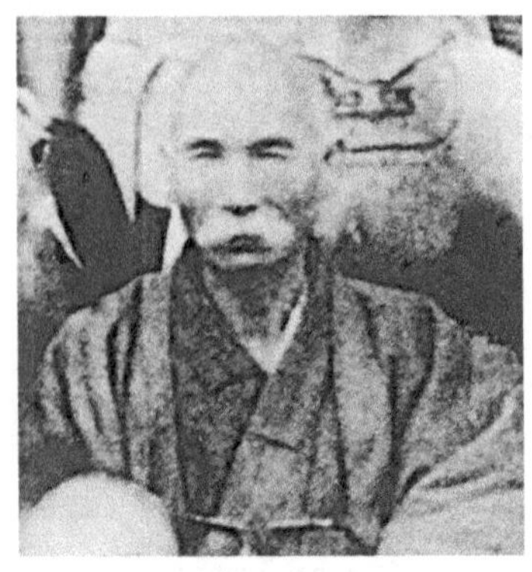

I expect that all advanced Shotokan, Shito Ryu, and Shorin Ryu practitioners must have heard of Anko Itosu (糸洲安恒, 1831–1915 [photo left]). Yes, he was the sensei of Gichin Funakoshi, the founder of Shotokan. However, I am afraid that not enough credit has been given to Master Itosu for what he did to modernize karate and to bring it to the public eye. In this chapter, I would like to introduce him so that all of us can remember his great contributions that helped build the modern-day karate that we have now. I will also share the valuable teachings that he left in his *Tode Kokoroe Jukkajo* (唐手心得十ヶ條, '*Ten Precepts of Karate*' [1908]).

Instead of creating a biography of my own for Master Itosu, I will quote from *Wikipedia*:

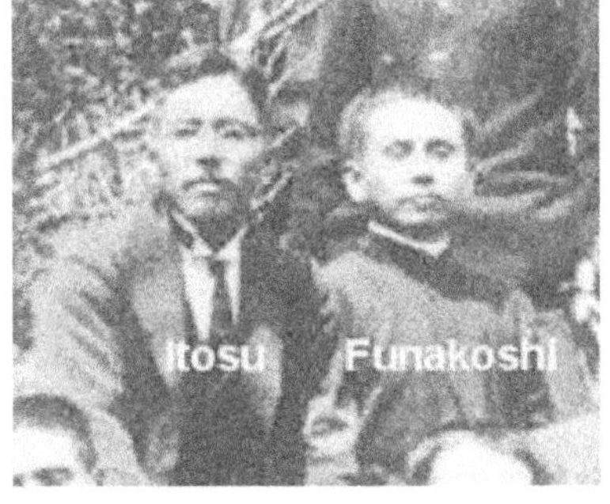

> Anko Itosu is considered by many to be the father of modern karate, although this title is also often given to Gichin Funakoshi because the latter spread karate throughout Japan.
>
> Itosu was born in 1831 and died in 1915. A low-rank Ryukyuan Pechin, Itosu was small in stature, shy, and introverted as a child. He was raised in a strict home of the *keimochi* (a family of position) and was educated in the Chinese Classics and calligraphy. Itosu began his *tode* (karate) study under Nagahama Chikudun Pechin. His study of the art led him to Sokon Matsumura. Part of Itosu's training was *makiwara* practice. He once tied a leather sandal to a stone wall in an effort to build a better *makiwara*. After several strikes, the stone fell from the wall. After relocating the sandal several times, Itosu had destroyed the wall.
>
> Itosu served as a secretary to the last king of the Ryukyu Kingdom until Japan abolished the Okinawa-based native monarchy in 1879. In 1901, he was instrumental in getting karate introduced into Okinawa's schools. In 1905, Itosu was a part-time teacher of *tode* at Okinawa's First Junior Prefectural High School. It was here that he developed the systematic methods of teaching karate techniques that are still in

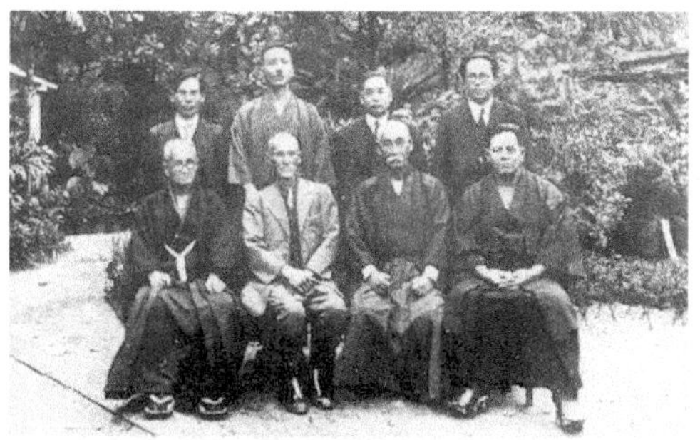

practice today. He created and introduced the Pin'an forms (*Heian* in Japanese) as learning steps for students because he felt the older forms (*kata* in Japanese) were too difficult for schoolchildren to learn. The five Pin'an forms were (allegedly) created by drawing from two older forms: Kusanku and Chiang Nan. Itosu is also credited with taking the large Naihanchi form (*Tekki* in Japanese) and breaking it into the three well-known modern forms Naihanchi Shodan, Naihanchi Nidan, and Naihanchi Sandan. In 1908, Itosu wrote the influential "Ten Precepts of Karate" (*Tode Jukun*), reaching beyond Okinawa to Japan. Itosu's style of karate, Shorin Ryu, came to be known as *Itosu Ryu* in recognition of his skill, mastery, and role as teacher to many.

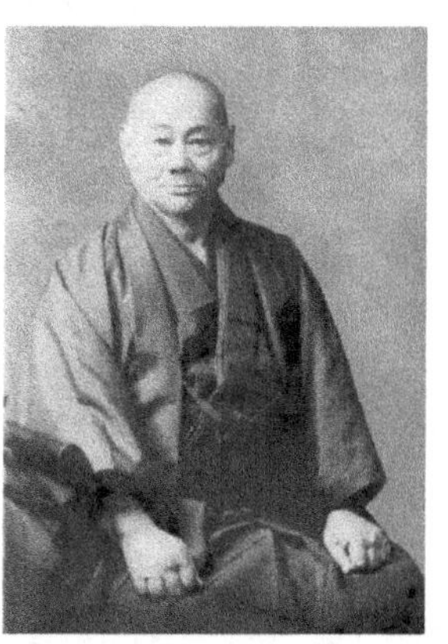

While Itosu did not invent karate himself, he modified the *kata* (forms) he learned from his master, Matsumura, and taught many karate masters. Itosu's students included Choyu Motobu (1857–1927), Choki Motobu (1870–1944 [photo right]), Kentsu Yabu (1866–1937), Chomo Hanashiro (1869–1945), Gichin Funakoshi (1868–1957), Moden Yabiku (1880–1941), Kanken Toyama (1888–1966), Chotoku Kyan (1870–1945), Shinpan Shiroma (Gusukuma) (1890–1954), Anbun Tokuda (1886–1945), Kenwa Mabuni (1887–1952 [photo below left]), and Choshin Chibana (1885–1969 [photo below right]).

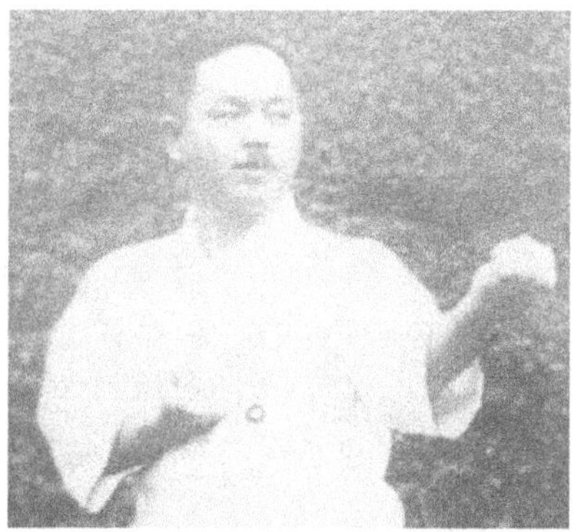

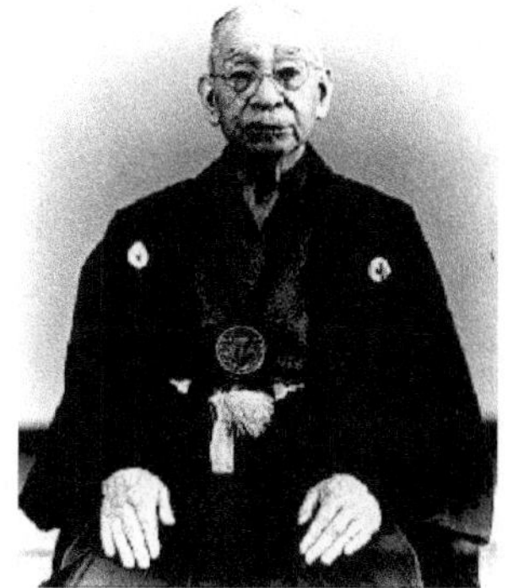

If you wish to learn more about Anko Itosu, here is an informative URL: www.historyoffighting.com/anko-itosu.php.

Below is a letter written by Itosu Sensei in October 1908. This letter preceded the introduction of karate into Okinawan schools and eventually into the Japanese mainland. The English text that I have attached below each section is my own poor translation of the original Japanese written by Master Itosu. Please note that this is present-day Japanese, not the old Japanese used in the early twentieth century. I take full responsibility for any possible (but unintended) mistranslations.

前文

空手は、古代中国思想（孔子の教え）である儒教や、古代インド発祥（釈迦開祖）の仏教から出たものではありません。その昔、中国より昭林流と昭霊流という二つの流派が、琉球（沖縄）に伝えられたものだと聞いております。この二つの流派はそれぞれ特長がありますので、このままの状態を大切に守りながら伝えていかなければなりません。そのためには、自分だけの思惑で、型に手を加えないという心掛けが肝心です。それで空手の修練の心得とその効用を、項目ごとに行を改めて書き記してみます。

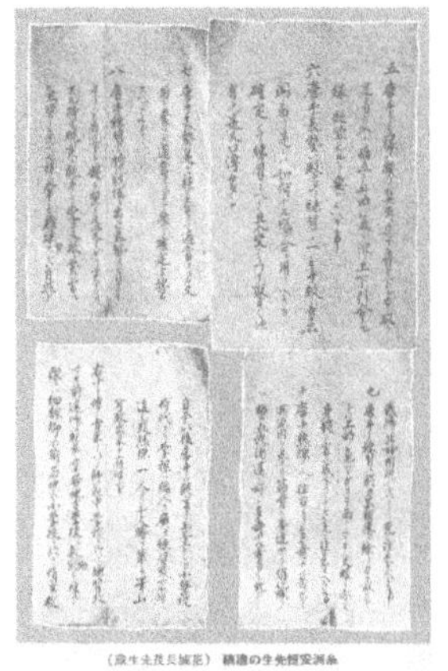

Preamble

I do not believe karate came from Confucianism (the teachings of Confucius), which is from ancient Chinese philosophy, or Buddhism (founded by Buddha), which was brought from India. What I understand is that, in the past, two schools, Shorin Ryu and Shorei Ryu, were brought to Ryukyu (Okinawa) from China. These two schools have their own unique and strong points; thus, we must take great care to preserve them in their current state when transmitting them. Therefore, we all must remember that the moves in the *kata* must not be changed or modified according to our own thoughts or tastes. I wish to write down the important points and benefits of karate training in ten different precepts.

一　空手は、個人としての体育の目的を果たすだけが、すべてではありません。将来主君（国）と親に一大事が起きた場合は、自分の命をも惜しむことなく、正義と勇気とを持って、進んで国家社会のため、力を尽くさなくてはならぬ、という名分を持っております。ですから、決して一人の敵と戦う意図はさらさらありません。かような次第ですから、万一暴漢や盗人から仕掛けられても、平素の修練の成果により、なるべくこれをうまく捌いて退散させるよう仕向けることです。決して突いたり蹴ったりして人を傷つけることがあってはなりません。このことが、本当の空手精神であることを、強く肝に銘じて欲しいものです。

1. The main purpose of karate is not merely to practice for your own physical benefit. It must be used with courage and justice to protect your family or master (country) when you encounter a serious situation, even if this means losing your life. It must not be practiced to fight against only one assailant. Therefore, in the case that you are attacked by a villain or a robber, see if it is possible to avoid a fight and manage the situation peacefully. Never think of harming another person with your punches or kicks. You must never forget that this attitude shows the true karate spirit.

二　空手は、専ら鍛えに鍛えて筋骨を強くし、相手からの打撃をも跳ね返すほどの強さにすることが理想です。このように理想的に鍛え上げれば、自然と何事をも恐れず、自分の信念もまげずに振る舞う、逞しい行動力と強い精神力が備わるものです。それにつきましては、小学校時代から空手の練習をさせれば、いつか軍人になった時、きっと他の剣道とか銃剣道のような術伎上達の助けになる効用があります。以上述べましたようなことが、将来、軍人社会での精神面と術技面への何かしらの助けになると考えます。最も、英国のウエリントン候が、ベルギーのワーテルローでナポレオン一世に大勝した時にいいました。「今日の戦勝は、我が国の各学校のグラウンド及びその他の施設で広く体育の教育をやった成果である」と。実に格言というべきでしょうか。

2. The ultimate goal of karate training is to make your body as hard as a rock so that it will deflect the assailant's punches and kicks. If your karate skills are excellent, you will have a strong spirit and be able to have confidence. This means you will fear no one and will be able to conduct yourself without compromising your

principles. If children start karate training while in elementary school, this will help them master other martial arts, such as kendo and jukendo, when they go into military service. I believe that the things mentioned above would be of some help to the spiritual and technical aspects of the military community in the future. Remember the words attributed to the Duke of Wellington of Great Britain after he defeated Napoleon at the Battle of Waterloo in Belgium: "The Battle of Waterloo was won on the playing fields of Eton." I consider this saying to be very accurate and relevant.

三 空手は、急速に熟練しようとしても、なかなか難しいものです。「牛の歩みは、馬と比較して、より遅いけれども、歩き続けていれば、ついに千里以上の里程を走破することが出来る」との格言があります。そのような心掛けで、毎日一、二時間ほど精神を集中して続けますと、三、四年の間には通常の人と骨格が違うばかりか、空手のかなり奥深いところまで到達出来る者も数多く出るのではないかと思います。

3. You cannot become an expert in karate quickly. There is a saying: "The cow walks more slowly than the horse, but if it keeps walking, in the end, it can cover over a thousand miles." With this in mind, and if you train diligently for at least an hour or two every day, then in three to four years, you will have a much healthier body than the average person. In the end, you may be able to achieve a good level of karate but only after such training.

四 空手は、拳足を鍛えることが主体ですから、常に巻藁などで、十分練習を重ねるように努めねばなりません。その要領は、両肩を下げ、胸を大きく張り、拳に力を込め、さらに踏まえた足にもしっかり力を取り、吸った息を臍下丹田（下腹のことで古代中国思想で気が集る所）のところに沈めるような気持ちで練習するとよいでしょう。また、突いたり、蹴ったりする回数は、ともに片方で百回から二百回というところが効果的と考えます。

4. Firming up the hands and feet is important in karate training, so you must train thoroughly on the *makiwara*. I advise you to keep your shoulders down, open up your rib cage, firmly grip your fists, stand solidly on the floor, and sink your energy into your *seika tanden* (the lower belly, where ki collects according to ancient Chinese ideology). To be effective, I suggest you punch and kick one to two

hundred times on each side.

五　空手の立ち方は、腰を真っ直ぐに立て、重心の平衡が崩れないよう両肩を下げ、力が体重全体に平均に及ぶような心持ちで、しかも両足も力強く立ち、吸った空気を臍下丹田に集中させ、上下の腹筋も丹田に引き合わされるようにして凝り固めることが大事な要点です。

5. Regarding karate stances, it is critical to keep your back straight, keep your shoulders down so that you don't lose your balance, spread your strength throughout your body, firmly stand on both feet, concentrate the air you've inhaled in the *seika tanden*, and stiffen up to pull your upper and lower abdominal muscles into the *tanden*.

六　空手表芸である形は、数多く練習した方がよいのです。が、漠然と練習してもそれほどの効果はありません。練習の効率をよくし、本物の技を身につけるには、形のなかにある一つ一つの技（手数）の意味を正しく聞き届けるだけでなく、その技はどんな場合に用いるか、ということを確かめて練習しなくてはなりません。さらに、形の中に出てこない特別な突き方（入れ）、受け方（受け）、腕や襟を取られた時の外し方（はずし）、関節の決（極）め方（取り手）などの高度な技があるけれども、それは秘伝になっておりますので、多くは師が弟子に対して口で伝えるようになっております。

6. *Kata*, the visible form, should be practiced many times. However, there will be little benefit if you practice without knowing the meaning of the techniques. In order to make your training meaningful, you must learn the meaning of each technique. In addition, there are other special techniques that are not found in the *kata*, such as different punches and blocks as well as grappling and joint techniques. These techniques are considered to be secret techniques and must be taught in a face-to-face training session with your sensei.

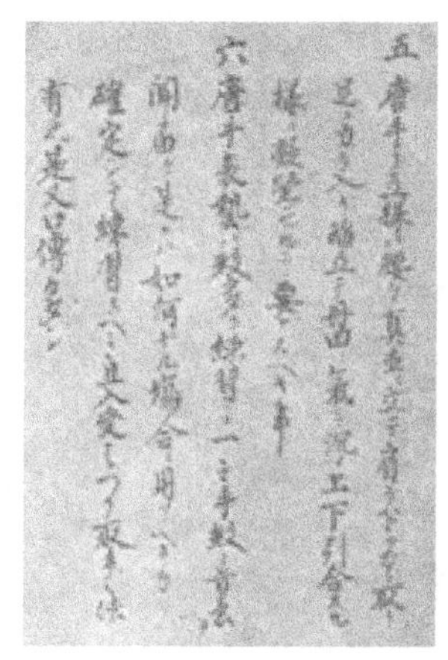

七　空手表芸である形は、その技の一つ一つについて、この技の目的は「

体」即ち体育（基本鍛錬）のために有効なものか、「用」即ち実用（応用技）として練習するのに適切であるか、あらかじめ確実に理解し、目的と方法を確定して練習しなくてはなりません。

7. Before training in *kata*, you must clearly understand whether its techniques are for the body, that is, for physical training (strength training) purposes, or for application, that is, practical use (*oyo* technique) purposes and determine a training method and objective.

八　空手の練習をする時は、ちょうど戦場に出かけるような意気込みがなくてはなりません。目はかっと見開き、肩を下げて、体に弾力性がつくように固め、また、受けたり、突いたりする技の練習でも、現実に敵の突きを受け、蹴りを払い、体当たりしている実戦さながらの強い意気込みでやらなくてはならないのです。このような練習をすれば、自然と他ではまねのできないすぐれた成果が、形となって現れるものです。以上のことをしっかりと心掛けて欲しいものです。

8. When you train in karate, you must have the same spirit as if you were marching onto a battlefield. Your eyes should be open and alert, your shoulders kept low, your body solid but elastic, and even though you are practicing punching and blocking, you must have the mind-set of actually fighting instead of merely punching and blocking the air. If you train like this, an excellent result that cannot be learned in other sports will become apparent in your *kata*. I really want you to remember and apply what I've explained above.

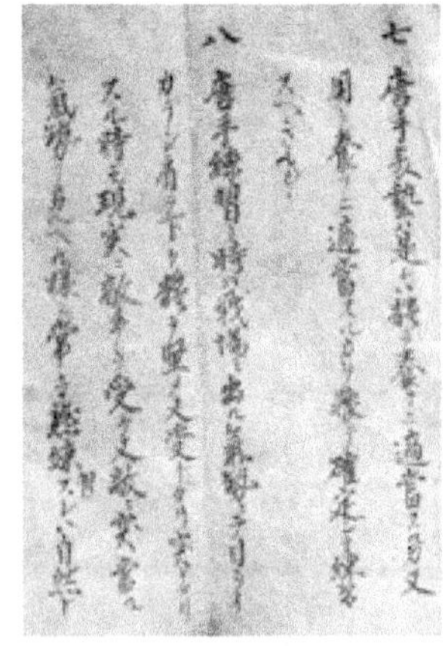

九　空手の練習は、自分の体力不相応に、力を入れて気張り過ぎると、上気して顔も火照り、目も充血して体の害になるものです。以上のことは、どんな視点からみても、健康のため有害ですので、しっかりと肝に銘じたいものです。

9. If you overexert yourself in karate training, the blood will rush to your head, your face will become flush, your eyes will become bloodshot, and your body will be

harmed. No matter how you look at it, such training methods are dangerous to your health; thus, these must be avoided.

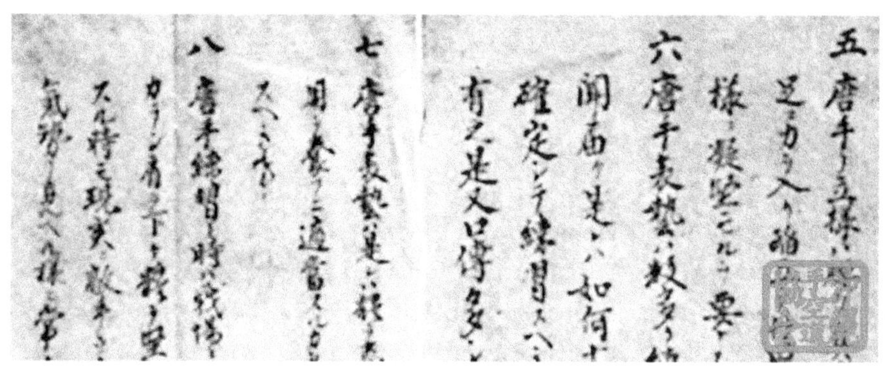

十　空手に熟達した人は、昔から長寿の者が多いのです。その原因をよく調べてみますと、空手の練習が筋骨の発達を促し、消化器を丈夫にして、血液の循環をよくするので長寿者が多いということです。それで、空手は自分以後は、体育の土台として小学校時代から、学課に編入して広く多くの者に練習させていただきたいと思います。そうすれば、おいおい熟達する者が出て、きっと一人で一度に十人の相手にも勝てるような猛者も沢山出てくることと思います。

10. Many of the karate masters have enjoyed long lives. If you research the cause, you will find that karate training builds a strong body and exercises the digestive and circulatory systems, thus resulting in longer lives. Therefore, I strongly recommend that karate training be incorporated into the physical education classes of our elementary schools. Once it becomes a part of our school program, we could train many students. Such a program would make it possible to produce some experts in the future who would be capable of defeating ten assailants at once.

後文

右の十ケ条の意図で、師範学校や中学校で空手の練習を行い、将来師範学校を卒業して各地の小学校で教鞭をとることになったら、その赴任に先だって、十ケ条に述べました空手教育の意図とその効用を、細かく指示し、各地方の小学校でも不正確な点が少しもないように指導させれば、十年以内には、全国的に普及するはずです。このことはわれわれ沖縄県民だけのためでなく、軍人社会においてもきっと何らかの助けになると考え、お目にかけるために筆記致しました 。

明治四十一年戊申十月
糸洲安恒

Closing Statement

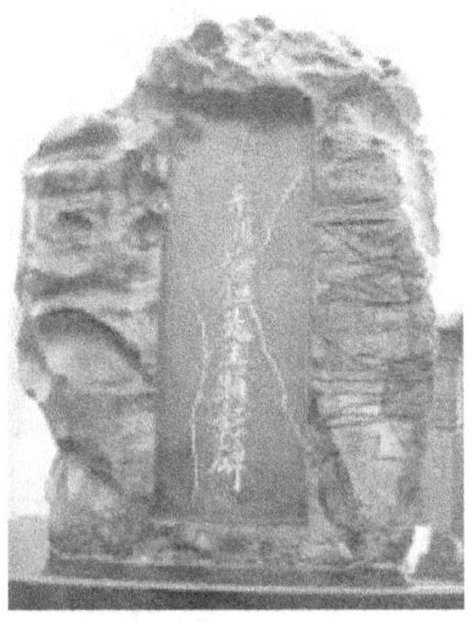

I further wish that the students of all high schools and universities practice karate according to the ten precepts described above. Then, some will attend the Okinawa Teachers University with their karate experience. In this way, after graduation, these teachers can teach karate correctly in the elementary schools with the right attitude and appropriate training methods. I believe the benefit of karate will spread across the nation within ten years. The great benefit is meant not only for the citizens of Okinawa Prefecture but also for those of our entire nation. With a strong belief in this, I have written this letter and these precepts for your review.

October 1908
Anko Itosu

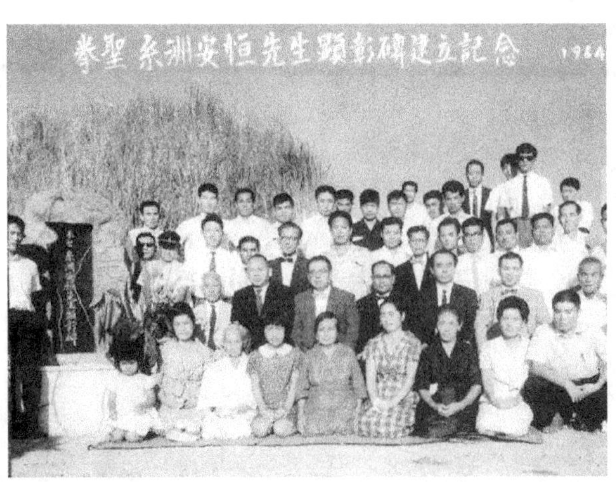

離

www.ingramcontent.com/pod-product-compliance
Lightning Source LLC
LaVergne TN
LVHW020712110826
845149LV00012B/2229

9780998223612